Small Wonder

The Story of the Yale Puppeteers
and the Turnabout Theatre

by Forman Brown

Foreword by Ray Bradbury

The Scarecrow Press, Inc.
Metuchen, N.J., & London
1980

Part I of this book was published by The Macmillan Company under the title, *Punch's Progress*. Copyright © 1936 by The Macmillan Company.

Library of Congress Cataloging in Publication Data

Brown, Forman George.
   Small wonder.

     Part I originally published in 1936 under title:
Punch's progress.
    Includes index.
    1. Yale Puppeteers. 2. Turnabout Players.
I. Brown, Forman George. Punch's progress. 1980.
II. Title.
PN1978.U6B7 1980   791.5'3   80-17815
ISBN 0-8108-1334-3

For Roddy

who received the least acclaim

and deserved the most

SINCE WE HEARD THAT MAGIC WORD:

TURNABOUT!

a fond remembrance by Ray Bradbury

It is not often given to be able to pay off old and special debts. But a love remembered is a love that must be nailed down on paper, and I'm given my chance here.

Back when the Turnabout Theatre began, I was still a young man in my early twenties selling newspapers on a street-corner in Los Angeles and making, when the sales were good, about ten dollars a week. Some of that money bought me my first ticket to see Forman Brown, Harry Burnett, Richard Brandon, and Elsa Lanchester, and all their marionette friends.

It was just about the fastest love-at-first-sight that any theatre-prone fan ever experienced. When I could afford to buy more tickets, I dragged relatives and friends along to see Frances Osborne bray-trumpet Forman Brown's fabulous take-off on *Die Valkyrie*, watch Lotte Gaslar stomp and grump her way through "Disgruntled," Dorothy Neumann doing a half-funny half-sad monologue or Harry Burnett lost on a desert island, holding a telephone directory in his hands and gloomily singing "Look at the Book That I Took."

It was all grand, it was all warm, it was all fun, and they were, though they did not know it, my family.

In all, I must have attended the Turnabout Theatre some 35 to 40 times over a period of at least ten or twelve years. The memories are still with me and are very special and fine.

If I were to have one wish at this time in my life, it would be to have someone put me in some sort of backward-turn-backward slipsteam device and mail me off to 1946 or thereabouts, to sing the magic word "Turnabout" and see my old friends pull strings or hear Elsa lilt her way through "If You Peek in My Gazebo," or "I'm Glad to See You're Back, Elaine."

For an evening like that, I think I would pay just about any price, and to hell with reason.

For now, there is this book, a memory piece by Forman Brown, who put the words in the mouths of Elsa and all his fellow actors.

My only regret is that you don't have *my* memories, as you read it.

April 19th, 1980

Table of Contents

Preface

In 1936 *Punch's Progress* was published. It was an informal tale of the doings of The Yale Puppeteers through their college years, their growing involvement in puppetry, the establishment of their theatres in Los Angeles and New York, and their return to Hollywood for a brief encounter with "the movies." Since then there have been scores of books written about puppets: books historical, technical, instructional, but none, I think, detailing the true adventure of a company of puppeteers, their successes, their failures, their frustrations and their triumphs.

Punch's Progress did precisely that, but it has been long out of print and has, indeed, become something of a collector's item. Meantime The Yale Puppeteers have gone on to win acclaim on the concert circuit, and to found and operate for fifteen exciting years, that unique Hollywood institution, TURNABOUT THEATRE. Thus this book, Part I of which consists of a complete revision of *Punch's Progress*, makes that story once more available, and Part II brings it up to date. So now it is not only the story of an adventure, but of its ultimate reward.

List of Illustrations

Part I

The Yale Puppeteers

1.

Who made the first puppet I suppose we shall never know, but I venture to guess that he was someone very like my roommate. He was a realist from the soles of his very certain feet to the tip of his unruliest hair. He had a positive phobia for abstractions. He had square-fingered hands that were made for carving and whittling and modeling and mixing—delicate, strong, sure. He had always a troupe of neighboring youngsters shrieking about the door of his cave, his igloo, his wigwam, to see what amusing toy he might fashion next. He had a humorous eye. He had many friends. He was, in other words, an advance copy of Harry Burnett.

How I came to room with Harry has no part in this account. He was a distant cousin, and there was I. And we managed. He thought my interests, save music, quite unaccountable, and I thought his extremely amusing. He knew the best places to hike, and how to fry bacon to brown perfection with the most breathtaking simplicity. I, in turn, could write the somehow necessary concluding paragraphs of his sociology and history theses, beginning, "It may therefore be seen from the foregoing that...." Rhetoric themes, too, on occasion, were my willing contribution to his college education.

The puppets provided a more interesting field of collaboration. A touring marionette company came to Ann Arbor. Must I confess that in those distant days—1920—marionettes meant nothing to me? I believe I even labored under the illusion that they were somehow worked by electricity. The company appeared in the Natural Science Building, as unlikely a theatre as could well have been found, for the seats veered up from the stage so sharply that the small proscenium seemed at the bottom of a chasm. The play, however, was charming. Harry shared my feeling, it seems, for a night or two later I was confronted on the stairs by the absurdest creature ever conceived. It was a gangling marionette, with thin legs, a lumpish head stuck full of dun-colored hair, and a carriage inspired surely by St. Vitus. "Here's Hamlet!" said Harry.

Hamlet, be it said, would have horrified any bona fide puppeteer, but fortunately in those early days (and in the history of the revival of puppetry in America they *are* early days) bona fide puppeteers were very scarce. His controller was a tennis racket, through the interstices of which threads ran down to the alleged joints of Hamlet, with a ring at the end of each thread to prevent its slipping through. Needless to say, Hamlet's creator had never seen the "workings" of a marionette. He had relied solely on his own ingenuity. The head was of melted wax, and the puppet, consequently, had a peculiarly post-mortem complexion. But his rickety antics were convulsing. He made the rounds of the neighbors and all the Ann Arbor friends, and he inspired, shortly thereafter, letters, researches, questionings, experiments, all of which resulted in some information as to the uses of papier-mâché, the rudimentary anatomy of the puppet, and the method of his control. Ingenuity, natural skill, and a good deal of patience finally resulted in some puppets that were worthy of the name.

The play was the thing. The only difficulty was in deciding what the play should be. We wavered for some time between pantomimic presentations of "When You and I Were Young, Maggie" to Yeats and Lord Dunsany. Neither of us had considered The Puppet—his capabilities, his heritage, his temperamental limitations. A play was a play; a puppet was something to do a play with. To end the controversy I wrote a play myself. It was, as I remember, called "Moon Magic." It was highly rhymed and romantic, and creaked with proper sentiment—a princess, a fountain, a moon (cut from a cigar-box) which rose on a gallows-like contraption and none too steadily, against a flannel sky. We further, to piece out our program, did "Little Red Riding Hood," with the assistance of Harry's older sister, Mary, whose role of the asthmatic grandmother still provides us reminiscent mirth.

The venture was a success. That is to say, we gave the show, and the neighbors and long-suffering members of the King's Daughters, who sponsored the performance, thought it "very novel" and "so different." "Little Red," as the more familiar opus was called by its perpetrators, had even a request performance or two. "Moon Magic" happily succumbed after a single showing.

Thereafter I seem to remember a lull in which life somehow managed to proceed about as usual, with classes to attend and papers to write, and the dim but certain glow within that meant "At any rate I've done something different from most of these people!" And we had. For puppetry is, I am convinced, a virulent disease, or perhaps an insinuating and narcotic habit that will not be denied. All my life I seem to have been fighting puppets, and yet at unpredictable but dismayingly regular intervals, when I have sworn myself free of them, and foolishly begun to believe that possibly I might really be—whisk!—and I'm back again. But of that anon.

The habit was launched. It was only a matter of a few weeks before strange sounds emanating from the basement workshop and a singularly preoccupied roommate told me we were off again. We were. "Little Red"—we were still disregarding The Puppet—seemed to indicate the sort of play we should next attempt. At the risk of my reputation in the Graduate English Room of the library, I began to go juvenile. Fairy tales of all times and all nations I read with reckless abandon. I occasionally asked for one volume or another of *The Golden Bough,* just to mislead the librarian, but this was only a ruse. At last we hit upon "Rumpelstiltskin." The word itself was appealing, and the story even more so. It opened golden vistas for Harry—vistas so golden, in fact, that it became my nightly duty to tarnish them with a little healthy skepticism.

The state of his mind in those days must have been a thing to marvel at. It whirled and buzzed with golden spinning-wheels, with coaches that really rolled by landscapes that really flew, of thrones and jewels, of forest caves and elves and all the curious paraphernalia of the fairy story. So, despite the indifference I struggled to maintain, "Rumpelstiltskin" grew quite beyond us. When it came time to put the show together it seemed Shubertian in its proportions. But it was at last put together. The basement was quite out of the question as a rehearsal hall, so we secured a vacant store. In one end the stage, an enormously clumsy construction of two-by-fours or worse, was set up. Inquiries and interviews with students active in various university dramatic societies netted us several assistants, and afternoons (there were no lights in the store) found us feverishly at it.

Rehearsals of a puppet show with trained puppeteers, let me interpolate, can be unbelievably chaotic and nerve-shattering. Rehearsals with untrained puppeteers are bedlam. The willing Thespians we had recruited would forget either their lines or their puppets, with the most peculiar results. Fortunately we had time—an ingredient professional companies too often have in very meager quantities—and at last the production began to take shape. The performance was but three days away when the chiefest of the recently acquired, arduously drilled puppeteers withdrew. The excuse offered was, I believe, a special examination. It may actually have been a nervous breakdown. At any rate the proverbial confusion reigned most despotically, and was dethroned only by the arrival of Robert, whose formal introduction I shall briefly postpone. The show went on, and a rollicking show it was, with purple velvet and gold fringe, with a spinning-wheel that span, with a truly regal and rococo throne room untouched and uninfluenced by Gordon Craig or the Russians.

The only flaw in the performance was one of those unexpected things that the veteran puppeteer is always expecting. To us it had the charm of a new and unique experience, and it serves as well as any incident I can remember to show how The Puppet may, on occasion, rebel against his Lord and Operator, and take things into his own hands. It is this ever-impending possibility that keeps the puppeteer alert. It was the throne room scene. The miller's daughter had become queen, as fairy-tale daughters have a way of doing, and was being very queenly indeed, when the prime minister, quite as regal in his way, in a sweeping gesture of prime-ministerial elegance, caught the queen's right foot and pulled her gently but firmly from her throne. Imagine the queen's position! And the prime minister's! And that of their respective puppeteers! But the court took no notice. Even the king was unmoved, and the prime minister, without even so much as an apology, continued his peroration to the end of the scene hanging resolutely to the queen's right ankle.

The show, however, despite this strange interlude of puppet psychology (a psychology, let me say, that no scientist has yet studied) was a success. That is to say it paid for itself in the single performance we had arranged for, and the local paper wrote enthusiastically of it. "Local boy, etc." It was even once revived. The stage we had evolved was never meant for traveling. It was clumsy and heavy, so the dream of invading near-by towns with "Rumpelstiltskin" died from undernourishment.

2.

Robert Henderson's advent into the company was significant. He was at the time seventeen, a freshman in the University, with a professorial father and a protectively ambitious mother. He was a precocious youth with a passion for the stage, and with Robert, Art came to our puppet show. Not, fortunately, to "Rumpelstiltskin." That was too far along to be aestheticized. But with "Rumpelstiltskin" behind us, we had a reputation to maintain, and another production was inevitable. Whose the suggestion was I do not remember. Perhaps it was Robert's. At any rate, early spring found us once more feverishly at it, with this time an enticing object in view. The idea was this: Harry was to build a show that three of us could operate and that could be transported easily. Robert's suavity and faculty connections were to secure us a week of bookings during the spring recess. My own humble contribution was to be such bits and interpolations as were not dictated by Robert's very superior knowledge of what-was-what in stagecraft.

Robert, it seems, as I recall those days, had a considerable part in every department of our venture. He did his booking effectively. Five engagements were secured, all in the vicinity of Ann Arbor and Detroit, and all accessible by that happy phenomenon of the twenties, the interurban car. He modeled the puppet heads. Harry's, he said, were "too realistic." So our new puppets began to sprout angular faces which, let me admit, were effective and "carried" well—always an important consideration in a puppet head. He had an important share, too, in the selection of the program. In its final form this program always began with a piano solo by Robert, played with feeling. It was always "The Maiden's

Prayer," and while a prayer at the start of any puppet show could hardly be amiss, something a bit more robust might have been more appropriate. The curtains then opened on a pensive Pierrot who announced in couplets (mine) Tony the Fiddler. Tony, dressed in blue satin knee-breeches and possessed of a permanent soulful expression, played (with the aid of a backstage Victrola), and his grace always won us a sympathetic audience. Following Tony came a skit which Robert christened "A Night in Delhi." It was a highly impromptu affair concerning two rival snake charmers, and a snake to be charmed. It was never written down, I believe, but grew slowly, performance by performance, and at last crystallized into definite shape. The haphazard evolution of this piece provided an excellent talking point for Robert: it was pure Commedia dell' Arte.

Not one high-school principal in ten knew what "Commedia dell' Arte" was, but she would never reveal such ignorance to Robert, no indeed! There was something regal in his youthful superiority that made one violently partisan. Most of the principals, fortunately, were impressed. The program continued with a pair of Negro entertainers—a gentleman with a banjo and a decidedly Topsy-ish girl with many lace petticoats. By present standards they would have been unthinkable, but that was fifty years ago, and Robert could assure everyone that they were "in the genuine puppet tradition." Then came a toe-dancer, favorite with the little girls; "The Three Wishes," which seems an inevitable choice of new puppeteers because of the scope it allows for tricks; and finally an opus by no less a genius than George Bernard Shaw—a scene from *Androcles and the Lion*. After having given dozens of performances of it, we discovered that we should, all this time, have been paying royalties for its use. As our receipts for the entire show were frequently much less than the sum of this royalty, we quietly let it drop from our repertory. We all regretted its going, for it is a completely successful play for puppets, and I am sorry, in a way, that Mr. Shaw was never told so—though he would no doubt have replied that he knew it all the time.

Such was the program. The puppets were much improved,

and the stage, considering the adaptability we demanded of it, was fairly satisfactory. The stage proper consisted of two oblong boxes placed end to end. These, when we packed, served as conveyances for our curtains and props. Besides these two boxes we carried a large old-fashioned telescope bag for the puppets, and a long pack of uprights, braces, etc., wrapped in a tarpaulin held together with trunk straps—four pieces in all. The puppets we used were about sixteen inches in height, constructed of wood and wire in the usual fashion, with such divergencies of pattern as Harry found desirable. An individual method of stringing the knees procured for them a lifelike gait, and provided us with another talking point. Our settings were simple—set pieces and cut-outs against a back-drop of black velvet. This setting proved so well adapted to puppet needs that we retained it, with variations, through all the vicissitudes of our puppeteering. There were only fourteen puppets in the whole production, so we relied to a considerable extent on lines and on the excellent behavior of our actors for our success.

3.

The spring tour was both encouraging and stimulating. It brought with it the excitement that can never again be quite so tinglingly poignant—the excitement of trouping for the first time. The tour had its inception at the Henderson's. For the occasion Robert's mother invited a houseful of guests, principally faculty members and their wives—guests whose presence was terrifying to Harry and me, unaccustomed to such a reversal of the established system. But we acquitted ourselves acceptably. The professorial parlor resounded with professorial applause, and the professorial dining room might, for all the glee it contained when the performance ended, have been back-stage indeed at a successful first night.

Fortified with the assurance of this applause we fared forth. Not without misgivings we loaded ourselves and our strange agglomeration of baggage onto the rear platform of the interurban car. The conductor may have had his doubts, but if so he kept them to himself, and let us, panting, aboard. Our destination was a village en route to Detroit. Here we dismounted. Confronting us in a drug-store window was a poster—our poster, its yellow expanse proclaiming that we, The Puppeteers, Students of the University of Michigan, would that night grace the boards of Hoop's Hall. A small boy at the curb pointed and whispered to a second small boy, and we were for a splendid moment that most romantic of all romantic things—an arriving theatrical troupe, freighted with a glamour of footlights and unreality, a glamour mysterious and slightly suspect.

Into the drug-store went Robert while Harry and I stood guard over the tarpaulined pack, the telescope case and the boxes.

11

"Can you tell me where Hoop's (he pronounced it so it
rhymed with 'soups') Hall is?"

"What say?"

"Hoop's Hall."

"Oh! You mean Whoops's Hall! Yeah! Right around the
corner and over the meat market."

Up the long and dingy flight of steps went the impedimenta,
and double doors swung open into "Whoops's Hall." It was a
sight that put a sudden tarnish on the glow of the previous moment. A high-ceilinged oblong room, its narrow windows were
streaked with dust and its walls crazily festooned with tattered
remnants of crêpe paper decorations, stained and faded. The
same discouraged streamers hung in tangled shreds from the
chandeliers. At one end was the stage, its curtain decorated with a
bilious sunset surrounded by advertisements for village stores,
sadly awry. The floor was littered with debris and dust. A stove in
one corner gave off a sooty odor which vied with the smell of
damp chips in the adjacent wood-box to give the place an aroma
entirely in keeping with its appearance.

Brooms were recruited, and buckets of water, and by show
time "Whoops's Hall" was clean and orderly, the show set up, the
puppets hanging stiffly on their racks, and the puppeteers, tired
but complacent, fidgeting behind the black sateen curtains, making tentative guesses as to the probable size of the house and the
caliber of the audience. The puppeteer on such an occasion is
prone to envy his puppets, hanging relaxed and ready all about
him, while he must worry for himself and for them too, knowing
that their behavior will depend entirely on his own skill and lack
of nervousness. They might be, indeed, were the puppeteer only
calm enough and philosophical enough to recognize it, sane and
silent models for his own conduct.

On this particular occasion, our first out-of-town engagement,
the calm of philosophy was far from us. Robert, in the role of
impressario, could stand importantly and teeteringly by the
wooden table at the door, selling tickets to whoever came pounding up the wooden stairs. But Harry and I could only peer
through the too-small apertures in the curtain, bite our fingers,
and pray for the best. The tumult on the stairs was not impres-

sive. Nor were the faces of the scattering occupants of the front seats. Indeed, it seemed to me as I looked them over with fearful and critical eyes that a more benighted and benumbed assemblage had never met together with a sullen dare to be entertained. My heart was lead, and my fingers ice; the whole venture seemed fore-doomed to inevitable and ignominious failure.

The minutes, however, ticked away, as even such heavy minutes have a way of doing, the number of unpromising faces increased to a scattered synthesis of lumpish boredom, and the show began. The lines of Pierrot that I had prided myself upon for their lyric niceness and subtle humor, seemed lifeless and unprovocative of the anticipated chuckles. Pierrot's walk, however, and his expansive gestures, were met with gales of laughter and adolescent guffaws. And so it went, from one unforeseen reaction to the next, and we learned our first great lesson in stage-craft—a lesson that can be learned in no other way—the lesson of emphasis and restraint—that the play must be accommodated to the audience, so that two successive performances of the same piece, with the same lines, may seem quite different things. The puppeteer, too, must train himself to a pitch of audience-sensitivity that is remarkably keen, for he is limited to his ears alone for information as to the success of his efforts. If his patrons simply smile, he cannot see. They must chuckle or laugh aloud. If they fidget in their seats he does not know. If they walk out, even, he is not aware, unless they walk so heavily that he can hear.

After the show there was the usual crowd of round-eyed youngsters and patient parents crowding about the stage for an explanation of its simple mysteries. They liked the show, it seemed, and we were somewhat reassured. The receipts were $18.35, which, when our expenses were deducted, left us each with two dollars for our work, but a vast respect for the showmanship of barnstormers everywhere.

The rest of the spring tour was relatively uneventful. The remaining auditoriums were far removed from the "Whoops's Hall" category, being auditoriums in modern schools, slick and convenient. But always I shall be grateful to Hoop's Hall and the initiation it afforded to us in our careers as troupers.

4.

When college opened again after the spring recess, we found that our five-day tour had paid for our stage and equipment and netted us a small sum besides. Furthermore, timid as it had been, it had whetted our appetite for more, and we immediately began laying plans for a summer tour. Locomotion was our principal problem, but fate solved this for us very neatly through the person of a scrupulous and adamantine interurban conductor. It was a warm Friday in May, Robert had gone ahead to make final arrangments for an evening engagement and to address the high-school assembly on the vast danger to their immortal souls should they miss the puppet show.

They very nearly did. For when Harry and I, in our usual breathless style, began piling our voluminous assortment of luggage aboard the interurban platform we were halted by a gruff and peremptory order to stop, desist, and, if I recall rightly, to "get the hell off of here with that junk—what do you think this is, a freight train?" Pleading did no good. This unobliging Charon pulled the bell-cord twice with a decisiveness that was eloquent, and we were left among our scattered possessions watching the car vanish around the bend.

There was nothing for it but to rent an automobile. I stood guard and Harry went forth in search of one. He returned with an ancient Ford Model T into which we loaded ourselves with a good deal of difficulty, and arrived at our destination a little late to find poor Robert in a flutter of managerial nerves. The proceeds from that performance went as down-payment on a second-hand vehicle of the same vintage, and subsequent week-ends assured us of the wisdom of our move.

Harry Burnett and Forman Brown tour Michigan resorts in style (1921).

Summer found us, then, eager to be off and adequately equipped for a tour. Robert had made such bookings as he could by mail, and for others we relied on personal contact later in the season. The tour carried us through a land new to us all, though we did not go beyond the boundaries of our native state. Beginning in the resort area north of Chicago we made our way by jumps of ten, twenty, thirty miles northward along the shore of Lake Michigan. Saugatuck, Macatawa, Muskegon, Manistee, Pentwater, Petoskey, Cheboygan, Mackinac. We played here a hotel (setting up our stage in a corner of the ballroom or casino if the hotel possessed one; if it did not, clearing a corner of the dining room after dinner was over, we ensconced our theater there), there a village opera house; here a summer camp, up

sandy difficult roads through the dunes, chaste and lovely as a
series of Japanese prints; again in a small-town movie theater
(each night a different place, a different set-up, a different sort of
audience.) Our days were full and happy. The mornings we
spent, as a rule, in chasing down prospects for new engagements,
in tacking up posters at some town a day or so ahead on our
schedule, or in handbilling cottages and hotel verandas.
Matinees were the rule, and this necessitated our being on hand
in time to set up our stage and get everything ready for the
afternoon performance. This we soon developed into such a system that all could be got ready in less than an hour.

The unpacking of the equipment was always the signal for the
congregation of all the children in the vicinity, peering and pok-
ing and asking innumerable questions. The masking curtains
would soon be set up, the lights rigged, the stage set, the puppet
racks bolted in place, and all in readiness for the emergence of
the actors. It was the event the children most eagerly awaited,
though it must be stated, in justice to all, that their elders were
not infrequently as eager as they. It was something of an event.
The straps of the bulging case were unfastened, the top, resisting
and complaining like an old bellows, pulled slowly off, and there,
in a seeming inextricable confusion, lay the marionettes, each in
its small calico bag. The perennial mystery of "keeping the strings
from getting tangled" seems never to be dispelled, though in
reality it is simple enough, for the strings of each individual figure
are fastened securely just above its head by the draw-strings of the
bag that contains it, and the remaining expanse of string, twisted
by giving a smart twirl to the puppet, is wrapped tightly around
the controller, whereupon the whole may be deposited in a trunk
with very little danger of tangling. In unpacking the reverse of this
process obtains; but to one who is not familiar with the ways of
the small actors the whole matter seems difficult.

Forth they would come, then, one by one, accompanied by
the Oh's and Ah's and Lookee's of the small circle of admirers:
the dainty ballerina, with her fluff of blue skirts and her sequin
bodice; the two Hindus, one fat and one lean; the woodcutter and
the woodcutter's wife, to whose nose, through the exigencies of

her very existence as a puppet was always fastened on her emergence from her bag, the string of sausages that would, in an hour or so, be the reward for her greed and selfishness; the dragon, befeathered and ferocious, who would bring her her evil fortune; the soulful violinist; the sad Pierrot; the opera diva, flamboyant with paste jewels and expansive bosom, and all the rest. All would be removed from their bags, twirled nonchalantly about to untwist their strings, and hung at last in swinging unconcern along their rack. Each would have to be tested then by a small trip across the floor to see that all its strings were attached and in proper order, and that it was in readiness for whatever tricks it would be called upon to perform. Sometimes a repair kit would be needed for a new string, a broken finger, a chipped nose, but for the most part they were seasoned travelers and required little attention.

A matinee. And then, if some small boy from the crowd of volunteers could be amicably settled on to stand guard over the small world, the three of us could have an hour or so to ourselves for a swim in the lake, a quiet hour lying in the sand atop the dunes, the lake wind running whisperingly through the stunted pines that struggled through the white drifts. Then dinner and an evening show, to a different group, this time—a group as really if not as vehemently interested as the children—many, in fact, brought back by the urging of the smaller members of the family, who, fascinated by their afternoon's introduction to the land of *les petits comediens en bois,* pleaded for a retarded bedtime in order that they might enjoy them once more before their departure.

It is always gratifying to the puppet showman to know that everyone likes his wares, and he is fortunate in the essential genius of his actors, for there seems to be something inherent in the puppet that gives him an immediate and impressive advantage over his flesh-and-blood competitor. It was to me, to all of us, on this first summer tour, a never-ending source of wonder and delight that wherever we went, whether our audiences were Milwaukee millionaires, Chicago telephone operators, or Michigan farmers come in to town on a Saturday night—people to

whom a marionette was as foreign as a Manet, and a puppet as
unfamiliar as Plato or Peru, in every case there seemed to be
something, some wooden quality in these small and angular figures that was universally compelling and amusing. So, at night,
when the show was over, there was without exception an interested audience to the "tearing down" and the packing up, the
loading of the small car, and there were nearly always, from the
hotel verandas, shouted good-nights and wishes for good luck,
and not infrequently someone left behind who had rather be
riding with us through the night of stars or driving rain, perhaps,
to the scene of next day's endeavour.

Finances were often precarious, but on the whole we fared
well. Occasionally we were permitted to charge admission, but
more often we simply passed the hat, stopping the show for a few
moments after what seemed a likely climax, when our audience
would be in high humor, collecting what we could, and resum-
ing when all the watchers had been canvassed. Sometimes these
collections were small indeed, but usually our patrons were
generous, so on the whole we did not badly.

So the summer went. We progressed bit by bit through July up
the tawny dune-country into the woods and rugged hills until
August found us in the blue and golden tip of Michigan's southern peninsula, a land studded with lakes and wooded bays and
pine-fragrant islands. Behind us was the pleasant memory of a
month of vagabonding—hard work, tired muscles, but fun and
health and new contacts and new ideas. We had played, during
July, one of our more memorable engagements. It was a Saturday
night, and having no other booking, we sold our services on a
percentage basis to a small movie house in a canning town in the
fruit belt. The owner, fat and unkempt, was dubious, but he was
willing, after some persuasion, to chance it.

His theater was combined with a fruit store through which the
audience entered, to divide, at the rear, in two sections and find
their seats in the dingy auditorium. When we unloaded in the
back alley we found to our surprise that the stage, which was very
small, was almost completely occupied by banana crates, fruit
boxes, wooden pails of candy, fruit wrappings, burlap, all in a

discouraging and evil-smelling confusion. We set to, cleaning and stowing away boxes and crates and buckets, and had barely time to set up before the feature picture, a Bill Hart western, flickered in crazy reversal on the thin screen which hid us from the audience. There was no getting out, and our uncertainty as to the length of the program compelled us to sit, Gargantuan shadows chasing across out faces, until it was over.

Then came the lights, and the proprietor's announcement that, as a special attraction, there would appear on the stage the famous "migonettes." The screen was hoisted on noisy pulleys, the lights went off again, and into the diminutive aperture of our stage stepped Pierrot, a tiny and no doubt surprising successor to the shadowy giants that had preceded him. He was greeted respectfully, and then, though we trembled at the prospect, came Pyramus and Thisbe. We needn't have worried. In the language of Times Square it "wowed 'em." These country people, some of whom had possibly seen Punch and Judy at the County Fair, laughed until they cried at Lion and Wall and poor lisping Thisbe dying her bloody death on the body of her rotund and protesting lover. We were a success, and the remaining two shows packed them in, for the people who went out, apparently, spread the news to the groups of gossiping neighbors that were gathered in front of the stores and at street corners. The impressario himself, proud of his attraction and interpreting our persuasion as his own, went forth into the street with a megaphone to shout "See the migonettes, folks—sompe'n you'll never forget!"

Our share of the proceeds surprised us, but what gratified us most was the reception our puppets had met with in so unlikely a situation. We discussed it at length in the enormous high-ceilinged bedroom as we counted our nickels and dimes after the show; and the advice of some traveling wit, scribbled on the wallpaper above the coil of rope, one end of which was attached to the radiator pipe—"In case of fire grab free end of rope and jump!"—seemed no more quixotic than our mood and our day's fortune.

August brought a slight change in our routine. Robert's parents had taken a summer cottage not many miles from Charlevoix, and Mrs. Henderson, certain that her son was being underfed and wrongly fed, and suffering in consequence, insisted that we make our headquarters with them. The resorts in upper Michigan are so close together and so easy of access that this was entirely possible, so for three weeks or so, with the exception of two or three over-night excursions, the Henderson cottage became our home. It was a bit crowded, and the enforced intimacy not conducive to the utter serenity the lake and woods provided so satisfactory a setting for, but we were fed and pampered unmercifully, and had it not been for the fact that Harry and I were expected practically at dawn every morning to man the oars while Professor Henderson trolled for bass for miles around the lake, the puppet bridge, I am sure, would never have been able to sustain the added weight. The drives, though, after performances, through the crisp pine-pungent nights, brittle with stars, the roads winding through the dark canyons of the woods, veiled, often with floating wisps of fog that one entered and slipped through and emerged from with a shivering delight, were chill and titillating inducers of sound and untroubled sleep.

The country was an unending joy. Its profusion of lakes, like blue gems dropped unexpectedly among the pines, the woods, silent with a more than cloistral silence, the mornings, all gold and glitter across the lake, the dark flight of bitterns, the clanging cries of the crow, the underlying pedal-point of white gravel crunching beneath swift-turning tires—all these mingled in such a pleasant unobtrusive way that the days fled by and autumn came on all too quickly.

There was, late in August, the big engagement of the summer—an engagement all the bother and unaccustomed preparations for which gave it a special importance to us all: Grand Hotel on Mackinac Island. The car had to be left behind, the paraphernalia entrusted to porters to be put on the tiny steamer, and then, on arrival, once more turned over to other porters until a horse and wagon could be procured to take it to the hotel. Never had our simple little stage invaded so imposing and palatial a home. Its corridors, down which we trod on reverential feet over miles of thick carpet seemed endless, and the rococo elaboration of the ballroom an unexpected elegance. We set up our equipment, which in contrast with all this gold and white and scarlet became suddenly shabby and almost impertinent. We left our theater to the hushed silence of the ballroom in charge of a nattily supercilious bellhop, and made our way back through the miles of corridor. The dining-room doors were ajar. "Gosh!" breathed Harry. "Two-fifty for lunch!"

In the village we found ourselves a cheap but clean and sunny room, and ate our lunch in a cheap but not so clean and sunny lunch-room. We pooled our resources, hired a carriage in the afternoon and took the drive over the island that delights all tourists, not only with the beauty of the views it unfolds, but with the quiet old-fashioned luxury of an open carriage and a coachman to drive it.

The evening's engagement, while moderately profitable, was much less gratifying from the standpoint of enthusiasm and inter- est than our less pretentious appearances, and the next night, in the little wind-swept town of St. Ignace, playing in a small movie-house half filled with villagers and lumberjacks, the old and proven democracy of Punch seemed much more genuine and vital. From St. Ignace we made our way to that lovely chain of islands, Les Cheneaux, lying along the southern reaches of Lake Superior like an emerald necklace dropped in a bowl of blue glass by loving, yet careless, fingers. There was a missed fork in the road one brilliant night which resulted in a fifty-mile drive through pine forests in the increasing cold, an empty gasoline tank, a halt beside a clearing where, clattering up to the pine- stump fence, an old white horse came like a goblin steed, whin- nying his curiosity, a disgruntled farmer, and, by chance, two spare gallons of fuel to carry us back to St. Ignace, rigid with cold, just as the steel-blue dawn was coming over the straits.

There was a hotel without electricity where we gave our per- formance by candle-light, the puppets making grotesque bur- lesques of themselves against the sateen backdrops. There was a performance given from the top of a billiard table, with the fold- ing doors of the game room forming the proscenium for the antics of our troupe. There was a day of mistaken directions, of storm, of delay, of nothing to eat, of arrival barely in time for a performance, and the ample reward of an audience generous with praise, applause and dollar bills. There were days when The Play was the thing, completely and joyously, and days when, tired and discouraged, the pessimistic implications of puppeteering were uppermost, and my own young spirit rebellious and, perhaps, jealously happy in rebellion. On a park bench in Traverse City, in such a mood, waiting for a mechanic to repair our heavily laden car, I scribbled on a stray envelope a sonnet, "Puppeteer," which going later into a volume of verse, won me many friends:

> I have played God, stood balancing above
> the yellow glow of lights and pulled the strings
> that make alive the tiny wooden things
> and felt not mercy, kindliness or love,
> but only aching fingers, eyes that strain
> to make the puppet pass across the stage
> and simulate the human heritage
> of pleasure that is masquerading pain.
> Some day I shall not make them act like men.
> I shall be God indeed, and shall not care.
> Ah, how I'll send them swinging through the air!
> Ah, how I'll make them leap and grovel then!
> Ah, how I'll laugh when they who watch the show
> whisper "He's mad!" He's God, I'll have you know!

5.

For the most part, however, there was slight occasion for philosophical introspection. The summer was over almost before it had begun, it seemed, and it was time for college again. It was at this time that the insidious pretensions of The Puppet began to make themselves felt in a practical way. For there is, as has already been said, in the craft of puppet making, in puppet manipulation, in puppet playwriting, however casual the association may be or however lightly it may be assumed, something persistent and subtle that grows and insists until it cannot be put aside. It is as if the small figures wove, in silence and in secret, the strings that animate them into a net to snare the unwary soul who gives them a moment's attention. I have known dentists to neglect their patients and real-estate salesmen to forget their prospects, so involved did they become in the mechanics of the puppet stage. I have known whole classes in playwriting to turn frantically and with one accord to the composition of puppet plays on the intrusion into their midst of one small puppet. And so it was with me. I found myself, in complete and blind disregard of the advice of my departmental head, turning down three excellent offers in the English departments of three highly reputable universities to accept, at a lower salary, an instructorship at Michigan which would permit me to continue, over week-ends and in such spare time as I might have, this association with my wooden friends.

Robert, because of college work and parental insistence dropped out of the company. The Theater had him, however, and he has gone on as actor, director, and husband of a revered British stage star. Our new member, Elwood Fayfield, had dis-

tinguished himself on the campus as Mr. Pim in Milne's play
of that name. He replaced Robert and was soon more proficient
than his predecessor, and much less temperamental.

And here might be inserted a word on puppeteers. A valid
criticism of the puppet show in America has been either that the
puppets are crudely made and badly worked, or that the voices
and interpretations are poor and amateurish. This is easily explained by the fact that the small amateur companies begin,
ordinarily, with the mechanics of puppeteering, and are willing
to let the play take care of itself; and that the large professional
companies recruit their puppeteers from the stage and consequently get people with good voices but with no skill or experience in their new trade. Versatility backstage in a puppet show is
more to be desired than any other quality, for on the puppet
stage, in miniature, appear all the problems of the legitimate
stage, and they must be met not by a great corps of trained
specialists in direction, lighting, acting, scene-design, costuming, etc., but by three or four persons who, among themselves,
must supply all these talents and more. Mechanical and electrical
skill, talent for writing, for music, for sewing, for speaking, singing, whistling, mimicry, painting, designing, business management—all these and more must be contributed by one or
another of the puppeteers, and the more talents there are combined in one person, the better for the show.

The show, then, with its new member, Elwood, went on
through the following winter, its "home" in the Burnett basement, where the stage was kept set up, usually, for rehearsals.
Engagements, of course, were largely restricted to week-ends and
to towns within easy driving distance of Ann Arbor. Many of
these engagements came through people who had seen us at
various places during the summer, or who had read of our vagabond adventure, and we enjoyed the sensation so dear to the
heart of a trouper, that of being known and recognized, in even
so modest a way.

Many of these dates were amusing indeed, for to many
localities a puppet show was a complete novelty, and the fact that
good people willingly spend their quarters and half-dollars for a

form of entertainment so mysterious and exotic speaks highly for their desire for entertainment, their courage, and their curiosity.

I think always of a Friday night we played in a village so small as to be on only the most detailed of maps. In fairness to the good people who provided us with so much fun, I can only relate that the name of the village was singular, terminating as it did in the letters "i-t-h" so that, whenever it was mentioned it gave one the sudden conviction that all its inhabitants must lisp. Such was not the case. We were to play for the Community Lecture Association, our appearance being the second in a series of five. The scene of our performance was the small white Methodist church that, standing at a crossroads, marked the center and indeed practically the whole of the village, for, deducting the church, there would have been left only eight or ten houses, each with its red barn, a general store, a grange hall, and a blacksmith shop.

We were to begin at seven-thirty, so we timed our arrival for late afternoon, allowing ourselves ample time to set up the stage and have an early dinner. But there were complications. The stage needed some additional raising, and, most disconcerting, the church was lighted by a system of gasoline lights which had to be pumped up by the janitor to a sufficient pressure. We solved the lighting problem at last by collecting all the spare light cords in town (the citizens were only too eager to help) and by stretching them perhaps fifty yards to the nearest house, which, fortunately, was equipped with its own lighting plant. It was six o'clock before we were through and so dark that the janitor, who was afflicted with athsma, had to be summoned from the recesses of the basement and set to work preparing the auditorium lights. It was a task diabolically unsuited to a man of his generous proportions and peculiar infirmities, for every complaining stroke of the pump handle, accompanied by a peculiar and lugubrious sucking-whistling sound, caused in the poor belabored breast of the pumper a sigh of such lung-withering, ear-shivering proportions that the church reechoed with the rhythmical and alternate puffings and whistlings of pump and janitor. It was well that the minister arrived when he did, for his gravity in the face of this ridiculous dissonance calmed our hilarity. We were to go, he informed us, across the road to Mrs. Whipple's for supper. We ran—and knocked at Mrs. Whipple's front door, out of breath.

"Oh, good evenin'!" said Mrs. Whipple in the darkened hall. "Come right in. Throw yer things on the divinport in the parlor. Supper'll be ready in a jiffy."

It was, bountifully. We ate in the huge kitchen, and ate quantities. Mrs. Whipple was talkative and obviously a-twitter, for she was entertaining the lecture folks. An extended conversation was difficult, though, for Mrs. Whipple's experience was limited. A cow mooed sadly in the outer darkness. "You see, I ain't lived in town long. Always lived in the country till this fall."

We had crossed a railroad track on the edge of the village.

"Where does the railroad run, Mrs. Whipple?"

"Well now! One end runs to Jackson; I know that because my niece, Emily, works there in a office. But I declare, I don't know where the other end runs—ain't never inquired, I guess."

Supper, happily, was over by six-thirty. Were we Mrs. Whipple's guests or Mrs. Whipple's boarders, or were we, by chance, guests of the Lecture Association? Mrs. Whipple gave no inkling, and we dared not ask for fear of offending her. So we simply told her how good her biscuits were, and ran back to the church. To our amazement it was surrounded three deep with cars, and along one side, under a row of maples, were arrayed seven buggies, the horses blanketed and docile along the pipe hitching-block.

Inside the church was full.

"They come to things early here," Mr. Hickock, the minister, explained, thrusting a bald pate through the curtains. At six-forty-five not another person could have been forced inside without the aid of a shoehorn. Every window-ledge bulged; chairs filled the entry way, and youngsters in starched gingham sat, giggling and impatient, on the floor in front of their elders. The whole place buzzed with anticipation. At seven the head of Hickock again appeared, incandescent with importance, and told us we might as well start, since they couldn't get any more in if they tried. He would make a few preliminary remarks. He did, while we, poised on the bridge, puppets ready in our hands, waited.

"Tonight," he began, "we have quite a novelty, one you'll all enjoy. But first let me remind you of the third number on our course, which will come three weeks from Thursday at the same hour—a home-talent play, 'Mrs. Wiggs of the Cabbage Patch.' And now"—we waited, tense for the gong and the extinguished light—"now it gives me great pleasure to present the Poopeteers, who will present their poopets."

A snort from Harry set us off, and the curtains opened on a twitching Pierrot, silent in the hands of a convulsed puppeteer.

There were other engagements as amusing, for to nearly every town or village visited we carried the revised gospel of The Puppet. Never a traditional figure in America as he has been for centuries in the rest of the world, he still was accepted with a heartiness which seemed to spring not exclusively from the joy of something novel, but from the dim remembrance of something almost but not quite forgotten. People wherever we went seemed somehow, though unconsciously, happy to meet the little wooden descendants of Punch and Kasperl and Guignol that had amused their forebears in some corner of Sussex or Bavaria or Brittany.

The winter sped by, and spring brought with it a disheartening telegram. A touring marionette company, presenting shows for large box-office returns, needing a puppeteer, and hearing of our work, wired Harry an offer of several weeks' duration touring with their company. Harry was frankly excited. He had never been away from home on his own, and this seemed an excellent opportunity for wider adventure, for contact with professional puppeteers (who were in reality less expert than he)—a glamour, in short, not to be rejected. There were only a few bookings ahead for us, and, after some consultation, it was decided he should go. We set to work at once finding a replacement. That anyone could really take his place was unthinkable, but we found a student who was at least eager, and spent a few frantic days training him before Harry's departure.

Harry left, and the few shows we gave without him filled me with dread at my responsibility, for my knowledge of puppets was only such as one could not help acquiring from associating with them. My bent was decidedly not mechanical, and I was continually harassed with the possibility of something going wrong that I could not right. Nothing did, fortunately, but the performances were hardly a joy, and I made no attempts for further bookings until summer.

Summer came, and brought Harry back from his tour, full of the wisdom of the road and proud of his experience, but tired out and eager once more to get at his own puppets and his own show. The touring company, using very large figures, had played in legitimate theaters, civic auditoriums, opera houses from the Mississippi west to Denver and south to Oklahoma, giving slipshod performances in places totally unfitted to puppet production, and Harry, using his own reaction as a test of the artistic rightness of their work, knew that he did not enjoy it and that something was obviously much amiss with it.

We began plans for the summer, and started out again, early in July, to cover the same route we had covered the previous year. It was, if anything, pleasanter than before. We had several new engagements, but there was the additional satisfaction of returning to places where we were recognized and enthusiastically welcomed, and where we renewed the casual acquaintances of the summer before. The tour ended in August, and it was an end none of us faced with much pleasure. For Harry, lured by a second contract for a more extended road tour with the same company, in which, this time, some of his own favorite bits were to be included as an olio, had agreed to go, and I, in one of my recurrent but never very permanent revolts against the tyranny of The Puppet, had signed a contract to teach English in a southern college. So the puppets were packed away, the stage stowed in a corner of the cellar, which acquired a sudden neatness and openness it had not exhibited for three years; we made our farewells and went our respective ways. Harry was obviously embarked on the career of a puppet showman, but I, free of their wooden fascination (so I ignorantly believed), I was to become something much more dignified and important as a schoolman and an author.

So we parted at the summer's end, not without, on my part, at least, a good deal of genuine regret, and frequent and suffocating nostalgia during the ensuing winter in a strange southern city, where I tried valiantly to exude a dignity and a seriousness I could put no credence in. This year and the next, so far as I was concerned, might well be dropped from this chronicle, and will be, save for these few lines. They were years, I see now, of an alien endeavor in a field to which persistence might ultimately have reconciled me. My patience, luckily, was not sufficient. I saved money, obsessed with the idea of a year in Europe. It was that goal that made those years endurable.

6.

During my first year in the south Harry toured for a considerable part of the season. As his experience widened he became increasingly conscious of his needs in the domain of stagecraft, and the following fall he enrolled in the newly organized department of drama at Yale University. He found there an environment for which he was peculiarly adapted, and into which he fitted easily and admirably. The whole department was in a state of experiment. Occupying a great old house among the elms of New Haven's lovely and dignified streets, its quarters were hastily and in a very impromptu fashion adapted to its needs. There was nothing academic in its curriculum. All was informal, and among the students, who were of all ages and from all parts of the country, a spirit of camaraderie prevailed that was more like that of Montparnasse than New Haven. They were frankly regarded by the conservative undergraduates as a strange assortment of freaks who had no business on the campus. The fact that this exclusion from the ranks of the collegiate bothered them not at all provides the most striking index to their character as a group and to their interests.

Harry's finances, despite his year of touring, were not sufficient to carry him through his course without augmentation from some other source, and the source for him was, obviously, puppets. It is here that Richard Brandon—Roddy—enters the story, and continues with it to the end in an important way. He had come to Yale after a year at Dartmouth and a year of uncertainty as to his future. He and Harry met, became firm friends, and together undertook the venture of reviving our old show. Roddy's talents were principally those of impressario. He could book en-

gagements and make routes and plans with all the assurance of a
veteran theatrical manager. Aside from this, his greatest contribution to the show was, and continues to be, an unbounded loyalty.
Harry's show was for him the only show. Competitors were to be
feared and fought and never trusted. It was a loyalty which sometimes seemed foolish and sometimes caused arguments, but
which has been so much more often a challenge, an encourage-
ment, and a prod to action which might justify it, that it has been
perhaps our greatest asset as a partnership.

Since I was not engaged in this revival I can write of it only
scantily and without, I know, a complete or just retelling of its
triumphs and failures, the difficulties it encountered, the enthusiasm with which the drama students received it, the puppet
plays, the scene designs, the costume sketches it inspired. So
pronounced, indeed, did the interest become that the head of the
department, George Pierce Baker, was forced to remind Harry

Brandon and Burnett in front of the Yale Drama School (1926).

that this department was, after all, a department of drama and not of puppet drama. My only intrusion into this year, so far as puppets were concerned, was at Christmas time. I booked Harry's puppets as a holiday attraction into the chief department store in the small Carolina city where I was teaching. He brought them down from New Haven, and for three days, on a temporary stage erected in one end of an impromptu theatre, we performed an incredible number of shows to throngs of children. There was again the old stir within me, and the succeeding post-holiday weeks of freshman English classes and theme-reading were tasteless and dull indeed.

For the rest my contact was by letter. Their difficulties were greater than ours had been at Michigan because they were more dependent on their efforts for their actual livelihood. They played, as we had done, schools and clubs in the vicinity of the college town. THE PUPPETEERS, STUDENTS OF YALE UNIVERSITY, their advertising read. It was too long a title ever to survive, and it became very soon The Yale Puppeteers in the casual way in which such changes occur, and has so persisted. Their show, which, with a few exceptions, was practically the same as the one of our Michigan days, was as popular in New England as it had been in the West. There was still, however, difficulty in booking enough engagements within easy reach of New Haven to pay the necessary expenses, and there were, I know, many meals of bouillon-cube soup and day-old doughnuts which were donated by a kindly baker downstairs. There were enforced fasts in order to buy enough gasoline to get the show to its week-end destination. There were bickerings and bargainings and sometimes feasts when a show was over and a check in hand. There was, above all, The Kennel, so named because it was the home of "The Pups." It was an apartment of three rooms located above the aforementioned bakery. Reached by a dark and narrow stairway, its rent was cheap and it offered distinct possibilities. Its furnishings came from wherever they could be had, either for the taking or at bargain prices. There was a studio bed, a profusion of masks and puppets and cushions (no chairs), a reed organ, and, prized possession, a white bearskin rug that once, it was insisted, had belonged to Eli Whitney, who had removed its head for reasons best known to himself, and left the slightly moth-eaten remainder to shed its hair on the floor of The Kennel.

It was essentially a rendezvous for the night-time, for then its makeshifts and imperfections, softened and changed by the alchemy of candlelight, melted into a dim and pleasant ambiance. Here the drama school would congregate. The puppets would perform, the organ play, budding poets would read their verses, plots would appear and vanish, and plans for the Great American Puppet Theater flourish and multiply with a lavish disregard for the practical that was in keeping with the spirit of the room.

That summer they made their first tentative expedition into the resort sections of New England. It was urged that I join them, but, still resisting the pull of The Puppet, I saw them off and returned to Michigan to await my long-cherished trip to Europe. Their tour, taken with little advance preparation, was modestly successful. The bookings were secured, for the most part, only a day or so in advance, and—so I gleaned from the hasty notes that were my share of the summer—New England was thoroughly, if sketchily, covered.

Harry's diary for the summer was kept each day in a few lines scribbled on the bottom of the poster which had been used to advertise that day's performance. I should like to quote them all, but a few examples will serve, not only to give a picture of the tour, but also some of the flavor and personality of their author:

July 10. Kineo on a fly date. Gala opening of The Pups. Lovely rainstorm on the lake. Not bad. $21.65.

July 13. Girls' camp. Surprise party for "we girls." One hour to set up. Girls out boating and had to stay there in the rain until we finished setting up. Staying at Elms Inn these days. Living on coffee and doughnuts and doughnuts and coffee. Bought our own tuna today so we could have a change of diet. Roddy filched 25¢ from me and with 10¢ he got God knows where a filthy pipe.

July 14. Another girls' camp. Blackberry flummery for dessert! Diet table next to us for "fats." This camp has three directors who spend their time directing each other. Saw some Kineo people in the ice-cream parlor in Bridgton after the show. $25.

July 15. Camp Kingswood, Me. . . . Electric lights, thank God! Swell performance. $25.

July 17. Biddeford Pool. Worst place yet for setting up. Show best of any yet. Eating at Walsh's roadside stand. Catsup bottle fell on the floor. We asked "Did it explode?" Mrs. Walsh herself, I guess, replied "Lord no! This ain't New Joisey!" (It seems that during our retirement into New England there were some big explosions there.) $37.50

July 18. Old Orchard Beach. Served us right for playing here on the Lord's Day. One lady with five kids put in a dollar bill and took out 90¢ in change. There were even eleven pennies. About 400 present—take, $20.01!

July 19. Sparhawk Hall, Ogunquit. Wonderful audience and wonderful place to play in. $75.75.

July 26. Gloucester. Lunched at Romany Marie's. Met her husband, Dr. Marchand, who shouted, when he knew who we were, "Are you those guys? Jesus Christ!"

July 29. Dennis. Drove all night from Boston. Arrive about 6:30, cold and hungry. $28.25.

July 30. Mataquason. Nice crowd of nice people. One woman said "Better than Sarg's." One woman always does.

July 31. Wood's Hole. Capacity house. Roddy sold tickets noon and night in the mess hall. 190 people, real ones. $95.

August 3. Bought a bathing suit and tried to get burned.

August 4. (On the Cape) Tippy table nearly upset with pups. New York boat passing through the canal drew the audience to the windows during Tina's dance. Swam in ocean and got badly burned. Bless God. $21.

August 17. Drove to Brewster in terrific rain storm. Front wheels began to wobble, engine choked and nearly died, we got soaked and that was all till a flat tire followed a little later. Fixed up our wobble in Danbury. Set up in Stockbridge in hotel full of antiques, mainly pitchers and vases. Scared to death to move suddenly without looking up, down and around. $38.

August 22. Had five blowouts getting to Lennox.

August 25. Hotel invited us to dinner, but put us way off in the corner with a plate of dog biscuits on the table. $38.

August 26. Hazlehurst. Lady saw us at Fort William Henry and got us to play at her home tonight. Roddy asked $50 and she never batted an eye. Set up in parlor and didn't dare tack anything so we had an awful time with curtains. Family went off to dinner in their motor boat leaving us with the servants, who congregated and we gave a show for them. Cook brought us lunch. Everyone nice to us.

August 30. Bretton Woods, N.H. We took morning train up Mt. Washington, one cog at a time. After hours of cog-itation reached a windy top. So windy we could hardly stand up. Got sandwich at Mountain House which broke us. Blew our steamy breaths a few snorts and descended. Luxurious black cloud prevented our seeing anything. Humph! Call that a view!

September 6. Sugar Hill. Drove to Robert Frost's, who knows Forman. Robert

not up, so we built fire for Mrs. Frost and waited. Showed him the puppets.
Edward Davidson there too.

On my departure for Europe, late in August, they arrived, I
remember, in New York after an all-night ride from Boston, and
for a day we were together, planning, talking, plotting. Already it
was decided by Roddy that the following summer the three of us
would take a better managed tour of the same territory. The
possibility seemed to me infinitely remote, for between it and this
hot August night in the hotel room, rumbling with the traffic of
Times Square, was a year of unpredictable happenings, a year in
which I might write a novel or a book of verse or a narrative poem
that would make my participation in such a scheme childish and
ridiculous. Roddy and Harry, perhaps, knew better. At any rate
they were sure it would be as they said, and the fact that it was,
justified their belief.

The ensuing year was a busier one for them and a fuller one
for me. For them it meant increased responsibility in their work
in the department, which permitted less time for puppets. For me
it meant new sights, new contacts, new experiences—a new and
totally enchanting world. Their letters told me of all their doings
and their plannings. Mine, I know, were full of the joy of my life
and the desire that they might share it. Harry became "prop man"
in the newly completed Yale Theater. Here he was in his element, with an endless list of things to make and an endless supply
of tools and materials to make them with. Small wonder, too,
that the puppets, multiplying with a fecundity remarkable in
creatures of wood and wire, began to crowd out the properties, as
papier-mâché heads became almost as much in evidence as
papier-mâché fruits and bushes and balustrades. Small wonder,
finally, that the ever alert pince-nez astride the nose of "G. P."
communicated to him that strange things were afoot, that Lilliputia was invading New Haven and setting up headquarters in
the drama workshop, with the result that the small intruders were
summarily banished to The Kennel, where they were visited and
condoled with by such dissenters in the folds of the drama as
stood loyally for Lilliputia. For Harry and Roddy, then, and

various ones of their fellow students who helped them out now and again, the propaganda went steadily on and plans persisted and matured for a summer tour.

For me too, as spring came questing into Florence shy and curious, growing bolder each day until at last it was in every cranny and runnel and cobbled stone, the plan for a summer of New England vagabonding became more and more acceptable. My carefully garnered funds were running low. There would still be enough for a few weeks in northern Italy and Bavaria and an April in Paris, and then I must go back to America. Through all my stay in Europe, wherever I went, if there was a puppet show to be seen I sought it out: a Punch and Judy booth at St. Giles's Fair in Oxford; Guignol in the Tuilleries and the Bois de Boulogne and again in Nice; Orlando in Naples; Kasperl in Munich. And my pleasure in all of them assured me repeatedly that I had not renounced The Puppet so completely as I thought.

7.

Our reunion in The Kennel was a happy one. Neither Harry or Roddy expected me, as I had sailed a week earlier than I had planned, and they were in the midst of a production at the theatre. In spite of their sixteen-hour days of sewing and painting and hammering there was yet time for a welcome-home party, and the retailing of plans for the summer. These were somewhat more ostentatious than they had been the previous year, and a good many bookings had already been made. The tour, as planned, called for a double circuit of shore and mountains. We were to start in the vicinity of New Haven and work our way northward along the Atlantic coast to Maine. Thence we would go west by way of the White and Green Mountains to the Adirondacks, thence south and east to the Berkshires, thence south once more to Long Island Sound. Then we would cover the entire circuit a second time.

Since it was not yet May, and our opening was scheduled for June 30th, I had a month in Michigan before returning East to help get the show ready for the summer tour. When I returned I found the anticipated turmoil. I wish I could do justice to the days that immediately precede the opening of a new puppet production. There seems, at first, ample time, and things progress nicely. Then, suddenly, the time is nearly gone, and one is surrounded by puppets half-finished and in various states of undress; one is buried beneath an ever-increasing pile of shavings and string and sawdust and gay rags that seem to multiply as one watches them. Needles disappear, scissors hide away in the most unexpected places; tacks are found in the fake hair, and glue in the feathers; tools can never be found; and then it all mounts increasingly to the consciousness of the dismaying shortness of time, and the attempt, while fingers stick and mouth is full of nails, to remember the lines of the new play and the cues for curtains and lights. There are rehearsals in which the Chinese princess, because she is not yet costumed, must be played by Topsy, and the Mandarin, her father, because he has not yet been strung up, by Bottom, or Wall, or Pierrot, or even the soulful fiddler, violin in hand. And, more than all, funds that seemed ample run low and one must bargain where one would rather demand, and eat bread and butter amid the chaos of the workshop when one would rather put on a clean shirt and dine at the corner restaurant.

The complications of this show were considerable, as two new plays were involved. We were persisting in the revue idea, as it provided a varied program—one which was easily adaptable, by addition or omission, to any occasion. So we carried four short plays and a number of divertissements, new and old. Two of the plays were mine. "Weather" we had done with success in Michigan. Based on the idea in one of Aesop's fables, it concerned Mr. Sunny, a brick-maker, despondent over a prolonged period of rain, and Mr. Rainy, an umbrella-maker whose business flourished. All ended happily when, after a pitched battle, they decided to cooperate. It was a play that appealed to both children and grown-ups, and is still being done here and there by amateur puppet companies. The other play, "The Lavender Elephant," had Japan for its setting, and, invoking as it did a trick and a surprise, it always could be depended on.

Two new plays were the work of one of the drama school students, Grace Dorcas Ruthenberg. Both were written in verse, and both were fantastic. "The Gooseberry Mandarin" was, in a way, a small melodrama in which a willow tree, dying for the sake of a princess, was the pathos-provoking character. We attempted the play with some qualms as to its success, for it was a new genre for us, and one which required a treatment very different from our noisier and more masculine material. Harry, however, did a beautiful job technically. The puppets were fragile and charming, the willow tree a masterpiece, and the

setting archaic and lovely. The pains we took with its production
were amply rewarded, for it became one of our most popular
pieces. To me fell the disquieting task of playing both the princess
and the willow tree since I could manage a falsetto for the one,
and my normal voice was adjudged best suited to the other. In
consequence I held long dialogues with myself, most of which
went well enough, though on one occasion I recall doing the
princess in a baritone and the tree in soprano, flusterd by the
giggles of an otherwise dignified lady who had chosen to sit on a
pillow directly in front of our stage where she could gaze discon-
certingly not only at the show but at our own frantic maneu-
verings as well. The second play, "The Poetic Whale," took the
Jonah story, and by making the chief actors not Jonah and his
sailor associates, but the dyspeptic and literary whale who swallowed him, and his worrying and slightly shrewish wife, gave it a
delightful and verbally diverting novelty.

So much for the plays. They required a good deal of painstak-
ing work and rehearsal, but what caused us most trouble was the
orchestra. This orchestra was the realization of Harry's long-
cherished ambition. "Symphony," he called it, and while it
scarcely merited so expansive a denomination, it was, as puppet
orchestras went, something remarkable. There were twenty-two
musicians, arranged in flanks and banks, without too careful
regard to position as to which musician was playing which in-
strument. They were, when completed, a temperamental-
looking crew, featuring bushy hair of all the shades available in
the make-up department. And they needed twenty-two dress
suits. We sliced and cut and cussed and folded and swore and cut
again, and were finally discovered in a state approaching hysteria
by the mother of one of our New Haven friends, who, taking pity
on us, took the twenty-two coats home and in some miraculous
fashion returned them two days later, trig and correct.

We were still assembling the show, I remember, on the morning of June 30th. Boxes had to be built for the orchestra, and to
me, least fitted of the three, the task fell. How I ever got them
together I do not know, but I did. In the meantime Harry and
Roddy were applying red lacquer to the new Ford station wagon

we had acquired—this time a Model A. At three o'clock, tired and hating the sight of one another, we were ready to start. We arrived in Litchfield and set up our stage. We should have rehearsed, but we were too utterly weary to do more than lie on the floor back-stage and pray for show time. Show time came, the audience was delighted, and we knew that, with a bit of smoothing, we had a good show.

We returned to New Haven after the show, and in the early morning, amid the litter and confusion, fell, still dressed, into unmade beds to sleep till the alarm clock awakened us such a very few hours later. Harry's diary for the ensuing day reads: "Spent all forenoon shoveling the apartment into the alley." And that, literally, is what we did. A few utensils and dishes were saved for friends who were returning to school in the fall. The rest was "shoveled into the alley." That night at one of the shore clubs was pleasant enough and remunerative enough to fortify us for our third engagement—an insane asylum. We took it because we needed the money, and they would pay $50. It was a singular experience. The huge bare hall was filled with the dull disconcerting faces of the inmates. Their applause, though quite beyond prediction and not always justified, was hearty. One poor soul who sat in the front row kept shouting with witless insistence at intervals of a few minutes, "I'm Mooney, I'm the one!" The hit of the show was the banana which the willow tree bore for the princess' father at the climax of "The Gooseberry Mandarin." This moment, the most moving in the fragile little tragedy, they greeted with shrieks and guffaws, and our initiation, we all felt, was complete.

To retell in detail the whole round of the summer would be wearisome and unneccessary. It was like the summers in Michigan save that the country was different and there were more people to entertain. Our routine was much the same, though more arduous, for the fact that the resort colonies were larger made the task of billing them more difficult. Bookings were easy. There were, during the entire summer, only eleven open dates, including Sundays, and it was fortunate the resorts were so close together, for it enabled us to play York Harbor, say, in the evening and to bill Ogunquit and "poster" Kennebunkport in the forenoon. It was a summer of hard work, and a most profitable one, varied and provocative as to experience and happy in coop- eration. For the three of us made a good team and a congenial one. Harry and Roddy came, sometimes, to perilous ground when they differed on matters of program or policy, but demands on all of us were so great that little time was left for dissension.

Out of these kaleidoscopic months a few moments, a few incidents, project themselves with particular brightness. Galli, our burlesque prima donna, sang Tosti's "Goodbye" in a Gloucester hotel to shrieks of laughter. After the performance a stern-eyed young lady demanded, in a tone implying more than casual curiosity, "Your opera singer—she's not supposed to be Mme. Homer, is she?"

I assured her to the contrary.

"I'm glad," she replied. "Louise Homer is my mother."

From New Haven comes a quotation from the diary: "Many people enthusiastic over tonight's show, including Isabel Wilder's brother. What a nice guy!" It was, of course, before *The Bridge of San Luis Rey.*

In Maine, a flat tire on the edge of the village. A gentleman with a walking-stick came by and stopped, asking many questions about us—our destination, our plans, our success, our methods of billing. When he left he gave me his card. It read "Daniel Frohman."

There was the rambling white hotel in the Berkshires which, when we arrived, showed a dismaying lack of patronage. A few old ladies, shawled in lavender scarves, rocked on the veranda, and we assumed, this being a collection date, that we were in for it. As we set up our stage in the late afternoon, however, two or three of the ladies we had observed rocking on the porch, ap- proached, questioned us and departed. That night they all turned out, perhaps forty of them, looking like forty sisters, and with them were a number of husbands who had been golfing or nap- ping or watching ticker tape during the afternoon, and pinned to every prim bosom and in every correct lapel was a rosette of Yale blue ribbon in our honor. Dollar bills were the rule, and their interest continued, not only throughout the performance, but afterwards, through the process of tearing down our stage, packing our puppets, helping with buckles and even with loading our station wagon. As we were about to start away, one of the primmest and laciest of the old ladies called crisply: "Young man! Puppeteer!" I went back to the veranda. She leaned carefully, like a fragile puppet herself, over the railing. "Young man," she said, "you have had, I want you to know, fourteen millionaires helping you pack tonight. I wish you good luck. Goodnight!" With a gallantry suggested, no doubt, by my inferior position, as she extended her small gnarled hand, I kissed her finger tips and hurried off, conscious for once in my lifetime of having done exactly the right thing.

There was Bar Harbor. We played at an exclusive hotel to a few guests who wandered idly in after dinner, and, amused, stayed to the end. One lady among them separated herself from the others after the show, and approached. "Your performance is charming," she said, "but it deserves much better patronage. Why don't you let me arrange a matinee for you at the Building of Arts? You'll want a list of patronesses. I'll start them off, and write a note to the others you must see. I'm Mrs. Anthony Biddle."

She was as good as her word, and next day, armed with her letter, we set forth in our red wagon to call on Mrs. Atwater Kent, Mrs. John D. Rockefeller, Jr., Mrs. Edsel Ford, Mrs. Stotesbury, and a dozen others. We swept majestically past hallooing and protesting gardeners and gatekeepers, through imposing gateways and up flower-lined drives. We ran the gauntlet of Muriel McCormick's police dogs and faced the shocked dismay of Mrs. Kent's butler, knee-breeched, white-stockinged, plum-coated, snowy-wigged. We conquered our amazement at two-dollar seats and twenty-dollar boxes, and behaved, we believed, as though this were the customary thing.

Other engagements intervened, but at last the matinee day came, clear and perfect. We set up our stage and waited, nervous and important. At two o'clock the two special police arrived who, we were told, were always on hand at such events. At two-thirty, hidden in the bushes flanking the classic sides of the auditorium, we saw the first limousine arrive. "Hispano-Suiza!" Harry hissed. Another three minutes, and another impressive crunching of gravel. "Rolls Royce!" said I. Now they came in rapid succession, and, hardly able to credit such good fortune and such singular importance to our small entertainment, we hugged each other ecstatically, and on hands and knees scuttled back to the stage door.

The performance started with the puppet orchestra performing a recording of the Second Hungarian Rhapsody, made by the New York Symphony, Walter Damrosch conducting. Its bravura passages, its melodramatic shifts of tempo, made it a perfect vehicle for puppets. Halfway through the piece a masculine voice, surely from the front row, shouted "Faster!" Harry obligingly made the small conductor agitate even more wildly his flying arms, his bobbing head, his gesticulating baton. A gust of laughter, reassuring and friendly, swept up to us through the bright aperture of the stage. "O.K., boys!" whispered Harry.

An hour later the curtains swung together on the dying willow tree. There was the usual flurry of applause. I stepped through the curtains to deliver my usual invitation to the audience to come back stage if they cared to do so. A beaming florid face, topped with snow-white hair, in the very middle of the front row, looked familiar. Recognizing it suddenly, I brought my speech to a halting end and plunged back through the curtains. "Ssst! It's Walter Damrosch!"

Another memorable occasion, though for quite different reasons, came a few days later in the White Mountains. We had made our headquarters for a few days in the house of a Whitefield woman who "took in boarders." Her house, on the edge of the village, was clean and comfortable, and our two connecting rooms were adequate. Our landlady was large, slightly deaf, and possessed of an expansive sense of humor and a tendency to asthma. These two characteristics in combination produced a frequent and disconcerting result—a laugh which was of such unfeminine and Gargantuan proportions that it set her whole fat body shaking, and yet issued forth as if squeezed through layers of resisting flesh in a series of steamy wheezes. Her husband, small and wizened, was as taciturn as she was merry.

We left her for a weekend jaunt through the mountains, planning to return on Monday, and requesting that she hold our rooms for us. Sunday night found us in Dixville Notch, with our pockets well lined with the returns from a series of engagements, and overhead a sky so clear and so star-encrusted as to set the towering balsams in steepled silhouette against it. "Let's drive down tonight," suggested Harry. It was only sixty miles, and the highway was good, so we went. We had hardly started when we observed that the sky was more luminous than stars could ever make it. An aurora borealis of such brilliance as none of us had ever seen was waving ragged streamers of pale green and lavender far into the sky. Pulsating, shifting, they mounted on every side, converging overhead. It was awe-inspiring, and our drive was punctuated by stop after stop as we all climbed out, shivering, to crane our necks skyward and marvel. It was, consequently, after one o'clock when we reached Whitefield. The house was dark. We knocked furtively, and then, since there was no answer, more

Our heroes at Whitefield, N.H. (1928).

insistently. A light flickered on and after several minutes the door opened and we were greeted by our landlord, looking less friendly than ever in a long striped flannel nightshirt, his toes curling from contact with the cold hall floor. "We rented your rooms, boys. Didn't think you'd be back till tomorrow." He was apologetic but annoyed, and about to close the door when there was a creaking behind him of a bedstead, and a solid thumping across the floor. It was the landlady. "I'm awful sorry boys," she wheezed. "I tell you! pa and me is sleeping in the sitting room, but there's a screen, and if you want to set up you can. I don't know where else you could get in this time of night."

We didn't either, so in we trooped. We were cold, and the haircloth furniture offered no very enticing prospect for a night's rest. However, as the lights went off and the bed behind the screen creaked alarmingly, the funny side of the situation struck Harry. He suddenly exploded in a snort of laughter, which, because he tried to stifle it, sounded the more surprising. It startled Roddy and then me, and then—unforeseen effect—Mrs. Houck. She wheezed three times, steamily. The bed shook and her husband whispered testily, "Oh, shut up, Emily!" All was quiet for perhaps a minute when another snicker tore through the silence like a pair of dull scissors through a sugar sack. It was all over then. Every snicker of ours, no matter how repressed, brought an answering series of spongy wheezes from behind the screen, till there was nothing to do but guffaw loud and long. Mr. Houck, scrawny and pathetic and blinking, peered around the screen and testily announced that maybe he could find us "somethin' to lay on." He returned, shivering, with the pad from a porch swing, and, pushing back the marble-topped table, spread it on the floor with a resentful bang. We regarded it with suspicion. All of us had our overcoats on, our caps and our gloves, and the mathematical division of that narrow pad into three spaces on which we might rest ourselves thus arrayed was, at that moment, beyond us. We did our best, however, with much shoving, pushing, whispered directions, knees in chins, fists in eyes, arms and legs cramped in strange contortions. It did nothing to allay our mirth, and by the time we were all quieted down it was well after two. All went well for ten minutes. "Godfreys!" breathed Roddy, straightening his leg and rolling us both on the floor, "I've got a cramp in my leg!" This called forth not only a scramble from us but a renewed spasm of tremors and pneumatic explosions from behind the screen.

We gave it up then, and went out on the front porch, where we sat watching the airy banners of the northern lights, fascinated in spite of our weariness until the dawn, steel-blue, dispersed them. At five-thirty we saw smoke from the lunch room down the street, and went down, dawdling over our coffee until after seven. The occupants of our rooms were gone. Mrs. Houck, still mirthful, was remaking the beds. We fell into them as soon as she had lumbered out, and slept till afternoon.

There were memorable personalities, too, during the summer—an afternoon spent with John Cotton Dana, humorous, scholarly, quizzical—with introductions to his Pheidippides, his wheel-barrow, to his specially contrived cat-holes for pet cats, to his amusing "Grecian" urn, which turned out to be an old Vermont churn, carefully painted in the archaic Greek style with figures whose peculiar antics became apparent only on close examination, to his Japanese prints, to his bird refuge, to his garden wall which confronted one with the oriental precept "If thou hast two loaves of bread, sell one and buy thyself a lily."

There were pleasant hours in the pine-circled cottage of Robert Frost, listening to his dry yet vibrant voice in anecdote after anecdote concerning his contemporaries, interlarded with shrewd aesthetic maxims so simply expressed that one only realized later that they formed the backbone of his own starkly humorous poems.

There was a private performance one night in Kennebunkport at the home of Booth Tarkington, with the wise and gracious novelist, guided deftly by his wife, holding a lantern in the garden while we stowed away our bags and cases, and waving us Godspeed with it, a tall, thin figure showing dim behind the arc of swaying light.

And there were other people equally interesting, if less well-known. I think at once of a librarian in the Berkshires who told us tales of the summer colony and the townspeople until our lunch-time had stretched to such an extent that we were nearly late for our matinee. I recall a dark road on a dark night when we, after a successful performance, were returning to our base with a con-siderable sum of money in our pockets, and the fright we were given by coming suddenly upon a car in the middle of the road, and a man waving us to a stop with his flashlight. I visioned a robbery. "How about a little gas?" said the voice of the signaler. "I can siphon it out." He did so. "Let me pay you," he said. "Oh, don't bother," said Roddy blithely. "We've got lots of money—had a good night tonight." He was an honest man. There was a Gloucester fisherman who in return for tickets for his two young-sters, took us sailing with breath-taking skill in an exchange which seemed to us grossly unjust to him. There was the Boston lady who thought our version of the Jonah story unforgivably blasphemous. And there was, to climax the summer, Mrs. H————, in whose music room we played to a suburban garden club, who had eight footmen in scarlet livery, and who, we were told, during the war lodged complaint with the govern-ment because of her inability to secure eight six-foot footmen who "matched"; Mrs. H————, living quite alone in her forty luxurious rooms with her thirty or more servants.

It was, in all, a summer rich and varied and kaleidoscopic. It ended rather late, and we took each his separate way—Roddy to an operation and a quest of health in Texas, I to Michigan to fill a vacancy in the English department, and Harry to his long-anticipated trip to Europe.

8.

In spite of the fact that the following winter saw us so widely scattered, and the puppets, our faithful wooden artists, stored once more in trunks, heel to head, toe to chin, and stacked, with an unfeeling disregard for their record as troupers, in a New Haven garage—in spite of all this the torch was carried on. Only I was the apostate and turncoat. Teaching in Ann Arbor was infinitely more congenial than it had been in the South, but it took only one semester to convince me that, pleasant as life was in the town I loved so much, the flavor, the bouquet of life was gone. Too, I missed my partners, and had always with me the martyred, mildly zealous feeling of the stay-at-home.

Roddy's lot was less pleasant than mine. Sinus operations, a futile trip to Rochester, Minnesota, another to Battle Creek, and finally, desperately, to San Antonio. There, nearly out of funds, he concocted a one-man puppet show and sold it to several schools. He pawned his clothes. He wrote three stories, and sold them, and his modesty has never permitted him to tell us more than this meager outline of his winter. Puppets, however, were a vital part of it.

Harry, long eager to visit Europe, and more than ever fired with the idea of a grand tour of the Continental puppet theaters by my own sketchy reports of what I had seen the year before, set off—and the burden of the story during these months is certainly his. He visited the puppet theaters that every tourist sees—in Palermo, in Salzburg, in Munich, but he also sought out a great many that are not familiar—tiny theaters hidden away in quarters of cities never visited by sight-seers—theaters, some of them, with a century or more of tradition behind them, still playing, despite the more glamorous cinema a few doors away, to eager crowds of men and boys. To one who had dreamed of the possibility of an American puppet theatre some time, all these places, no matter how crude or how primitive, were sources of live and eager interest. And since they all provided background for the ultimate realization of his dream, a few of them, at least, deserve description in this chronicle.

Naples—and only two blocks from the railroad station a marionette theater. It seemed too auspicious a beginning to be true, but there it was, its grimy façade displaying large and lurid posters, hand-painted by some bloodthirsty artist with gay spectacles of decapitated knights and scimitar-brandishing Saracens. And the lettering proclaimed it to be really a marionette theater: TEATRO CENTRALE—MARIONETTI. One lira admitted him to the crowded auditorium. It seated perhaps two hundred men and boys in parallel benches and in a horseshoe balcony so low that one must be careful, if he was not a Neopolitan, not to crack his head smartly against it when he rose from his bench. The air was blue and acrid with smoke, but through it one could see the dimly lighted stage, and it prevented not at all the surprising clatter of armor, and the thunderous barrage of rolling Italian periods to sweep against one's eardrums in an exciting surf of sound. Knights in full armor swung onto the stage, with no regard for Newtonian laws; they slapped and jabbed and prodded wildly, their every thrust accompanied by the thump of the puppeteer's foot back-stage. Hands—the human hands of the operators—appeared gigantically and unexpectedly, and disappeared again. Puppets leaned and lurched and flew through space, and, occasionally, at some particularly horrendous climax, a canvas curtain—on which was depicted a Georgian couple on a balcony in the light of a livid moon—would clump to the floor with the finality of fate, only to roll up again for the bowings of small, dark-haired puppeteers. This was not Harry's dream, certainly, yet it had a vitality and a picturesqueness one could not deny.

By next day Harry had located a second theater in Naples— one that seemed even older than the first, and had by dint of

many references to his pocket dictionary, persuaded the proprietor to let him back-stage during a performance. He was placed
precariously on a rickety chair in the wings, from which his feet
protruded onto the stage, but he was volubly assured that that
would be quite all right. He saw here what he had known from
the previous performance he must see. In the faint glow of two
twenty-five watt bulbs, which provided all the lighting effects the
stage boasted, the sweating puppeteer swung the heavy armored
figures on and off the stage with, apparently, the more clatter the
better. They varied in age, these puppeteers, from sixteen to
seventy, and they had in their work all the jealous pride of the
fanatical showman. The puppets bumped and rattled; the florid
Italian sentences flowed on; the creaking crudely painted drops
squealed up and down on antiquated rollers; two small boys,
squatting Arab-fashion in the opposite wings, smoking, suddenly
began fighting, and rolled onto the stage, to be booed by the
audience and reprimanded by the padrone. It was all strange, and
seemingly interminable, but it ended at last, and the puppeteers
gathered around him, eager for praise and voluble in gratitude for
the condescension this American visitor had shown in watching
the actual workings of their performance.

Later there was a similar experience in Palermo, with
marionettes shinier and productions more elaborate, because,
unlike the Neapolitan theaters which are hidden away in poor
parts of the city, and difficult of access to tourists, these Sicilian
theaters (one on the immediate water front) had become conscious of their ·picturesqueness, and catered largely to tourist
trade. One feature of these Palermo theaters, however, he found
particularly amusing. Each was equipped with a hurdy-gurdy—
the smaller theater with a battered and decrepit example of its
breed, wheezy and discordant, the more splendid theater with a
perfect masterpiece of a hurdy-gurdy, gilded and equipped with
bell attachments. Both, however, were turned continuously by
small boys, sweating and persistent, who keyed the velocity of
their grinding to the emotional tension displayed on the stage.
"Valencia" seemed to be the favorite tune. If the scene were
romantic or sad, it issued forth slowly and steamily, while if a

battle occurred, it blared forth presto, prestissimo, with an impetuosity that shook the walls.

In Rome Harry had hoped to find Podrecca's famed Teatro dei Piccoli, but they were on tour, and in this Italian capital not one marionette theater was to be found. True, in a corner of the vast Pincian gardens was a small Guignol show for children, but it was too like the ones of Paris to be of any fresh interest. Florence, too, was devoid of puppet shows. There were, to be sure, puppets, but they were hanging limp and lifeless in a dim and dusty corner of a Via Romana antique shop, just as they had hung the year before when I admired them, and had hung for I do not know how many years before. I had admired them, but Harry coveted them, and they were worthy objects for his enthusiasm. Twelve figures there were, straight out of the eighteenth century, and in a remarkable state of preservation. They had been used, it was thought, as a sort of puppet stock company for performing the comedies of Carlo Goldoni, probably in the home of some wealthy Florentine. There were nine male characters, all of the Guignol type (operated over the hand and fingers, like a glove), representing the stock figures of the Italian comedy—the Arlecchino, Brighella, the Capitano Spavento, the lord, the servant, the priest, the Moor, etc. The three women characters were differently contrived. Their bodies were carefully modeled and mounted on bamboo rods. Strings attached to each arm ran down through the body, and when pulled, raised and lowered the arms. The heads were mounted on a spring arrangement that gave them a surprisingly lifelike appearance. All twelve were exquisitely modeled, and costumed in brocades and laces, with tiny gloves, infinitesimal buttons, kercheifs, tiny swords, and all the accouterments of that foppish century. They were, considering their age and rarity, ridiculously cheap, for while not unique (there is a similar and slightly older set in the museum of Naples and one in Venice) they were extremely choice. A deposit held them, and the following season the proceeds from several engagements paid the balance. They were for many years one of our most prized possessions, and they are now in an American museum.

The businesslike Milanese, so surprisingly like Americans in appearance and manner, seemed to have little interest in or information about puppet theaters, and Harry was about to give up and go to the Scala when he stumbled, quite by chance, on the Teatro Gerolamo, only a few blocks back of the Duomo. Teatro Gerolamo, though giving no indication of great prosperity, still retained an air. It was like an impoverished old actor who still manages to achieve, though perhaps pitifully, a certain grand manner. The theater, seating perhaps two hundred-fifty people, was an opera house in miniature, boasting three horse-shoe galleries, dull now and shabby. Two tiers of boxes directly adjoined the stage, the proscenium of which had once been gay with nymphs and gilt paint, in the best baroque style, but was now really only a sooty frame from which the winged nymphs seemed to peer like soiled and disconsolate angels.

The performance as well as the theater seemed drab and old. The puppets, about twenty-eight inches tall, were shabby and badly lighted. Here was no Orlando and no clanging armor, but a vaudeville performance, with short sketches involving pantomimic representations of the trials and tribulations of Pierrot. The grand finale, a set depicting a lurid Bay of Naples, with four canvas ground rows depicting waves shoved from side to side across the stage, was so crude and so unconsciously caustic a comment on much of Italian stagecraft of the time that it was genuinely amusing.

It was in Turin, however, that the grandest of Italian puppet theaters was found—a theater designed to turn puppeteers the world over green with envy. It was, again, an opera house in miniature, with three horseshoe balconies and a gallery bright with gold and fluttery with angels—theater to the last impertinent dimple on the tiniest cupid's knee. There was a six-piece orchestra, and the show itself was one of those incredible marvels of mechanics that makes one wonder "What next?" In sober retrospect one could realize with chagrin that it was simply a skillful synthesis of hokum and trickery, but at the moment it held one with an almost breathless amazement. Ballet dancers twinkled their toes, aeroplanes roared across the stage, automobiles collided, cycloramas rolled past galloping donkeys pulling cartloads

of peasants, military parades marched smartly while puppet spectators in sidewalk cafes waved flags and applauded. And the audience applauded too, Harry loudest of all, for here was color,
glamour, mechanical skill, showmanship, something tangible to
which, with such personal reservations as he might care to make,
one could aspire.

Italy provided one more interesting puppet experience. The
Podreccas, as we have said, were on tour in Germany, but the
Yambos were touring Italy, and, as luck would have it, were
playing at Vigevano, a small city not far distant, on the next night
after Harry's visit to Milan. He took the first train, and his diary
must tell the rest:

I was about to enter the station with thirty or more passengers when two gen-
darmes picked me out of the whole mob and bade me wait. At least I gathered
that much from their stentorian voices. I waited and was meanwhile furnishing
amusement, evidently, for the station gang and the people on the train. After
vainly trying to guess what the officials wanted I produced my passport, which
busied them for several minutes. I discovered soon that they couldn't read very
well. Then I produced my letter of introduction to one of the members of the
Yambo company, and after studying the address for a few minutes he deigned to
read my letter. Then to further assure him I showed him my notebook wherein
is written my purpose in Italy, etc. Now a third officer has arrived and they agree
mutually to convey me somewhere. Instead of going through the gates where
have just passed the common herd, they lead me through another door into
what is apparently *their* office, and carefully unlock the door from which we all
emerge on the court towards the town. I repeated several times, "Carrozza"
(carriage), but evidently the one carrozza had left the station with some luckier
mortal, so a policeman was detailed to lead me down the street to I don't know
where.

I feared it was the jail, so at intervals as we passed the flare of advertisments
for Yambo, I'd call his attention to them and smile, hoping to determine his
intent. He was waxen. I tried a new phrase on him (I learned it today): "Fa
freddo" (it's cold). Evidently he was satisfied with the weather. We passed a
beautiful old palace on a square. He now spoke and said "Bel piazza." I agreed,
naturally, for it was pretty. I wondered if he was being ironical or anything. He
stopped to chat with a man for a few minutes, and then I was sure I was going to
jail because he was so playing with my important time. We continued, after the
potato crop was settled, and soon a building flamboyant with Yambo posters
appeared, and his highness took his leave after refusing a ten-lira piece. Mussolini must be on the trail. I found the mistress back stage, and she spoke very little

French, and that poorly, but she did dig into trunks and boxes and give me bills, circulars, etc. She showed me about the stage, an enormous affair with puppets hanging everywhere. She said they have 415 puppets in the company. Puppets quite large, nearly three feet, but not especially pretty. One man got on bridge and operated a puppet for me. Went with company to dinner and made arrangements to return Friday to see a show, also one on Saturday and possibly two on Sunday, as they change show every day, which is beyond me! Only small town, about 15,000. It must be the music that draws the houses. After lunch I was accompanied back to station to avoid further molestation by police and I further protected myself by getting a letter from the manager to the effect that I was returning in two days to stay the weekend. What a universe!

Later—after Milan:

Today I got off the train and the policeman greeted me with a smile. Dined with the contralto of the troupe and was soon joined by others. I was conducted to a seat in the orchestra by the directress. All these theaters must be patterns of the Scala, only most of the patterns lost their edges before the suits were made. Three circular balconies and gallery over all. Across orchestra pit extends red canopy bearing name YAMBO. This screen, I was told, hides both singers and orchestra. Back-stage again. Nearly all figures have moveable mouths. The puppets are terribly worn and, in some cases, colorless. Again, terribly rickety and antiquated lighting equipment. Here they actually use two ten-gallon-or-more water dimmers. Switches on light-board loose, single-pole, and very unsafe. I can see a New York inspector undoing in ten seconds what they have spent years building up. And they wish very much to come to America. I have been plied with a thousand questions about hiring singers in New York who can sing Italian, about actors to read lines, about wages, etc. Till now I have been rather optimistic with them, broadcasting the idea that we Americans are great opera lovers, but now that I have seen the crudities back-stage, the rickety packing arrangements, inadequate and dangerous lighting equipment, I begin to be conscience-stricken. I am seated back-stage. Curtain rises revealing maroon velvet marionette curtain and badly arranged curtain devices. Today I mentioned that the Teatro dei Piccoli had been in America. The directress said; "There are only two companies, Piccoli and Yambo." At least she shares honors with another.

There were other theaters, old and musty, new and bright, some dull and pathetic, but all speaking eloquently of the reality and universality of the appeal of Punch. In Lyons there was the original home of Guignol, that slightly more playful and less violent—in short more Gallic—vesion of Punch, still satirizing pomposity of every sort in a style so pleasing to Frenchmen. In

Germany there were theaters where Kasperl, the German Punch, still played in the charming plays of von Pocci, and still, as his English counterpart in some obscure country fair, hangs the hangman—here in Bavaria, thumbs his nose as Faust, his master, goes hurtling down the murky vastnesses of hell, proving once more the old, old truth that the clown may outplay the wise man, and that laughter may, after all, be the supreme wisdom. There were, too, in Munich the skillful and charming marionette versions of the operas of Mozart and Offenbach, operas in which the excellence of the music and the charm of the production were ample compensation for the lack of action that in any other form of puppet performance would have been inexcusably boring. Prague, too presented a surprise to this American puppeteer in the form of a state-controlled puppet theater under the jurisdiction of the Department of Education—modern, complete in every detail, from its charmingly decorated auditorium to its stage, equipped with the finest of lighting equipment, its fireproof costume and storerooms, its paint shops and rehearsal stages. Here, with the gratis assistance of singers and actors from the state theaters, were presented such examples of classic drama as *The Tempest, A Midsummer Night's Dream,* the comedies of Goldoni and Molière, the operas of Mozart, and native classics—a repertory, in all, of nearly 200 pieces—an institution to marvel at.

Harry also had an unforgettable afternoon in Vienna at the home of that remarkable man, Richard Teschner—mathematician, sculptor, artist in the completest sense of the word, whose puppets have attained, through the genius of his fingers, a liveliness, attenuated and spiritual, that lifts them into a dramatic realm all their own—a realm few puppets can achieve— a realm in which only the most fragilely imaginative plays of a Yeats or a Maeterlinck are adequate material. These figures of Teschner, so far from the tradition of Punch, serve, perhaps more than any puppets in the world, to show how much the soul, the inner and essential individuality of the creator instills itself into his puppets, making them really his own creatures, being really the god of a microcosmic but personal universe.

9.

Spring had brought Roddy back to the North, healthier and happier. He came to Ann Arbor to see me. My future was uncertain. I was not going to teach again, I knew that. And I was still adamant on the puppet project, which would involve another summer of touring. This resolution on my part seems illogical in the face of my dissatisfaction with my lot at the time, but it had a valid explanation. The previous summer, when we stayed for nearly a week in a small rooming-house in Franconia, New Hampshire, there had been a time for exploration. Up a lane which followed the banks of the Gale River (how so brawling and tumultuous a brooklet ever acquired so dignified a name I do not know) I came suddenly to an open meadow, flanked on one side by the fringing trees along the inner bank of the stream and on the other by a steeply mounting hill, thick-grown with pine and balsam, in which the occasional white trunk of a birch, slender and shining, stood like the ghost of a tree not yet in seed. At either end of the meadow was a house and barn. Both were weathered, and both in disrepair. Over the trees along the stream rose Mt. Lafayette and Profile Mountain, the dark groove between filled with puffing clouds. It was so quiet, so deserted, so friendly. I walked out along the disused road, the brook babbling along beside me and the thorns of the berry bushes catching at my sleeve. I met a small boy with very black eyes, and a fat bulldog, and an air-rifle.

"You been up to the Plantation?" he asked.

"Is that what you call it?"

"'Course it is!" His contempt at my ignorance was complete and withering.

The Plantation, it turned out, was for sale, and for a sum so small, when I considered its wooded hill, its brook, its sunny meadow, its peace, that it seemed a thing I could not let go. I drove out to Frost's. Robert came down, and together we tramped over it, pacing out its boundaries, flailing through the thickets for its spring. If Robert Frost said it was a bargain, it was a bargain, and such was his decision.

The deal was closed so near the summer's end that there was no time to do more than bask in the quiet satisfaction of ownership. Fifty acres of land mine! My woods, my meadow, my spring, my tamarack—ideas childish and absurd when we consider the dignity and immortality of trees and earth and water, yet ideas peculiarly gratifying to humankind. And so, all through the winter, compensating me somewhat for the drudgery of teaching, I planned for the rehabilitation of one of the houses—new sills, a new roof, partitions to be removed, a fireplace and chimney to be built, a flower-bed to be planted. The summer would be for that, not for another period of vagabondage with a puppet show. With Roddy, of course, it was different. He struggled as hard against the sedentary as I against the roving way of life. Harry had been strangely silent in his brief notes with their unfamiliar postmarks. For him the present, it seemed, was sufficient. But Roddy knew, of course, that summer would mean a third New England tour, and his mind was busy with tentative routings and advance publicity.

The day of Harry's arrival came, and brought simply a wire: LANDED SAFELY. HOME SOON. HARRY. A day passed, two, three. I was puzzled. Harry's mother worried, and Roddy was in a fever of impatience and supposings. He came, at last, thinner and more self-assured than I had ever seen him. Between unpacking bags full of puppets, posters, soiled shirts and programs, he told us blandly of his plan. The summer show was to consist of two elaborate productions—the finest marionette productions America had ever seen. For who was to design them but Norman Bel Geddes. Our amazement was too great to permit questions, and they were not neccessary, for Harry was so possessed by his idea that it bubbled out like water from a suddenly tapped spring.

The productions he had planned in Europe, bumping his way in third-class carriages from puppet theater to puppet theater. On the boat he had conceived the idea of securing Geddes as designer—and in no wise deterred by his complete lack of funds, he approached the great man. The idea must have pleased him,

HARRY BURNETT'S
MARIONETTES
FORMERLY
THE YALE PUPPETEERS
PRESENT

Hansel & Gretel at 10:30 a.m.--Bluebeard at 8:30 p.m.
Saturday, July 28, 1928
At the Guild Hall, Silvermine
Admission: Adults $1.00   ·   ·   Children $.75

for he agreed to design the two productions complete, sets, puppets, costumes, lighting, for a figure considerably less than his usual fee for designing a legitimate production, and the task certainly involved as much work, if not more. And so it was all settled in Harry's mind. For the first time in America a really fine artist in stagecraft would design a puppet production, and of course it would be an enormous success—who could doubt it?

Arguments followed, of course: the expense, the inadvisability of so ambitious a show for the summer circuit, the difficulties of transportation. Roddy, I know, had his doubts. I certainly had, but as I was not really concerned in the project save for writing the songs and incidental music, my admonitions had little weight. Roddy, won over at last by the glamour of the undertaking and his loyalty to Harry, plunged into plans with all the vigor and enthusiasm he had in such generous quantities. Money was raised—a sum that was dazzling considering our usual budgets of a hundred dollars or so, and the venture was under way. Roddy purchased an antiquated Ford. He had never driven a car. For two or three days he permitted me to give him lessons, and then off he started for New England. Harry returned to New York, where contracts were signed, a studio found on Bank Street, sandwiched in between stables where horses fat and thin peered placidly from second-story windows, whinnied dismally in the middle of the night, and tramped like distant thunder in the gray dawn.

My news was fragmentary indeed. From Harry I almost never heard. From his sister Mary, who was helping out, there was an occasional amused and hurried note. From Roddy letters infrequent, brief, and, I thought, not too pleased with the results of his booking tour. I knew he hated driving, and loathed the car he had bought, but it was not until later that I learned that when it turned turtle in Vermont, he left it in the ditch and never drove again.

When college closed, despite my eagerness to get at my cherished plan of rehabilitating The Plantation, I drove first to New York. The "Descent into the Maelstrom" would do feeble justice to my arrival at Bank Street. With the first engagement, at the far end of Cape Cod, only a few days away, there were more things to be done than could well be done in a month. Harry, working from blueprints, pounded like a demon in the low-ceilinged front room. One interrupted him only with prayers and trembling. In the back room, Mary, surrounded by mountains of colored rags, yarn, crepe hair, braid and ribbons, sewed and fitted and tacked, sketches and color charts propped before her, piles of gangling puppet bodies at her side. Two or three volunteers came in at various times. There was little conversation. Everyone was too preoccupied to talk. The clock went round and round, and its revolutions signified little save the scarcity of time. Somewhere between one and two in the morning and eight, there would be sleep, only half undressed, in a cleared space among the rags and sawdust. Occasionally someone would set aside the glue pot and brew some tea. Someone would run to the delicatessen and return with sandwiches, and there would be the briefest possible intermission for a meal. The grimy windows at the back of the room would grow gray and then black and the nightmare activity would go on. They would grow gray again, and white, and it would make no difference. The piles of scraps and remnants grew steadily, rising like a flood. A puppet would be finished, cramped legs would unbend, and it would be carried to the front room for stringing. But always they would return with another. Harry's capacity for work was appalling. His nervous tension drove him unsparingly. He was haggard and unshaven and short-tempered, and his mass of curls unkempt and long, but his energy made the best efforts of the rest of us seem clumsy, inept and inconsiderable.

Underneath all this tension and drive there was, like the buzz of some persistent, annoying insect, the constant financial worry. The venture was costing double what Harry had planned. Details which he had not foreseen, but which were essential to the production, kept arising, and those essentials he had counted on were costing much more than the sums he had assigned to them. It was all so different from our usual production, in which, if the thing we wanted was too expensive, a makeshift would have to do. All was informal, and somehow we managed. Here every costume, every prop, every piece of scenery had behind it specifications which must be met—blueprints and drawings and color charts which must be followed.

The cast arrived to rehearse, and there was nothing to rehearse except lines, so they set to work pounding, sewing, gluing, while I made a few unhappy attempts to teach them the songs. There were three who, with Harry, were to make up the company. Bob Bromley came from New Haven. He was to be general handy man, to manage the lights and to drive the truck. George Cotton, from one of the New York drama schools, had been chosen because of his voice, which was not only excellent in quality, but remarkably adaptable. The third recruit was a girl, Dorothy Scott. She too came from a drama school, but had had stage experience in several short-lived Broadwy plays. She was very tall, very statuesque, and very handsome. Had she been an opera singer she would have been a perfect Brunhilde. She was truly a magnificent creature, possessed of a voice proportionate to her size, and a sense of humor as expansive. All three plunged into the work as though it were the ultimate aim in life, despite the fact that it must soon have been apparent to them all that the finances of the company were precarious indeed.

Time never seemed to move so relentlessly toward a dreaded day and hour. Bob was sent off, paint smeared and unshaven, with a borrowed three hundred dollars to buy a truck. The understanding with Geddes had been that the whole thing was to fit into a one-ton truck, and so Bob's instructions were to get the best one he could find for the sum given him. It was not his fault that he came back with the most temperamental vehicle that ever set demented tires on the roads of New England. She was roomy, and seemed sturdy and sound. Her eccentricities developed later. For the splendid moment she stood, breathing regularly and reassuringly at the Bank Street curb while all within deserted benches, needles, and glue pots to form an admiring circle around her. Roomy as she was, we all had qualms that she would never hold the two shows, for they seemed already to fill the better part of three rooms. And two days later our qualms were justified, for when the show was carried piece by piece to the sidewalk, and we tried stowing it away in the dim cubical body, a dismaying number of drops, set-pieces, props, and the inevitable impedimenta were left on the sidewalk. We tried again. And again, sweating and profane. At last, in despair, it was agreed that the only thing to do was to strap the back-drops, which were mounted on twelve-foot poles, to the sides of the truck, and to rope as many of the flats as possible on top. This was a decision forced by extremity, for it was obviously ridiculous to expose all this expen-

sively designed scenery, on which the paint was barely dry, to
dust, rain, or whatever tormenting factors chance might direct
upon them.

The truck was a surprising sight. There was no room for personal baggage save in the driver's cab, and little enough there. It
was obvious that another car would be needed for the company,
but just at present, with the first engagment only a day away and
the treasury practically empty, that was unthinkable. Dorothy
volunteered to go by train. Bob, George and Harry squeezed
themselves as best they could. Work and worry and sleepless
nights, fatigue-drugged bodies and taut nerve—and now a difficult drive in a top-heavy truck to an engagement for which no
one was prepared. The truck purred along through the traffic of
the Post Road with disarming steadiness. It was not until they
were well into Connecticut that she choked, sputtered, and died.
She was, with difficulty, revived, and coaxed on to Cape Cod,
but, protesting and coughing, her progress was slower and slower
until, in New Haven, long past midnight, she sighed steamily
and expired. Harry and Bob walked a block to the Green and fell
asleep on park benches. George accommodated his six feet to the
crowded cab of the truck as best he could. Cold and very little
rested, they sought, as soon as there was any sign of life, a garage.
The diagnosis was not promising. Wires had to be sent to the
Cape cancelling the engagement, and to New York to someone
who had not yet contributed, a plea for funds.

If any of the three could have foreseen how disastrous a summer this breakdown foreshadowed I doubt they would have had
the courage to continue. The failure of the venture, from a
financial standpoint was due, of course, to other factors than the
caprices of the truck, but it was these very caprices that began and
augmented a series of events that can only be classed as bad luck.
The truck was christened a week or so later "Camille," because
she broke down in every town, and indeed she had much the
maddening temper of a touring prima donna. She inevitably
collapsed on the outskirts of the village one hoped to enter
grandly, and one was instead towed ignominiously in by the
village repair car. Date after date that Roddy had booked had to

be postponed or abandoned entirely. Managers and sponsors were disgruntled, and still Camille malingered, and there seemed nothing to be done, for every mechanic who had a hand in her repair guaranteed without limitations that he had effected a cure. She was, though, incurable, and at last was abandoned, and a deal made with a trucking company for a truck and driver. The fee was high, but compared with the expense of maintaining Camille, it was modest. It at least involved the expenditure of no large sum at one time.

The show itself, when it achieved its première at Woods Hole was, neccesarily, a ragged thing. There had been in New York not only no time for rehearsals, but not even an opportunity to set up the stage, try out the sets, plan the lighting or shifting of scenes. None of the three new members of the company was an experienced puppeteer, and the burden of the performances fell on Harry. One cannot puppeteer and hold a script at the same time. The efficient operator must be so familiar with his lines that he can devote all his attention, all his ingenuity, to the actual manipulation of his figures. Consequently the first performances were unsatisfactory. To Harry, so tense, so proud always of the perfection of his work, and so conscious now of the importance of the undertaking, they were heart-rending. And there was so little time for rehearsal. The two productions required three hours' strenuous work to unpack and set up, and better than two hours to tear down when the show was over. It was an impossible schedule. The elaborateness of the production was its greatest drawback. From the first, much seemed superfluous, and many of the set-pieces, unavoidably broken through the exigencies of packing, were tossed onto the roadsides, and New England must have been sprinkled with Moorish arches and fountains and columns, and witches' gardens and operatic fences. Mr. Geddes would have writhed at the destruction wrought in his careful designs. He would probably even have prevented their being displayed, but he did not know, and since the fault was in considerable measure his own, the company felt only relief as some other piece was pitched into a daisy patch or a clump of elderberry bushes.

I saw the productions only toward the end of the season, when they were going more smoothly. They seemed to me then, as they still do, pictorially the loveliest settings I have ever seen on a puppet stage. To their creation Geddes had given all the dramatic sense, the color, the feeling that have made his designs for the theater incomparable. They were, however, not puppet sets— they were living-theater sets in miniature. They took into consideration none of the limitations, none of the peculiar demands of the puppet and the puppeteer. They were, in short, impractical, and hence, as designs for a puppet production, bad. The plays, too, were a little heavy, it seemed to me. A little conscious of the burden they were carrying, as if they said "Here is all this splendid scenery. . . . We must try to be worthy of it." The long play which must sustain the interest of the audience for an hour and a half or more is at once a handicap to the puppeteer and a considerable problem for the puppet playwright. For he must have novelty, novelty, novelty; action, action, action; surprise, surprise, surprise. He cannot, like the writer for the theater, build up so strong a sympathy for a character that that character may sit in a chair, like Candida, or on a bench, like Hamlet, and talk. For his character is, after all, only a small wooden figure, relying solely for his dramatic effectiveness on a few basic and simple gestures and such vocal sympathy as his operator is able to project through him. Puppet drama is drama at second hand—the intimate sympathy of the man on the stage and the man in the pit does not exist, and the long play is the supreme test of the puppet-playwright. Such plays, even the best of them, have always seemed to me tedious and constrained, and these two, "Bluebeard" and "Hansel and Gretel," were our last attempts at plays of such length as well as our first.

A word should be said, too, concerning the puppets. They too were carefully made from the Geddes sketches, and they were lovely to look upon, but they were dolls, not puppets. Ariane, archaic and graceful, Bluebeard, fat and irascible, the witch in "Hansel and Gretel" a perfect realization in wood and cloth of everything witchlike. But here again it had been a vast mistake to follow the designs of an artist, fine as he was, who had probably never made a puppet and who knew little or nothing of puppet anatomy. In order, for example, to achieve the stiff and oriental beauty of Ariane, who was nude to the waist, it was neccesary to make her head and body all in one piece. The modeling was exquisite and the figure in repose charming, but when it was required to move about the stage one realized how much the "puppet temper" had been sacrificed by such construction. The "muscles" of the puppet had been paralyzed, and half its charm destroyed.

The season dragged on. The abandonment of Camille eased the situation considerably. There was no more sleeping in firehalls, as the whole company had been forced to do one night in Maine when Camille had made them lose the booking they had counted on to pay the night's lodging. There were no more broken engagements after that, but the whole thing had got off to a bad start. And there were still back-breaking hours of readying the shows and repacking them day after day, a task which seriously hampered the publicity campaign of billing, and this was of vital importance to the success of the venture. But this department had to be given up entirely, entrusted to small boys, or limited solely to a circuit with a Ford touring car on the back of which rested a hurdy-gurdy, which had been found in Boston. Bob, silk-hatted, would turn the crank. Harry would drive, and George and Dorothy would distribute handbills to the gaping spectators. It was a curiosity-provoking sight. The car was painted vivid red. The costumes of the puppeteers usually consisted of sweaters and knickers (the topper excepted), and Dorothy, magnificent even in Khaki knickers, shouting and cajoling and urging the world at large to attend the most remarkable of puppet shows.

Many did attend, but not enough to pay the expenses of four people, a driver, a truck, and a battered Ford, and the tour became simply a protracted effort to pay the daily expenses and somehow, by the example of persistence if in no other way, to appease the creditors. It was a sorry prospect when they reached the White Mountains. The Plantation, luckily, was ready for them. Dorothy alone had to stay in a near-by farmhouse. The three boys and Roddy, who had now joined the troupe, made their headquarters with me for the few engagements in the mountains. I hope I was an agreeable host, though in thinking back on the time I am afraid I was a little disgruntled at the intrusion of this problem into my quiet summer. The scholastic mold was not entirely broken, and while this mess was really no affair of mine, it was a very bitter one for my two dearest friends, Harry and Roddy. I at least refrained—of this I am certain—from saying "I told you so."

The whole sorry venture had at least been a lesson to Harry, and to us all. It taught us that the puppet show must be the product of the puppet artist, not of the stage artist or any other. It is a lesson that has since been reinforced many times by observation of other puppet shows, notably one on the west coast designed by a talented artist which, considered pictorially, was beautiful, but, considered as entertainment was dull with the excruciating dullness only a bad puppet show can generate. The old formula, the old tradition, the puppet as comedian, as a piquant and robust criticism of life and manners, that was the thing for us. Puppets as picture, as purveyors of heavy philosophy, as symbols, as prophets of the New Theatre, might do for attic aesthetes, but for an American audience, Mr. Punch was the fellow.

10.

There is a wine one buys in Tuscany called "Est Est Est." The story goes that a Florentine merchant of great wealth sent his servant forth to find the finest wine in the kingdom. When he found it he was to write on the label, "Est"—"it." When he had tasted this wine he wrote "Est Est Est!" The air on a New Hampshire autumn seemed to me like that wine—pale golden, like honey, and with a bouquet all its own. And autumn had come. There was no doubt of that. One woke to crisp mornings, to find the grass stiff with crystalline frost. Birch leaves in the woods behind the house dropped their small leaves like thin-foiled coins of beaten gold. The maples here and there among the pines flamed like torches. The blackbirds wheeled and clattered. There was a skin of ice on the washbasin that one must push his hands through, and gasp and sputter as thin flakes of it clung for a moment to his tingling face. One could almost see the spring site, so many leaves had fallen.

Dorothy and George had gone back to New York, like the good troupers they were, making no fuss about unpaid salaries. Bob had gone to New Haven. The three of us glumly packed away the remains of the show in the barn and in the attic of my small house. Roddy, I could tell, was brewing some scheme or other. Harry, who more than either of us should have worried about the future, was least concerned of all. Though he probably never read the verse, the Biblical injunction to "give no thought for the morrow" was more perfectly exemplified in him than in anyone I had ever met. The inevitable "meeting" was held one cool gray morning as we sat around the fire on improvised benches and cushions drinking our breakfast coffee. Roddy had his plan worked out in such detail that the only obstacle he had to overcome was my determination to have done with puppets. His eloquence was never more moving, and finally, as we had both known I must, I yielded. Indeed there seemed no other way out for Harry than the one Roddy proposed. This was, briefly, to get together once more, and as speedily as possible, a small show which the three of us could handle, and start out on another tour. There were already a few good dates booked for the Geddes show, and Roddy was confident that his persuasive powers were equal to the task of convincing the neccesary club chairmen that our substitute performance would be far better than the one they had bargained for. We could get a week of bookings, enough to pay our initial expense, in schools in New Hampshire. Then we could go south, in the meantime booking as many dates as we could by letter. Once I had yielded, our chief difficulty was transportation. All we had was the Ford, battered and infirm. Roddy was sure it would do. It would *have* to do. The show would have to be built to fit, there was nothing else for it.

Harry and Roddy left at once for New York to bring back the neccesary tools, materials, and paints. I stayed at The Plantation, tramping through the yellowing fields and thinning woods by day, hugging my fire by night, concocting as best I could material which would be bright and amusing, and at the same time simple to stage, transport, and operate. The result was two new one-act plays, each of which had only a few characters and was built around two or three "tricks" which I knew Harry had been waiting to work out. We retained our opera singer, and "The Gooseberry Mandarin," and from the lovely eighteenth-century chamber orchestra which had been the curtain-raiser for the Geddes show, three of the choicest musicians who made up a trio that has become famous. These three dapper gentlemen in tie-wigs, white silk breeches, red velvet coats, and lace necker-chiefs have from that day to this opened practically every perfor-mance we have given. They have been our mascots, our trademark, etched by Gustave Baumann, sketched by Cecil Beaton, and, I devoutly believe, responsible in no small measure for such success as we have had. It is a steadying thought to be sure, without the slightest qualms or questionings that, in the magic moment when you are poised on the bridge, when the gong sounds its soft, deliberate "pong, pong, pong," when the lights in the theater fade out and the clatter of voices suddenly dies, when the curtains sweep apart, to know that the dark oblong before you conceals faces that are at once charmed and in utter sympathy with the small wonder you have created. And it is always so. The

The Haydn Trio

sketched by cecil beaton

slightly supercilious pianist, the violinist, alert and responsive, the cellist bending to his bowing with a quaint absorption, uniting together in the familair G major Haydn Trio, the presto movement, have never failed to win the admiration of an audience. How many recordings we have worn out I cannot tell. We have played it many hundreds of times. The musicians have had at least three changes of costume, and though the cellist some years ago was stolen by some misguided soul, his two survivors still stand ready to play with all their accustomed skill—a skill that comes, no doubt, from the extreme limitation of their repertoire.

But I am ahead of my story. The boys returned, we set to work at once, and I think I am safe in saying that we broke all records for speed in the preparation of a professional puppet show. The old figures were remodeled. As much of the Geddes stage as was of any use, Harry used, and his ingenuity was never given more scope. In ten days the show was built, rehearsed, and ready for opening night. We had our "dress rehearsal" at the Plantation. We set up the stage at one end of the living room, arranged benches and cushions as best we could, put reflectors on the oil lamps, and awaited our guests. They were villagers whom we'd met in various ways during the summer, and with some of whom we had become firm friends. There was the neighboring farmer who supplied us with milk and butter, and his wife; the garage man who had kept our Ford intact in some marvelous fashion, and his wife (you never know about these New Englanders) who wrote for *The Atlantic Monthly*; the postmaster and his family; the pastor of the Congregational church; the proprietors of the lunchroom and gas station; the professor from Armour Institute in Chicago who summered across the river—a diverse, but appreciative audience. They loved the show, and their mirth reached a hilarious climax at an unforeseen point. Thinking to enliven the prima donna act which one or two of audience had already seen, we added a second singer, and the two joined in "Whispering Hope," Harry and I, in the most affected falsettos, supplying the voices. Our choice of that particular number was wholly innocent, but we learned later that it had been for years the *pièce de résistance* of the village's most persistent and durable duo, a mother and daughter who, on the slightest provocation, whether the occasion was a funeral or a church supper, sang it soulfully, defiantly—some might even say, spitefully. So its issuance from these small figures released a spring of village mirth that had never been released so publicly before, and our guests took full advantage of their favorable position to set the small house ringing with laughter.

It was a good omen for the success of our hastily planned tour. Our schedule filled with surprising rapidity. We worked our way south into western Massachusetts. In late October we were in northern New York state, and then, for nearly a month, Boston became the base of our operations. There were private schools galore, expensive ones, money was plentiful, and we were soon paying off the indebtedness which was Harry's heritage from the summer's folly. It was a difficult tour, packed full of engagements, with many long jumps neccessitating hard, cold drives by night, hastily snatched meals and little time or energy left for finding comfortable places to sleep. There was little novelty in it. Crowds were always pretty much the same, having the same reactions, asking the same questions, making the same comments. The difficulty was augmented by a return of Roddy's illness and his enforced absence for some weeks. The bookings, fortunately, were fairly complete, and Harry and I managed, though it seemed at first impossible, to do the entire show ourselves, securing in each town some eager youngster to pull the curtains on cue, shut off the Victrola, etc.—all this to be learned in a half-hour's rehearsal just before the performance. We got along surprisingly well. Only twice, I think, were cues bungled and curtains wrongly timed, and only once did our piano soloist blare forth surprisingly with "The Stars and Stripes Forever" played by Sousa and all his brasses—an effect which must have had, at least, the charm of the unexpected and illogical.

As the weather grew colder, trouping became harder. It was impossible to put the side curtains on the Ford, for pipes, poles and packages protruded from the rear, and curtains would have been of small protection anyway. So on we went into Pennsylvania and over and through the Alleghenies, now snow-mantled and bleak, and that, in the twenties, in winter, was no minor feat. I recall with particular horror a trip from Wilkes-Barre to one of the suburbs of Philadelphia where we were scheduled for a matinee the following day. It was a considerable drive, and we could not be too sure of the car, so after the evening performance we loaded the show and started off. The night was bitterly cold, and the sky clear and brilliant with stars. The thermometer stood at five degrees above zero, and going lower. We wrapped ourselves as best we could and started off.

Maps are deceiving. The road we were to follow was shown as

fairly direct, straight and well-behaved. Almost immediately, however, we started climbing and winding, up and up, the cold growing more and more intense. The motor chugged slower and slower. We went into low gear and finally reached the summit in a cold that our coats could not keep out. On we drove. There would be a town soon where we could get coffee and a warm room, one of the towns shown on the map. But they were, when we reached them, only clusters of small houses, a store or two, all dark and inhospitable. So we went on, shivering and miserable, through air as keen and cutting as a knife. On a curve the front wheel of the car slipped off the macadam and broke through the ice of a roadside puddle. There was a sharp, crackling spatter, and our windshield was coated with ice. We could not clean it off, so Harry, who was driving, was forced to lean out for the rest of the trip in order to see the roadway ahead. We were nearly to Mauch Chunk, and we could certainly go no farther. It was two o'clock, and we were numb with cold.

Mauch Chunk, Pennsylvania, may, perhaps, in some seasons of the year belie its name, and be a civilized community. Approached on such a night and under such conditions, it was a diabolically contrived hell. It is reached by a steep and circuitous road which dives down, abrupt and sinister. It is a dark and twisted town, squalid and black, I should imagine, even in July. One garage was open. With chattering teeth we asked for a lunch-room. All closed. We asked for a hotel. Around the corner. We ran to it, just to keep ourselves warm. A clerk, surly and half asleep, shuffled up dirty stairs in scraping carpet slippers and escorted us to a high-ceilinged, bare room, with a chair, a brass bed, a dresser, and left us. We could see our breaths in the room. I turned on the radiator. There was no answering hiss of steam. Harry turned on the faucet marked "hot." A faint, icy trickle emerged. Still dressed, we got into the hard bed and pulled over us the insufficient blankets, piling on top of them overcoats and sweaters. It was no good. We were still cold. We shivered, sleeping fitfully, till five in the morning, dawn only faintly promised, tidied ourselves as best we could, and were on our way again. It was a crystalline morning, and as our laboring car topped the hill that shut Mauch Chunk from the sun, it seemed, there in the valley, black and sprawling, no more attractive than in the dark of night. The sun helped some, though the weather remained glacial. We reached our destination at noon and went at once to the home of the chairman who had arranged for our appearance, knowing she would be uneasy at our late arrival. She, good soul, had in readiness a steaming dinner, hot water galore, and a crackling fire in the library. I have forgotten her name, but her hospitality I shan't forget.

Roddy came back early in December, quite well again. We had done better than we expected, financially, Harry and I, and now we celebrated by buying a new car, a small paneled truck. It was shiny and new and held our small show, our personal luggage and ourselves neatly, with no flappings or bulgings or protrusions, and our pride in it was mighty if somewhat adolescent. We had it photographed, standing carefully at either end, knowing full well that we were only the incidental and unimportant supporting members of the cast to the real star of the show, the new Ford.

Christmas drew near. Roddy, using contacts we had already made, recommendations, and our most commendatory pressnotices, had booked the skeleton of a very decent tour, starting in Washington shortly after the new year, and taking us thence through private schools in Virginia and the Carolinas. We were all looking forward to it eagerly—new territory, pioneering in a new field. Christmas came, with a private performance on Long Island and a memorable one in a Fifth Avenue church, where we were preceded by a vested choir that, holly-crowned, sang carols before the appearance of the puppets. The audience, select and made up of elderly ladies and gentlemen of Unquestioned Refinement, made only the faint well-mannered murmur of conversation that the occasion and the edifice permitted. We too, back-stage, moved on tiptoe and whispered our comments to one another. It was a very special occasion, and it presaged, we hoped, a pleasant and profitable season to come.

11.

We each went home for a brief holiday, and met again the day before New Year's. There were depressing tidings awaiting us. An epidemic of influenza, news of which had filled the papers for days, had elected to stage its most persistent bout in the South. Four of our eleven bookings were cancelled. Next day, by wire, a fifth was cancelled, and then a sixth. We were glum enough. Fortunately our current engagment was a lucrative one, calling for three appearances of two shows each in Washington, Baltimore and Annapolis, all under the sponsorship of the Maryland League of Women Voters. So we were assured of a modest capital. It seemed unlikely, however, that it would be sufficient to tide us over the vacant periods, and there was no reason to suppose that "fly-dates" in schools which we had counted on as fillers would be easy to book in view of the epidemic which they all feared and which was closing many of their doors. Again Roddy became enveloped in the gloom fog of taciturnity that always preceded the announcement of some new plan of action. It came the night of our last performance, which had been a gala one, and we received it sitting in our hotel room, considering our disrupted itinerary chart.

"What about Florida?" said Roddy suddenly. From his tone I knew very well that he had worked out a plan and was ready—indeed anticipating—an argument. To his surprise there was no objection. His suggestion was seized upon so avidly that I believe he must have thought there was something wrong with it. I do not know when The Puppeteers had been so unanimous. Our capital, we figured, now that the current series was completed, would be sufficient to take us to St. Petersburg and keep us until a few dates could be booked. The manager of one of the leading hotels there, we knew. Indeed he had often urged us to make the trip we were now planning. It would be easy sailing once we arrived there.

"When'll we start?"

"Why not in the morning, good and early?"

And so it was settled. I don't know which of us was most eager.

Roddy, as always, was anxious to be on the move, to play again, and in new territory, the careful game of the booker. Harry, restless as always, had visions of sandy beaches and palm trees. I, having acquired a cold in the head, was completely ready to leave the cold rain of Washington for a bit of sun and warmth.

En route, intoxicated with our suddenly planned trip to Florida, someone suggested California. It sounded logical. Our plans after February, which would take us north again, were uncertain, and in the same glow of venturing that had set our wheels rolling south, we decided then and there that they should, thereafter, roll west.

Through the interminable pines of Virginia; lunch in Richmond; more forests of pine, with clay roads as red as garnet. North Carolina. More cultivation, more frequent towns, a night in a palatial hotel in Greensboro. More pines and rolling hills where gashes showed soil inconceivably red. Orchards, leafless now, cotton patches, cabins sending their ribbons of smoke into the winter sky. South Carolina: bad roads, and for me, peevish with a sore throat and a temperature, empty and monotonous. A doctor in Columbia sent me to bed with a hot lemonade, but in the morning we were off again through more stretches of dusty road and deserted country. Georgia: my head would hardly stay up, and at Brunswick we had to stop.

What occasion, what series of colossal events, what Olympian tournament, what international congress prompted the construction of Brunswick's leading hotel, I do not know. There it was, however, monumental and enormous. The bed in which I was placed was, I found, occupying only an infinitesimal corner of a vast chamber. To my feverish eyes the dresser seemed as far away as St. Petersburg, the ceiling as high as St. Peter's dome, and myself in my corner as insignificant as his least communicant. Another doctor. "Stay in bed tomorrow and you may be able to go on the following day," he said. This time I did not object.

Next day I was, definitely, better. The fever was gone and I had only the languid vacuity that was its aftermath. Roddy, however, in his own cavernous chamber adjoining my own, was ill, and voluble in his opinion of the hotel, the ailment, the local physician, the oranges, myself—who had passed on the germ— Florida, puppetshows, and all humankind. Harry, meantime, convinced from the profusion of fiestas, senoritas and palm trees displayed in those Los Angeles Chamber of Commerce effusions which had found their way to the hotel lobby, that at least half the population of California must speak Spanish, had bought a Spanish grammar and immersed himself in it with a thoroughness that made its removal, by force or entreaty, something to be twice considered.

Three days passed before we could proceed. On the second and third of these days I was able to summon enough energy and interest in life to get about a bit, to see for the first time the lovely and funereal beauty of live-oaks hung with Spanish moss, and to sense some of the slow and pastel insinuations of the marshes, pale and luminous and quiet, as if they had caught in their watery expanses so much of dawn and dusk that dawn and dusk tempered their whole day.

Our enforced vacation provided an unfortunate beginning for our Florida trek. Roddy had been left with infected sinuses, and his temper was not of the best. Our funds had run low, too, thanks to hotel bills, doctors, and all the rest, so we reached St. Petersburg with barely enough money to provide us with meals until we could earn some more. Our room, fortunately, we were not required to pay for in advance, and food in the cafeterias was ridiculously cheap. What was even worse for our company morale than our lack of money, however, was the unpleasantness of the weather. It was dismally cold, and we had all looked forward to warmth and sun.

It was our immediate task to see what could be done toward

arranging a performance. I went to the hotel manager we had known in New Hampshire and was cordially welcomed. He booked us at once for a performance in the ballroom on the next evening but one, gave me letters of introduction to the papers, lists of guests who might be approached with a request that they lend their names as patronesses, and within a few hours arrangements were complete. "By the way," added the manager as I was leaving, "I'll want you three chaps to have dinner here that evening, so don't forget." As if we could!

The dinner was bountiful, the show went well, the "take" was generous, and in complete cooperation, next morning the weather turned warm and sunny, and we drove aboard a small ferryboat in much higher spirits than we had enjoyed since leaving Washington. Our spirits were, as a matter of fact, much higher than our situation warranted. We had canvassed the large hotels in the St. Petersburg area thoroughly, and while the managers were cordial, there were no guests in the hotels. One, with four hundred rooms, had exactly seven. Another, thirty-five. We were armed with letters of introduction from our St. Petersburg friend to several managers on the east coast, in Miami, Palm Beach, and Daytona, and it seemed advisable to get there as promptly as possible. Our drive south was leisurely and pleasant. The air, hot and tropical, was unlike any air we had ever breathed, an air freighted with hints of swamp and scarlet flowers and white sands and waters blue and somnolent.

It was dark when we reached Naples and the western end of the Tamiami Trail. We ate in a lunch-room beside the highway whose sign informed us in its modest fashion that it was our "last chance." Then off we drove through the soft darkness to Miami. In the Twenties the Tamiami Trail was a monotonously straight two-lane road thrusting itself through a hundred miles of swamp and semitropical vegetation. It was, we felt, perhaps more of a delight after dark than by daylight. We stopped once or twice, turned off the car lights which picked the white roadway so sharply out of the night, and the darkness rushed in on us, soft and inevitable, and full of the sound of insects and frogs. A great heron rose once from the reedy shelter and flapped its leisurely way into silence. It was overpowering, somehow, and desperately lonely.

Next morning, in Miami, that carnivalesque and unreal city, we set out as early as we dared to present our letters of introduction. The first hotel we approached was palatial, but like a palace that had been deserted, for there was not a guest to be seen. The manager was cordial enough. "It just wouldn't pay you boys— you can see for yourselves. We've fewer than fifty guests in the house. Now if you are back this way in a month or so. . . ." We tried a second hotel. The story was the same. A third. We were, apparently, a month too early in a wretchedly bad season. We exhausted all the possibilities in Miami in a few hours—hotels, the recently organized little theater, the "university," struggling hard to appear important in its barracklike buildings. Our room we had optimistically taken "for several days." There was nothing for it, however, but to go on north to Daytona, trusting that somewhere en route we would find enough people gathered in one spot to warrant our setting up our theater and giving a performance. Our funds, which had already been reduced by paying our rooming-house bill in Miami, were once more running low. We learned, before leaving, of Hollywood-by-the-Sea, a hotel reported to have a goodly number of guests. Its manager was another acquaintance from another New England hotel, and on this we pinned much hope.

Hollywood-by-the-Sea. The hotel, looming across a waste of paved but now broken and neglected streets, with here and there a small stucco house, dwarfed any other hotels we had seen. It was as amazing, standing here in what was obviously the sad awakening from some realtor's dream, as the Pyramid of Gizeh would have been. We approached with fingers crossed—and got our date for the next night but one, a Sunday intervening. There were only some sixty guests, to be sure, but the manager believed, apparently, that something should be done to keep them amused, and we were grateful. Outside again, we took stock. We still had two nights shelter to secure and meals for two days. Our total capital was $4.28. It was my idea that we drive on to Fort

Lauderdale and find ourselves accommodations, American plan. This would give us both room and meals, and our bill would not have to be met until after the performance. My partners agreed, and we drove on through similar country, looking like the dumping ground for some theatrical producer who, having more stucco bungalows, drug stores, and lunch stands than he could use, had set them down in this forgotten plain to crack and peel and weather and be slowly devoured by creepers and moss and the green decay of the land. It was only a few minutes' drive to the town.

My plan, we soon learned, could not be carried out, fine and simple as it seemed, for the reason that no hotel in Fort Lauderdale in those days had ever heard of the American Plan. We went once more into a huddle, and did the only thing we could do— took the cheapest room the hotel afforded, and tried to budget our pitiful fund. For breakfast next morning we spent fifteen cents each. Then we made a discovery. Just around the corner from the hotel was a house bearing a sign "All you can eat for 50¢." We decided to put it to the test, and promptly at noon we descended on the unsuspecting landlady like wolves on the fold, though not without some regret for the havoc we were about to wreak. We might have spared ourselves, for we were confronted by a table so loaded with things to eat that its leaves sank and its legs seemed in imminent danger of collapse. There was an enormous platter of roast beef, another of pork, and a third of pork chops. There was a Gargantuan tureen of mashed potatoes and another of boiled. There were bacon and eggs. There was cauliflower, creamed carrots and peas, macaroni and cheese. There were small dishes of jelly and jam and pickles. There was, at last, hot apple pie, rice pudding, chocolate cake and applesauce. The reason for all this was apparent. The boarders, eight in all, were section-hands on the railroad, and ravenous as we were, our efforts seemed pitiful and repressed in comparison with those of the train crew. It seemed incredible that such quantities of food could be stored away beneath denim and corduroy. We were, at last, full to bursting, and chastened in spirit. We still had $2.23 left. We were not hungry again until long after dinner time. After some discussion we appropriated twenty-five cents for a large sack of oranges. These were our dinner and our breakfast. At noon next day we once more visited this miracle of prodigality and ate as much as we could hold. We had left fifty-eight cents. We drove then to the hotel to set up.

We were to perform in an enormous lounge overlooking a glistening strip of sand and the pounding surf of the Atlantic. We dawdled and took more time than we needed. A guest would occasionally stop, look curiously, ask a question or two and stroll on. Twice the manager came by to look us over, and each time we listened hopefully for an invitation to dinner. We strolled along the shining beach, we returned and read the magazines in the lounge. Dinner time came. The salt air had made us hungry. The dinner gong chimed. We gave up then, sought our car and drove to the nearest drugstore. With dismay we saw that there was not enough gas in our tank to get us back to the hotel. "Shall we eat first?" asked Harry. "No, we'd better get a gallon of gas." Roddy's answer was heroic. With thirty of our thirty-eight remaining cents we bought each a chocolate milk shake, and with five of the remaining eight, a small package of very stale cookies. Our meal over and our hunger not appeased, we took our last three pennies and got weighed. It was slight satisfaction, when we got back to the hotel, to have the manager greet us with "Where'd you guys slip off to? I was going to ask you to dinner." Hollywood-by-the-Sea netted us $38.00. We paid our hotel bill and went on north. Palm Beach was as deserted as Miami had been. At Daytona we found our third engagement in a charming older hotel with an audience of charming people who were generous as well as appreciative. On the sum collected there we started north again. St. Augustine was empty, Jacksonville, nothing. We got, that night, to Savannah, strange and mysterious in a pearl-white fog that hung heavily in the wide streets and floated like twisting scarves among the moss-hung oaks and the balconied façades of the houses. The Biltmore, outside town? A little early. Come by again in two or three weeks. Next day we drove, like demons, through South Carolina in dust and in such mud as we had never seen, past sun-baked fields of cotton stalks, dilapidated cabins and tobacco sheds, green forests, deep and dark, rivers red as blood. At dusk we had reached the border of North Carolina, which meant miles of concrete highway, and through the gathering dark we sped along their curving ways, through rolling hills, pine-scented. Southern Pines was our goal, and we made it and found rooms and welcoming beds. Florida behind us—Florida where we had hoped to play for a month and had fled in a week. For the first time since the days of the Geddes show we were forced to wire home for money. It was only $30, and we determined that should be our last such request.

12.

The Tarheel State and the Tarheels themselves I found much more interesting viewed through the eyes of a puppet showman than through those of a teacher. We had, during the ensuing month, only three engagements definitely booked—one at the college where I had previously taught, one at the State University in Chapel Hill, and one at Hollins College in Virginia. We recouped our finances slightly, but providentially, at Southern Pines, where we found one of the hotels reasonably well filled with vacationists who seemed eager for a little diversion. The money we got from this engagement took us to Greensboro, where I had formerly been a college instructor. Though I reentered town in a dusty show truck, though the single room we secured was in a part of town my former dignity would never have permitted me to inhabit, though I had no assurance of a liberal salary check at the end of the month, and though I was regarded by all but two or three of the faculty people I had known as, no doubt, a sorry example of one who had fallen from the narrow path of scholastic rectitude, I was, I knew, richly recompensed by a freedom as complete as is allotted to most humans in such demanding times. If I wanted to walk down the main street in broad daylight in slacks and sweater I could do it. If I wanted to laugh openly at the college president whose chief diversion was bridge and whose favorite drama was "Abie's Irish Rose" I could do that too. It was the elation of independence I felt, and I was happy in it.

Our procedure was simple and logical. We started out, our first morning, with some reasonably sized town as our destination. Whenever we passed a school that looked large enough to provide us with an audience, we stopped, and Roddy went in to test his salesmanship. His task was not easy. The first school we tried was an imposing building set just outside a small town. Harry and I sat in the truck anxiously awaiting Roddy's return. He was gone a long time, and when he emerged at last, his face was red and his heels bit into the hard clay of the playground.

"It's no good," he said. "Let's drive on."

The superintendent, it seems, was a florid individual who had heard of Punch and Judy. Nothing could impress him: pictures, feature stories from the *New York Times* and the *Christian Science Monitor*, letters of reference from college professors in New England, names of patrons and patronesses. "I don't care what this Walter Dam-Damrush thought about your show. It don't cut ice with me. Now if you get me a letter from somebody here in Rockingham County, okay." His latest show had involved a monkey whose antics, Roddy gathered, had been more than a little disruptive, and he was not to be persuaded or cajoled into taking another chance. Roddy tried a number of schools, and at last got an engagement in that twin city whose name should delight any who revel in incongruous nomenclature, Leaksville-Spray. Roddy put the proposition to these schools on a strict percentage basis, and set the admission price at whatever figure the superintendent or principal thought advisable. It was an experiment, but if we could pick up even fifteen dollars a day, we could live until our definite commitments came or our luck changed.

We played Leaksville-Spray in the afternoon, immediately after school, and the large auditorium was jammed with children. We had got permission to visit each room in the school earlier in the day to advertise. Our advertising bore fruit. Harry and I would make the excursion as a rule. We would take two or three of the gayest of our troupe, hang them over our shoulders, and rap at the shiny oak door labeled 1A. The door would open, and the teacher bid us enter. Behind her would be a lively panorama of peering faces, pointing fingers, bobbing heads. I would therupon, concealing the puppet as best I might, tell them of the show that afternoon, ask them to bring their nickels or dimes, and explain in whatever language their age seemed to require just what a puppet show was. Most of them had never heard of such a wonder, and even Harry's demonstration which followed—a clown juggling his silver ball on top of the desk of some small boy in the front row, who would be awed perhaps, perhaps delighted, and perhaps even shy and a bit frightened at this sudden intimacy with a small creature that by good rights should never be so lively or so friendly—would do little to dispel their dismay. There would be shrieks and questions and waving hands and wriggling bodies and always pleas to "do it again."

So we would go, spending only two or three minutes in each room, until the entire school had been covered, and our efforts would usually result in a well-filled auditorium and a clamorous and enthusiastic audience. It was so in Leaksville-Spray. After the performance one small tow-headed youngster of nine or so came up to Harry, solemnly thrust out a grimy hand, and remarked "I sho' did lak' y'all's show. Why, hit's wuth a heap more'n y'all charged fer it! Reckon hit's wuth a—a quattuh at least!" It was heartening insurance. We had brought these children a small miracle—a land of people too small to be flesh-and-blood, yet too agile to be simply wood and wire. The mystery of The Puppet was never more profound than to these intent, wide-eyed, underfed children.

With the banners of our Leaksville-Spray success flying, it became comparatively easy to book other schools. While Roddy concentrated on them, I turned my attention to possible evening engagements in colleges, for club benefits, etc. The club was not the fertile field in North Carolina it had been in Massachusetts, but the colleges were immediately interested, and there were many colleges. We played in Quaker colleges, Baptist colleges, Methodist colleges, Moravian colleges, until one began to wonder if the much talked-of "common ground of intellectual attainment" was either very common or very intellectual. The sectarian differences of these seats—precarious seats, some of them—of learning, however, mattered almost as little to us as to our wooden actors. We could smile at the provincialism of some and admire the age-softened charm of others without fear of offense or criticism.

These were busy days, with performances in strange places and at strange hours. One school, operating from eight in the morning till one in order that the children might work in the fields and orchards in the afternoon, accepted us on the condition that we give our show before school began, at seven in the morning. The principal would guarantee, he said, that the children would come. The admission was five cents, but there were over four hundred children. It meant leaving Greensboro at four-thirty, setting up our stage in the gray dawn, and playing to a crowd of children whose early morning temper we had no means of foretelling. We took the chance, and our audience was neither sleepy nor peevish, but quite as delighted as though the hour had been a more conventional one.

Our most genuinely appreciative audience in the South was at Bennett College, a women's college for blacks. The girls here seemed far superior in keenness of perception and in understanding the art of puppetry as we purveyed it, to the usual groups of college girls to whom we had played. The number that found highest favor with them was the little Javanese dancer from the Geddes show. Gauche, stylized, utterly unrealistic in the attenuation and extravagances of her modeling, she was too often met with snickers, or frank boredom. But to these girls she was an animated pattern moving to music, the subtle spirit of a dancer, a distillation, an essence, and they could not have enough of her.

Of all our Carolina performances, however, the one that gave us most pleasure added not a penny to our exchequer. It was a compliment to my old friends, the Thom sisters. That designation had not, when I knew them before, been strictly accurate, for there had been at that time not only Miss Minty, Miss Angie, and Miss Liz, but Mr. John as well. Mister John, however, had rocked himself calmly and beautifully into eternity some months ago. Miss Minty, Miss Angie, and Miss Liz remained.

I had first met them as a trespasser on their ancestral acres. We picnicked often, Eleanor and I. She was a Bostonian who taught piano at the college. It was a joy for us to don old clothes, forget classes and papers and prying faculty members in the pungent fragrance of the Piedmont out-of-doors. We happened one such day on the Thoms, and had been so taken with them and their seclusion that we visited them again and again. One followed the pavement out of town for some miles, and then left it abruptly for a clay roadway, red as ground garnets, winding through pine woods. One left this scar on the land's greenness for a smaller one, almost hidden by the trees. This road, narrow and rutty and full of pine roots, grew fainter and fainter until it ended at last in a small clearing among the pines, thick with brown needles. Here one left the car and took a faintly traced path to the bank of a wide though shallow creek, shining with pebbles and murmurous with the gently flowing water. Here one was confronted with the choice of taking off his shoes and wading, or trusting himself to a six-inch log of peeled cedar which spanned the brook, holding meantime to a single hand rail cut from a younger tree. Once across the brook one climbed an easily sloping green bank hemmed on either side, at a distance of only a few feet, with pine forest but broken here only by an enormous cottonwood tree, a pile of stones marking a spring-site, and a rudely constructed kiln for the "trying out" of soft soap. At the top of this knoll was a high rail fence which one entered by a sagging gate hung on thongs of leather and almost hidden by the most magnificent boxwoods, I am convinced, in America, trees so high and thick and so redolent of the peculiar, ancient and acrid pungence of box that one knew they must have grown there for much longer than a century.

Inside the gate the earth was scratched bare of grass by the chickens, and rounding another boxwood so large that it all but concealed the cabin, one came upon the home of the Thom sisters. It was built of logs, lifted a foot off the ground on heavy piles. Its roof, covered with heavy warped slabs, extended in front, supported by four hewn timbers, over a narrow porch, the floor of which was so worn and broken that it provided precarious footing indeed. Inside, the house was divided into two rooms by a cavernous stone chimney, the fireplace in which was tall enough and deep enough to accommodate a large man standing upright. The room to the left was papered with yellowed newspapers, and almanacs dating back to the Civil War. Most of the space was taken up by three spindle beds, covered with woven coverlets. There was one low rocker, a few cracked dishes on the mantel, a clock with a painted dial, long since in disuse, and little else. Through the chinks of the clean-scrubbed floor came cracks of light and the sound of scratching, clucking chickens. The other room one could never enter or see into.

But as a matter of fact one never approached the Thom sisters in so logical and direct a fashion. One endeavored, even while crossing the brook, to shout in an unnecessarily loud voice to his companion, or to whistle a tune or sing a snatch of song. One talked loudly on his way up the green bank. One coughed and rattled his picnic basket at the gate, and said "Shoo, shoo" to the chickens. And even then, sometimes, he would round the last boxwood in time to catch a glimpse of Miss Angie's gray calico swinging into the forbidden room, and to hear strange mouse-like scurryings and rustlings from within. In former times it was Mister John one greeted, Mr. John sitting in a spindle rocker at the far end of the porch, his old blue-denimed back bent, his hand, like a knotted root, clasped over the end of a gnarled stick, his eyes very blue in his ruddy face bordered by short white whiskers.

But this time when we came, following the accepted routine of shoutings and bangings and whistlings, the chair was empty, and only the scurryings within indicated that the sisters were at home—where else could they be—and preparing themselves for visitors. We waited the required moments until the bustling seemed somewhat to have abated, and then rapped on one of the sounder boards of the porch. In a moment the door swung open on Miss Minty. Miss Minty was of uncertain age, probably fifty-five or sixty. Her face was like a wrinkled russet apple, her sandy-straight hair cut short in the neck, and her voice the heartiest, healthiest I have ever heard. She was dressed, always, in a faded and patched calico dress, very full as to skirt, very tight as to sleeves and bodice. She was barefooted, so we knew that the heavy men's shoes, caked with clay, would encase the feet of Miss Angie, who immediately followed her, peering around her ample form like a timid mouse. For there was, apparently, only one pair of shoes. If Miss Angie was wearing them, as she was, one always winced in sympathy for the torture she must be enduring from her swollen, arthritis-twisted feet. Miss Angie, much older that Minty and much more shrunken, had a small sallow face like those of old women in Flemish paintings. Her thin gray hair was drawn tightly back over her skull. Her dress was a smaller replica of her sister's, and the hand she always extended so graciously was swollen and painfully cramped. Her hospitality, however, was unfailing, genuine, and in spite of her poverty, or perhaps augmented because of it, a thing dignified and impressive. The one worn chair would be pushed forward, and apologies, never too profuse, would be made for the lack of chairs for the others.

Today I had brought two newcomers, Harry and Roddy. Finding the sisters ready, we ran back to the car, and with many precarious balancings conveyed several puppets, our portable Victrola, and a box of records back to the cabin. The Victrola having been opened on a corner of the porch, the puppets were brought forth, and the amazement, the pathetic glee with which these old ladies watched the small figures was prodigal pay for our trouble. Even Miss Liz, whom one almost never saw, sidled into the doorway and allowed herself a shy and toothless smile. When the dragon was brought out, its wire claws scraping madly on the floor, its green feathers flying, its red mouth clacking, old Angie drew her poor crippled feet hastily up beneath her skirt, and Minty, shouting with the almost hysterical glee of a child, flew into the house. Their interest was so divided between the puppets and the mysterious music issuing from the leather box that, like children, they hardly knew which way to look. It was all a breath-taking marvel. I had been away "out thar" (anything outside their own post-office of Julian, be it Raleigh or Rome, was "out thar"), and I had brought back with me these two friends who were some kind of friendly sorcerers. They had never heard a Victrola. They had never ridden in an automobile. They seldom, now that they were so old, even ventured across the log any more to the other side of the stream. Their nearest neighbors, a full half-mile "up the branch" brought them, when there was money, the things Minty could not raise in her garden. They had a cow, a mule that looked as old as Minty herself, and a few chickens. The house, built by their grandfather, was decaying slowly beneath and around them, and the boxwood was encroaching every year a little more upon it, but it would, they seemed to trust, last as long as they, and in the meantime they could be grateful for the puppets, the music, and the few groceries we had brought them.

13.

So the Carolina interlude ended, and it was time to start north. This prospect, in mid-February, was not one of unalloyed pleasure, but we had a week or more of lucrative bookings in Indiana and Michigan before starting for California, and we dared overlook no possible source of income just now. So we played our date in Virginia, and from Roanoke followed what the highway map told us was a U.S. TRUNKLINE. As a road, the less said of it the better, but as a vantage point for viewing some of the loveliest country imaginable, it was more than adequate. We climbed hills at incredible angles through clay so soft that it folded in behind the tires leaving no track to show that we had passed. We forded a dozen streams varying in width from a dozen to forty feet, where the road simply came to an end in muddy water and continued on the far side. Faith in the State and the gods of the highway department was surely never stronger than in these times of sickening descent into waters that might, to all appearances, be as deep as the Red Sea, and were certainly as murky. We met no cars, only occasionally a mountaineer, corncob pipe in mouth, astride a raw-boned, muddy-legged mule, before and behind him, as if to hold him on, bags of corn meal from some grist mill hidden in the piney wilderness. We emerged at last into Kentucky. Next day brought us to Indianapolis and a series of performances prearranged which, while they lacked the color and the romantic uncertainty of those we had been playing in the South, did give us the reassurance that we were, at least, adaptable, and our knowledge, steadily growing through the years, that The Puppet has charms to soothe the civilized as well as the savage breast. For here we were fêted. College dramatic clubs gave dinners for us, there were faculty receptions after the performances, and one delightful after-theatre party in the home of a grateful chairman.

The weather, fortunately, was mild, but as we set out for Michigan we encountered first snow and then the worst blizzard of the season. Ann Arbor was a welcome refuge, though the weather prevented seeing one's friends or doing much but sit indoors and watch the steadily dropping temperature. The day of our performance it cleared, though the cold held. The snow, dry as powder, lay in curving drifts everywhere, so brilliant in the sun and against the blue sky that it burned one's eyes. The performance, in spite of the cold, was a huge success. For Harry it was "playing in the home town," with all the friendly publicity. My turn was to come next day. We were thankful for our snug truck in the sub-zero weather through which we drove next morning to Otsego. My experience there was much as Harry's on the previous day in Ann Arbor. After the evening show we did our final packing, and next morning were off to California. We had two engagements en route, one in Terre Haute for a junior college, and one for an art colony in a suburb of St. Louis. At Terre Haute, however, our plans changed slightly, thanks to the influence of friends we had made a few days before in Indianapolis. They had arranged two appearances for us under Junior League auspices, the first in Tucson ten days later, and the second still a few days later in Pasadena. We were elated, of course, for these two dates would swell our capital considerably.

We left St. Louis in a driving rain, and our trip across the continent from that point became principally a whir of wheels and a rumble of the truck. The puppets were unprotesting. The three of us, crowded in the front seat by the addition of new pieces of baggage adjudged neccessary for so momentous a trip, made the best of Oklahoma mud and an Oklahoma hotel, and the overpowering and apparently endless expanse of Texas. This expanse was broken for us most interestingly by Big Spring. At the risk of incurring the wrath of its inhabitants, I cannot refrain from setting down a modest monument to that remarkable city as it appeared in 1929. It was then relatively unknown save to tourists en route by motor to El Paso, salesmen, and oil prospectors. It rose from the limitless horizon just at the crucial moment, the moment when, some three hundred miles from the reassuring modernity of Dallas, one had despaired of ever again seeing a living soul. It could be seen for miles, and the effect it made on the effete easterner was heightened by the fact that it was so definitely an oasis. Approaching by way of a hard and dusty highway that could be seen stretching miles ahead, and, if one looked back, for miles behind, it took shape finally into a surprising city. There, standing up like the proverbial sore thumb, was a ten-story hotel. To its left was an enormous and box-like movie palace, decorated in the most approved Hollywood manner. Farther to the left on a low hill was an imposing high-school building, white, expansive. The rest of the town, in comparison, seemed flatter than it really was. No building then had dared raise its roof higher than a single floor. And the construction of the other neccessary structures, shops, homes, offices, in contrast with the magnificence of the hotel, the theater, and the school, seemed doubly shoddy—mostly sheet-iron, tin facings, wooden fronts and tar paper. One instantly knew that all the tales he had heard of Texas wind must be pure invention—otherwise this town could not have endured.

We went immediately to this hotel, and found some difficulty in parking among the dusty Fords and Cadillacs. The lobby offered an amazing sight. Done in the same style as the theater façade—style which here found its outlet in red plush, tapestry hangings, Spanish furniture, and ornate lamps, it was a singularly incongruous setting for the men who crowded into it. Every elaborate chair, every divan was filled with men of a type I had supposed existed only in fiction and the movies—men moustached, ten-gallon-hatted, booted, and spurred. The air was thick with tobacco smoke and noisy voices and bitter with the smell of stale beer. From a back room came the click of chips and the clink of glasses. There was, we were told, but one room left, on the ninth floor. It contained only a pair of twin beds, but an extra cot could be put in. It was eight dollars, take it or leave it. The price, in those days, seemed shocking. We took it, with the help of a more than usually cordial bell-hop who offered to supply us with whatever we might like in the way of liquor or

entertainment. We took our entertainment, however, at the
movie palace, which was crowded, and on the two principal
streets of the town, crowded too, and exhaling, it seemed to me,
both nervous vitality and ill-repressed tension. When we returned
to our room the streets still swarmed with men and a few flashily
dressed women, and far into the night the shufflings and shoutings and bickerings of this strange town kept me awake.

We arrived the next night in El Paso just in time to see the
mild fringe of a Mexican revolution. The international bridge
had been closed at sunset, and we stood for hours, it seemed,
watching the single line of Mexican men and women seeking to
return to Juarez, or to enter El Paso. The language was strange to
us, but the faces of these people and their pantomime was
eloquent. For the first time we caught a glimpse of a part of
American life entirely new to us.

We reached Tucson through an unforgettable evening down a
road that seemed to be dipping through purple water. The desert
tints, a chromatic of pastels, yet bold and masculine. Slate blues,
purples, magentas, incredible violets, and all synthesized in a
melting gray that yet had nothing of mist, nothing of obscurity.
Here and there a giant saguaro would raise the awkward, ungainly pattern of its arms into the upper blue. We were two days
ahead of schedule, but our sponsors, hospitable souls, saw to it
that we were amused in the interim. We were introduced to our
first Mexican dinner, preceded by tequila cocktails, whose po-
tency certainly made no less impressive the dark shadows of the
Mexican quarter, its low adobe houses, its dusty roads, its "wish-
ing corner," where on a vacant lot, earth baked hard and still
warm from the desert sun, flickered a dozen or more candles
placed there by lovers with what whispered wishes for the success
of their amorous undertakings. There was, best of all, on the
second night, a long drive through the desert to Casa Grande, a
fire, a broiled steak, coffee, and then the Indian dances, dances
so impressive, so dignified in their pantomime that all the gaping
white people in their awkward clothes, and the outer circle of
automobiles that had brought them there, became an impertinence in the face of the dancers, feathered and beautiful under
the high stars.

14.

California at last. There was a mild disappointment, perhaps, that orange and palm trees did not crowd eagerly up to the very state line, but there were compensations: a desert such as one had read about, a veritable Sahara of a desert with dunes and drifts of tawny sands, undulant, clean and lovely. Then a final ridge of mountains through which the road curved and twisted among live-oaks and rocky dells and occasional small lakes of crystalline beauty. There was the slow descent into the California one had heard about, the California of orange groves and small, trim bungalows set among flowers of almost garish brilliance. There was San Diego, and the ocean, glimpsed for mile after mile as one drove up the coast, more than compensating for the barren-ness of much of the land. But then, alas, came the twenty miles from Long Beach to Los Angeles, with factories, oil and smoke, the thunder of trucks, and the pathetic suburban towns. Nowa-days a Freeway not so much eliminates all this as ignores it.

We sought out our old Michigan neighbors, the Siples, people who had been the most intimate friends of my family, and whose son Allen, now an architect, had been my companion and friend until college days. They had moved to Los Angeles a sufficient number of years before to be firmly entrenched. They had bought a spacious house which might, save for the palm trees in front of it, have been transported intact from Zanesville or Peoria or Grand Rapids, and their hospitality was as generous and sincere as it had always been. They welcomed us and for several days we were their grateful guests. Our Pasadena engagement was still some days away, but awaiting us was an invitation to tea next day from the Junior League chairman. The address was Orange

The Hollywood influence (1929).

Grove Avenue, which meant nothing to us, but we got ourselves in the best outfits we could, after days of traveling, entrusted our car to an amazing auto-laundry whence it emerged shining, and at the appointed hour glided expectantly up a long and imposing drive to our destination. An ivy-covered wall, a baronial lodge-house, and a veritable English park slid past the astonished nose of our truck, and three glittering Rolls Royces turned glittering backs on it as we came to a stop beneath a Tudor porte-cochère. A liveried butler appeared and waved us on. "The delivery entrance is around the garage." But behind him emerged our hostess. "Puppeteers?" "Yes," we breathed, "puppeteers." "Oh, how utterly delightful! Do come and look!" whereupon several more ladies appeared, cooing and exclaiming as the butler, chagrined and, I am sure, more than a bit disgusted, faded from view.

The tea became, after the first flurry of correct excitement at our arrival, a strictly divisional affair. All the ladies, teacups nicely balanced and wafers daintily fingered, sat admiringly around one Ellery Walter, who had just written "The World on One Leg," giving him a momentary glamor of which they were sure, whereas ours was still of untested quality. The few gentlemen present retired to the dining room, where the host, very tweedy, dispensed whisky and soda, and the low rumblings we heard were all of yachts and horses. We departed, at last, prepared for something rather special in this Pasadena date.

And something rather special it was. Held in the ballroom of the Hotel Huntington, it turned out to be a hospital benefit, with prices attuned to Pasadena wallets. The evening was encrusted with diamonds, and we considered our California debut a most auspicious one. Our own fee, however, was modest, and it was necessary to live. We began hunting at once for some place suitable as headquarters for our activities. It was, as such hunts always are, a tiring business. Finally, through the intervention of a young painter, Casey Roberts, to whom we had a letter of introduction, we found an ideal spot.

The Hollywood of the twenties no longer exists. Then it offered some of the most charming retreats in the world at the most reasonable prices. I call them retreats advisedly. For behind the city hills rise sharply, hills creased with innumerable small valleys and glens, so it was possible—and still is—to live within easy walking distance of the garishness that is Hollywood Boulevard, and still be in a spot as quiet and secluded as though it were a dozen miles away. It was in one of these glens that we found our house—a tiny wooden affair built into the side of a steep hill. One entered by way of the drive, skirting another small house which stood sedately on the level to find, half hidden by an enormous pepper tree, our house. The "ground floor" was literally that—simply a storage basement. The living quarters were above, walling in on two sides a small secluded garden, whose third wall was the steep hill itself, and whose fourth was a simple latticed fence, its gate giving access to garden and house. Our expenditure for furniture was nothing, save for springs, mattresses and a few necessary dishes and utensils. Harry and Allen Siple contrived tables and benches of redwood that were solid, serviceable, and attractive. Paint and colored cotton curtains did the rest, and we found ourselves with a comfortable and charming house and an adequate place for a workshop in the storage space below. And the rental was low enough to fit our budget.

Once we were settled, the next step was to get engagements. The field was relatively free. Our only competitor was a woman whose company had toured up and down the Pacific coast for years with two productions. She prided herself, and rightly, on her record, but the fact that our material was fresh and hers was staled by repetition, gave us a distinct edge. "This isn't Cinderella, is it!" the school principal would demand, and we could gleefully assure her it was not. So within six months of our arrival, our only senior competitor packed her two productions and took them to New York, with what success I do not know.

Roddy, once he got his stride in this new country, booked a number of engagements, both in the local schools and in outlying districts. They were not highly remunerative, but our living expenses were so low that we managed comfortably enough. Our greatest disappointment was that our appeal was so exclusively limited to children. We had battled in the East for adult audiences with enough success to feel we had achieved something worth doing. Here the resistance was harder, and the opportunity for reaching the sort of audience we felt we deserved was almost totally lacking. Furthermore, summer was coming, schools would soon close, and from what we could learn of California summer resorts, our chances of tiding ourselves over those lean months seemed slim. Roddy conceived the idea of himself taking a touring show back to New England, to territory we knew so well, where our name and reputation were firmly established. His plan involved finding someone to take my place at the piano, and, as a third member, the same Bob Bromley who had helped out on the ill-starred Geddes productions, and was still in New Haven. It seemed in some respects a rash undertaking, and yet, from other angles, a wise one. Fall prospects, we felt, warranted a further try at California, and so it was decided. Harry and I were to stay behind, prepare material for a new show, and make such contacts as we could for fall. Finding a substitute pianist was not easy, for he must not only play—and from the sketchiest of scores—but sing, manipulate puppets, drive a car, and be of an appearance and behavior suitable to our "image." Want-ads brought us a sorry and discouraging parade of disappointed juveniles, hoping vainly for the break that was to get them on the screen, loath to leave Hollywood for fear of missing the Big Chance, and yet forced by necessity to find work. We finally settled on a college boy who, though not ideal, seemed most likely of all the applicants, and forth, one fine morning, they went in our small truck, the new puppeteer and Roddy.

The summer was one of such unequal effort that our debt to Roddy can never be paid. In the California sunshine Harry loafed unconscionably, while in New England Roddy worried and slaved at a tour that was at best makeshift, lonely and miserably unhappy. We did, Harry and I, cooperate on a new play, one which marked a distinct departure for us and which has dictated the trend of much of our work with puppets since that time. Its success, of course, was still entirely provisional, but the idea seemed worth our best effort. So when, at the end of summer, Roddy came home, thin and ill and pathetically glad to be back, we were more or less ready for him, and the three of us plunged into preparation for the new season with a will.

I had titled our new opus "My Man Friday." It was a miniature musical comedy, and as such a genuine innovation in puppetry. Taking its departure from the Robinson Crusoe story it twisted the plot unmercifully but amusingly. It had its torch song, "He May Be Your Man Friday, but He's My Man Saturday Night," sung by a torrid dusky heroine; it had a chorus of jungle steppers; it had its quota of ridiculous beasts, two of whom, the Ostrich Sisters, subsequently became perhaps our most popular performers; it had little plot but much absurdity, several songs, and opportunity throughout for a colorful production which challenged Harry to quite outdo himself with puppets and sets. The workshop was hardly adequate for his designs, and totally inadequate as a rehearsal hall. Through the cooperation of the landlord we were able to remodel the basement, and we found that by digging out some of the dirt there would be room at one end for an adequate stage, and room even, in the workshop proper, for a few spectators, provided they were willing to sit on benches and cushions and the work-bench itself.

The new show progressed rapidly, and was ready for its "world première"—to use the Hollywood denomination—before a state convention audience of fiteen hundred teachers. It was a vehicle utterly unsuited to such wholesale consumption, but it was well liked. We were glad, however, to take it back to the tiny workshop for polishing and revision. And then in burst Casey, the friend through whose good offices we had found our house. After weeks of idling he had a commision, and a good one. His roommate, Bruz Fletcher, had been hired to write an act for the vaudeville debut of Esther Ralston, who was at that time a popular screen star. Bruz was to act as her accompanist, and Casey was to design the set and travel with the act. He wanted, before they set out, to entertain them with a performance of our new show in the workshop, and he further wanted Harry to make up portrait puppets of Esther and Bruz, as a surprise. We set to work. Casey did the heads, exaggerated but amusing caricatures, and attached to the bodies Harry had made they were surprisingly lifelike creations.

The party was a great success, and our ears rang with the praises of our guests. They were show people, and they liked the place quite as much as they liked the show: the small dim workshop with its benches and cushions, the door through which they must stoop to enter, the great pepper tree hung with lanterns, the drive lined with flickering candles.

15.

The possibility of making our impromptu rehearsal hall into a real puppet theatre was, after this party, too obvious to be overlooked. We finally decided that if it could be arranged legally we would try giving regular performances of the new bill, with the addition of some portrait puppets of prominent stars in the movie colony. We soon discovered that to call it a theater was out of the question. It was in a residential zone, and it complied with none of the city regulations as to construction, exits, seats, or wiring. The solution, we decided, was to call it a club, and to call the fee we should claim not an admission fee, but a membership for an evening. So, within a week, smart-looking cards went forth to such a modest mailing list as we had been able to acquire and as our friends had been able to provide us with, announcing that Club Guignol would be open each Saturday and Sunday evening, by reservation, with membership at one dollar each! There would be, we promised, entertainment that was distinctly different, and coffee and cakes in the Green Room.

We awaited opening night with trepidation, for here was a venture new to us—our own venture from first to last, and while we were not depending on it as our principal source of income, we zealously wanted it to succeed. Yards of sateen were bought to cover the rafters and the hillside excavation and plumbing. Two new benches were built, and pillows covered with various colors of sateen. By seating people on the workbench at one side, on trunks at the back, and on cushions directly in front of the stage itself, we could, we thought, accommodate twenty-five people. Upstairs, the small living room and the corners of the dining room were hung with marionettes and foreign posters. We

The Yale Puppeteers—Brown,
Brandon, Burnett—with willing
helper in front of their first
Hollywood studio.

bought a huge coffee pot, and in the Japanese section, inexpensive mugs. All we needed now was an audience.

We awaited the results of our mailed announcements with an eagerness that was hard to brook. Then a reservation came in, for six, and another for four, and before we knew it our house was sold out. It was a gala opening, midget style. The sky had never been more spangled with stars (this was B. S.—Before Smog), the candles had never thrown such grotesque shadows, the pepper tree never arched more protectingly, nor had an audience of ours been more charmed. The whole experience was to them so novel, and gave them, in addition to their delight in the puppets, so genuine a thrill of dicovery, that they were a joy to play to. Our working force had been augmented by Buster, a neighborhood youngster of twelve over whom Harry's magic had cast its customary spell. He pulled curtains, adjusted lights, and at the proper moment, about midway through the show, scrambled through the small window which was our only back-stage exit, scurried around the house and up the stairs and put the coffee on.

After the performance the audience and the puppeteers went upstairs and for an hour or more stayed crowded into the small rooms inspecting the foreign puppets, the Geddes sketches, the posters, asking many questions, and feeling that here was something romantic and unspoiled, and—wonder of wonders—still untouched by the gilt extravagance of Hollywood.

So we were launched. On our second night a small girl wrapped in a huge coat appeared from nowhere. It was Colleen Moore, scouting. She came again and again with parties of her friends, and others of the movie colony soon followed. Before we knew it our small basement theater had become so popular that we were turning people away. Mae Murray, on mincing feet, swathed in ermine, was voluble in her chagrin at finding no available place. Others were amused, and came back.

Harry set to work at once creating new portrait figures. He made no attempt at caricature, striving always for as good a likeness as possible, and relying on the inevitably humorous actions the resulting marionette would have for its appeal. They were built to scale and carefully costumed by Eddy, a young man who,

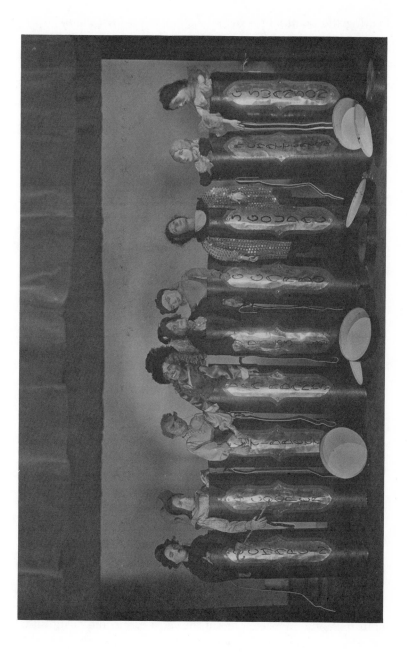

hearing the commotion in our back yard, which adjoined his own, came over to offer his services. He was a professional designer and dressmaker who had worked in the costume departments of several studios, and he had just the proper flair for the work in hand.

Colleen Moore emerged, piquant in a short evening gown of flaming red. Then came Jetta Goudal, at that time a star just approaching her zenith, regal in black and sequins. Gary Cooper followed, in checkered shirt, ten-gallon hat, chaps and boots—a costume that became him more in 1930 than it would in his later days when the Bond Street influence superseded that of the Great Open Spaces. And last of all in this early series came perhaps the greatest actress of them all, Aimee McPherson.

Each of these figures except that of Cooper brought us its own set of experiences. Miss Moore, with all the enthusiasm of a child, adored her small puppet, and saw in its antics a smart way of entertaining the guests at her housewarming. So we set a price—much too low a price, we found later. A scenario writer provided us with some tentative scripts, each involving two or three of the evening's guests, one concerning Elsie Janis and her mother being the most daring. In the elegance of Miss Moore's limousine we rolled to her new home to inspect the theater it contained, and on the eventful night, to an audience of Hollywood luminaries more than one hundred strong, the marionettes performed. Old puppets were metamorphosed by means of a bit of padding, a new wig, a hat, a stick, into figures that, thanks to the pointedness of the skits, could be taken, with a bit of imagination, for the guests they were supposed to represent. The hilarity was never more genuine. It was a triple triumph—for Miss Moore, for the new house, and for the puppets. We left them dangling on their back-stage hooks, surrounded by throngs of celebrities, and carried back to our small studio the knowledge that we had "crashed Hollywood." It was still another new field for Mr. Punch, and again he had done himself proud.

The small replica of Jetta Goudal had yet another chain of amusing consequences. One of the most exotic and beautiful of women, she had won for herself a reputation for temperament.

Judged by puppet standards the figure Harry contrived of her was a thing of beauty, expressive, and owning through his skillful manipulation the same slow and languorous charm that set her apart as an actress. So proud of his creation that he could brook no delay, Harry slipped off early one evening, presented himself at her door, and when she appeared, thrust into her astonished gaze this smaller image of herself. Her amazement was natural, and while she was still wondering what sort of maniac this might be, her friends gathered round her in the entrance hall, begging her to let this wonder in. With misgivings she did, and for a few moments Harry put the puppet through its paces to the delight of all save Jetta, who still could not be sure what new persecution might lie behind it.

"But ze gown! I nevaire wear ze gown *comme ca!* Ze coiffure! *Mon Dieu! Ce n'est pas de moi, cette coiffure!* I don't know! Maybe I sue you! But no! Meester de Mille! I 'ave no *monnaie!"*

It then occurred to the lady that the puppet must have an act of some sort. Harry explained that there was a song.

"A song? Seeng it to me!"

"I'm sorry, I can't. I'll have Mr. Brown send you a copy, though."

And this was the report Harry brought gleefully back to the studio.

Next morning while I was just considering typing off a copy of the lyrics to send to the actress, the phone rang.

" 'Allo! Thee is Mess Goudal. I 'ear you 'ave a song about me."

"Yes. I'm sending you a copy this morning."

"No. Zat ees too slow. Seeng it to me!"

"Now? Over the phone?"

"Of course! W'y not?"

And so into the unsympathetic rubber ear of the telephone, and with the feeling that the ear at the opposite end of the line might be quite as unsympathetic, I began;

"I am the screen's most temperamental lady.
I always play. . . . "

"W'at you say?"

Portrait puppet of Toscanini (1929).

Two Disraelis—George Arliss and his marionette portrait (1930).

Martha Graham with Harry Burnett and her puppet portrait. Below, portrait puppet of Greta Garbo as Mme. Cavalini in Romance *(1929).*

*Helen Hayes as she
appeared in* Victoria
Regina, *with Harry
Burnett and Victoria in
miniature.*

*Harry Burnett with
Ramon Novarro and
portrait marionette as* The
Pagan (1931).

Marie Dressler with portrait puppets of herself and Garbo as they appeared in Anna Christie *(1930).*

The tension in the voice was not reassuring. I cleared my throat and began again.

"*I am the screen's most temperamental lady. . . .* "

There was a singular muttering on the wire which rose promptly to a highly intelligible climax with the words ". . . an' I am not temperamental!" Then an unequivocal bang, and silence.

Sister Aimee was an entirely selfish idea. Quite apart from the fact that a puppet of "Sister" would offer fine possibilities for satire, it would prove too, we felt sure, a certain source of publicity. No one in the vast gangling city of Los Angeles has ever been more consistently "news" than the woman we planned to copy.

Harry started proceedings by visiting the Temple, that amazing institution that was Capitol and Whitehouse of the Foursquare Gospel. Here without much difficulty he met one of the strange company of her followers, Karvina, a girl who until a recent injury had been a trick rider with the circus, and who now, without sacrificing any of her breeziness, and without being in the least taken in by the mysteries of the Temple, was quite willing to submit her own personality to the extraordinary one of Mrs. McPherson, and to act in the combined capacity of bodyguard, personal agent, page, jester, and go-between. This enthusiastic girl proved exactly the contact we needed. She sneaked pictures of Aimee from Aimee's desk, let Ma Kennedy into the secret, and through her secured one of Aimee's costumes of lustrous white satin with the customary Foursquare symbol on its bosom, which our friend Eddy promptly and exactly copied, and in a few days Aimee was modeled, jointed, gowned, coifed with auburn tresses, given a small wooden Bible, strings attached, and ready to perform. This she did with the greatest charisma. She knelt, she bowed her carefully marcelled head, she raised her arms in supplication and waved them in exhortation. She was, in short, an excellent copy of the original. Her "number" was easy. It consisted of numerous verses outlining her many exploits, with hints not too subtle of the financial persuasion that was her so astonishing gift. In preview she was a tremendous hit; it remained to see what the original would think of the copy.

This too was arranged by the bareback rider. We were assured that on a certain Tuesday evening, without fail, the Great Evangelist would appear in our humble theater and pass judgment on our daring. Little impressed as we were by the McPherson aura, the thought of Aimee herself, in person, was a little terrifying, and all of us put in a bad evening made no easier by a delay which prolonged itself to such a length that we had nearly given up hope of her appearing at all, when she came, in a limousine which out-Hollywooded Hollywood, a limousine whose chauffeur was smartly liveried, and whose tonneau gave forth the strains of a radio—this in 1930, when auto-radio was, we supposed, the exclusive possession of Paul Whiteman's aluminum Isotta. Three women emerged—our horsy friend, a rather stout woman, middle-aged, red of hair, obviously Aimee, and a much smarter, younger woman, who was decidedly blonde. Her we gave little heed to. All three were seated, and, somewhat breathless, we began. The lights went down, the two doors that served as fire curtain swung slowly open, the inner curtains glowed to dull scarlet and parted, the Haydn Trio played, and then out strode Aimee, singing the outrageous verses that had never seemed other than funny before.

It was over, and we issued forth. All three were smiling, and Harry, braving her possible wrath, approached the older woman. "It was nice of you to come, Mrs. McPher. . . . " But he was interrupted by Karvina. "This," she said, prodding the blond young woman, "is Mrs. McPherson."

Just then we were too astonished to do other than stare. But next morning the auburn hair came off and was replaced by hair as blond as that of Hollywood's latest sweetheart. To the Temple, again through Karvina's intervention, went Harry with the puppet to get what we most coveted—pictures of the two Aimees in amicable juxtaposition. Not until then were we adequately impressed with the full and complete miracle that was Aimee Semple McPherson. Her sermons, whatever one may think of her theology, were carefully tailored with an uncanny instinct for the dramatic, and there were several to be prepared each week. There were songs and oratorios to write and direct, classes to teach, the

Evangelist Aimee Semple McPherson poses with puppet and portrait and its creator (1929).

whole complicated organization of the mother church and sub-ordinate churches to keep running smoothly, reporters to face, an emotionally unstable family always at hand to upset things—and the whole precarious stability to be maintained of a structure that founded on unstable emotions bound only by the enormous

energy, the dynamic and compelling force of one personality—
her own. Hers was a task, whatever, again, one may think of its
social or religious value, that few could have accomplished.

It was into the turmoil of such a life that we came, one more
small complication, begging photographs, and it is small wonder
that we had to wait, a great wonder that we were finally·received
so graciously. While we waited we observed. The corridors of the
large building flanking the Temple itself were bare and smelled of
disinfectant and sanctity. The office was institutional and suspicious. The classroom where we finally found ourselves was large
and filled to the walls with followers—nondescript young men,
young women whom beauty had passed by, old men, frayed and
fanatically hopeful, old women plump and thin, but all zealots.
And there stood Aimee expounding the gospel as one might to
not overly intelligent children. This at nine o'clock in the morning. As the lesson drew to a close she complained of being tired,
and spoke of a vacation recommended by her physician. Sympathy swept like a wave through the sad assembly. An old man
rose and in a cracked and quavering voice insisted: "Sister, sister,
I know what ails yuh! It's them radio waves. Yuh stand too close
to thet radio machine! Them waves goes right through yer heart,
sister!" There were scattered "Amens."

Later, at the Temple, the pictures were taken, and did their
share in publicizing our small venture. And as long as we continued in Los Angeles the puppet of Aimee remained a favorite.
Her every escapade, her every bout with Ma Kennedy, her every
marital experiment, was celebrated by a new verse. She had to be
cleaned and recostumed, rewigged and refurbished several times,
but she was worth it.

And so through the winter and early spring the weekend performances at Club Guignol continued. They came to be the
bright spots of our week. Other activities, which included such
engagements as we could secure in suburban towns, and a quantity of lessons in puppet-making which Harry undertook during
the week—these seemed dull indeed beside the small inevitable
flurry that was Saturday night and Sunday. Some of Harry's
pupils provided us all with amusement. They were mostly grade
school teachers, no longer in the bloom of youth, were "simply

mad about puppets," and were, in their zeal to learn the mysteries of the craft, a little pathetic. It was as though in puppets they were seeking to find a substitute for instincts and emotions too long repressed. With maiden-ladies who "do puppets" it always seems so. One, certainly well past thirty, never came to our studio without her mother, a grim, stout lady who sat just outside the workshop defying Bohemianism to tie any strings to her child. Another, to our delight and Harry's disgust, insisted on putting elaborate underwear on all her small figures. Though it made their joints stiff and their motions ungainly, they were at least "proper."

But in the weekend performances there was rare satisfaction. Our audiences were discriminating, and so small that the after-theater coffee was always an excuse for interesting contacts and conversations. But the inevitable fly appeared in the ointment. This time it was a very fat and frowsy fly—a woman who lived next door. None of us knew her, but she was obviously one of those meddlesome people with stunted imaginations, suspicious natures, and an instinct for trouble-making. Our audiences, it seemed, disturbed her, though all was dark by eleven o'clock, and she found a convenient weapon in the city zoning ordinance. We were, she reported, running a theater in a residential zone, and an inspector arrived one morning with legal notice for us to desist. Punch being an old hand with law enforcers, executioners and such, we talked ourselves out of it by insisting, with all the proof and all the vehemence we could muster, that we were a private club. The inspector left, grumbling. We heaved a sigh of relief, but, alas, too soon, for our neighbor, in addition to her other unspeakable traits, was doggedly persistent, and in a week a second inspector appeared. The fire hazard, he told us, was too great, and this time not even the wiles of Punch sufficed to rescue us. The Club Guignol "folded," in *Variety* parlance. But the course of events never seems to stop for long, and before we really had time to seriously bemoan the catastrophe, something had arisen which occupied our minds to the exclusion of troubles that were over and done with.

16.

Los Angeles had a history, but nothing to pin it to. As a pueblo it was too slatternly to care; as a wild western village, it was too careless; as a growing tourist town it was too busy; and now, in 1930, after more than a century and a quarter, as a city with a million or more inhabitants, it was too late. Or so it seemed. California climate, despite its widely advertised beneficence, was singularly unkind to primitive architecture. Adobe walls melted and crumbled and cracked, and besides, their sprawling construction was entirely too prodigal of space to suit the tastes of the most recent invader, the Realtor.

So, when an energetic Native Daughter, Christine Sterling, rediscovered Los Angeles, the Realtors, the Chamber of Commerce Boosters, the California Claque may perhaps be pardoned for its surprise and its inability to realize, all of a sudden, what the rediscovery meant—what lush new adjectives, what romantic new photographs, what inflation of civic pride. It took them some time, and even now the adjectives seem a trifle forced, the photographs a little contrived, the inflation a little uncertain as to names and dates.

It all began when Mrs. Sterling discovered, in a neglected alley leading off the old Plaza—once the center of the pueblo but now only a small square flanked by Mexican grocery stores, pool-halls and Chinese curio shops—an adobe house, crumbling and forsaken, its roof caving in, one wall demolished, overrun with rats, littered with debris, and properly enough, it seemed from its appearance, condemned by the city fathers to demolition. Being not only energetic, but a woman of great initiative and originality, and imbued with an evangelistic spirit, Mrs. Sterling, indignation burning in her breast, went home and painted on a large board a brief history of the old house: Built in 1818 by the powerful Avila family; for a few days the headquarters of General Stockton during the American occupation; Los Angeles' oldest house, forsaken and now condemned. She hammered her sign to the sagging veranda of the old house, called all the newspapers to ask whether any had observed this strange sign—and waited. The reporters came, cameras clicked, editorials burgeoned, and shortly a movement was under way not only to preserve the old house, but to restore to its original state the alley, and to make its long neglected name Olvera Street once more significant.

The plans included closing the street to traffic, paving it with red padre tiles, planting a few trees, taking over some of the old buildings for restaurants and shops and installing in the street itself Mexican vendors who in their awninged ramadas could sell the crafts of their native land. To us in our hillside studio and ex-theater came Mrs. Sterling. What more ideal for such a street than a puppet show? Under her enthusiastic guidance we inspected the street. It charmed us from the first. Already the paving was under way and the pepper trees set out. Already, in the basement of a great square house opposite the Avila House workmen were building a fireplace and installing a kitchen for a Mexican cafe. Already the old adobe itself was rousing from its long decay. Already one optimistic trader of that happy breed that delights in antiquity and surrounds itself, by gradual accretion, with a dismaying array of old and discarded things, sat, plump and benign, chewing a long cigar, before the door of his improvised shop—a room crammed to its high ceiling with old books, old buckles, old bottles, old baskets, old beads—in short, with every old thing imaginable whether it began with a *b* or any less convenient letter of the alphabet.

It didn't take half an eye to see that this was what we wanted. Los Angeles had been a city with little atmosphere—a gangling, overgrown town inordinately proud of its size and growth, shouting its culture too loudly so that the culture it actually had became suspect. There had been no odd corners, none of those quaint remembrancers of things past that give so many American cities their distinction. Here was something that promised to supply, even though in a small and artificial way, that lack.

There was but one feasible location. Its dimensions were ideal—a long, broad room with a high ceiling, but otherwise unprepossessing indeed. The building included, beside this room, another of similar size parallel to it, and three smaller rooms in the rear, and on the second floor, flanking a long corridor, a number of rooms that had once housed the family who built it, but in the gradual deterioration of the area, it had become a cheap rooming-house, a brothel, a hide-out for transients and bootleggers. Downstairs the two rooms had been variously vacant, or occupied by cheap restaurants and poolhalls. The walls, in fact, still bore the mottled blue and pink nausea that had been some restaurant owner's idea of decoration. The building was now unoccupied save for a few decrepit beds and dirty mattresses in the upstairs rooms, and by the optimistic trader who had installed himself in one of the three small rooms facing what had been for years, until its present rejuvenation, a back alley.

We could hardly wait to get started. The rental was fixed, and we were on our way. The street itself was to make its official bow to the public late in April, but we, obviously, could not hope to be ready so early, for we would have not only to prepare the theater, but to prepare a new show as well, "My Man Friday" having served us all winter. Those spring days were busy ones, particularly so for me, who, in addition to work on the theater and a new play, undertook to fulfill a dream I had long had by establishing, in one of the small rooms adjoining that of the optimistic trader, a bookshop. Since this room was located just beside what would eventually be the entrance to our theatre, it was agreed that the phone should be installed in the bookshop, which would also serve as box-office for the theater.

Of the bookshop this chronicle need only record that it achieved a character quite its own, that it attracted its quota of book lovers, and that in its modest way it prospered. Meantime the new show was taking shape. It was to be, we decided, a burlesque in the vein of "My Man Friday" of that redoubtable

American classic, "Uncle Tom's Cabin." As "Uncle Tom's Heb'bn" it took rapid shape, and to our particular brand of spoofing it lent itself admirably. The underlying humor of the situation lay in a complete reversal of the characters of Topsy and Eva. Eva became a sophisticated flapper, fresh from boarding school, and Topsy the pure and maligned heroine. In a snowy second act, where Eliza crosses the ice, her baby, a modern mite clad in red diapers, perched jauntily on an icecake and sang "I'm a Little Red—(in places)," and Horace and Evelyn, the two pursuing bloodhounds sang a hilarious duet en route across the river. But it was the final act that gave the piece its name. It was Topsy, of course, who expired, not Eva, and here in a field of cotton, with a chorus of cottonpickers, she ascended, a white-robed angel with black wings, and fluttered about the throne of a black St. Peter. It was an elaborate idea, and Harry plunged immediately into the making of the more than forty puppets it required.

The street meantime had its official opening, and the throngs that crowded into it seemed to augur well for our new venture. The great bare room that was to be our theater we kept open, painting the walls with announcements of our opening in May, and displaying a number of marionettes to the gaping crowds.

In the usual tradition of the puppet show, or at least of *our* puppet shows, there were not enough days in which to do all that had to be done. Harry worked like a madman at the new puppets and stage. The rest of us undertook to make the room we had acquired resemble a theater. Our funds were, as always, limited, but by careful management we contrived. Our greatest stroke of luck was finding, in a salvage store, hundreds of yards of faded velvet that had once adorned a Masonic temple. It had originally been a stately maroon, but now was a rusty brown, streaked with lighter shades and darker. We bought the whole lot for sixteen dollars. It filled our truck to the limit, and we had enough, we found, to drape the walls and ceiling of our small auditorium, the two boxes we had built into the rear corners, and to mask the stage. Hung in billows from the ceiling, and softly lining the walls down to the broad dado of wall-board, which we painted brown and used as a background for posters and photographs, and lighted dimly by two parchment shaded lanterns, it gave the room a strange air of age and eccentricity that we could have acquired no other way.

For seats we had a carpenter build us seven benches, each designed to hold ten occupants. Each box would accommodate five, in a pinch, so our seating capacity was eighty, and our signs and preliminary advertising soon read, with justifiable exaggeration, AMERICA'S SMALLEST AND SMARTEST THEATER—ONLY EIGHTY SEATS—ALL ONE DOLLAR. The benches were stained dark brown, to attune them to the whole shadowy ensemble. The only focusing point of brightness was, properly, the proscenium itself, a proscenium flanked on either side by a gilded Corinthian column, placed, in the usual topsy-turvy style of The Puppeteers, bottom-side up. They had come from a wrecking company at a total cost of thirty cents, and many were the architects who in the ensuing months must have writhed inwardly to see these two fine columns standing blithely on their heads.

Between these resplendent columns hung our "asbestos." We commissioned a Mexican sign painter who had set up a shop in a basement under the bookstore to paint it, providing him with a piece of canvas of the proper size. He was a small, thinfaced fellow, Jesus by name, and his forte, so he said, was the depiction of bullfights. So our curtain emerged a dazzling scene where a slightly bulbous matador in green trousers and purple jacket was on the point of plunging a sword into a russet bull of peculiar physique. Both matador and bull were shown from an angle which concealed their faces, for Jesus was not good at faces, human or bovine. It was a curtain as absurd as the theater, and we hung it gleefully. It even suggested a name for our new theater, for in Jesus' proud designation of our playhouse as the "Teatro Torito," or theater of the little bull, we found such an alliterative melody and such humor that we promptly adopted it.

While all this was taking place, activity behind that eclectic curtain was reaching its peak. The stage was being built and equiped with the numberless hooks and battens and wires and pulleys and flies and curtains and spotlights that a puppet stage, to function fully, requires. A sound wall had to be built, a wall which would serve the triple purpose of making the rear of the theater into a workshop, of excluding traffic noises from the street, and of providing in its smooth plaster surface, kalsomined a pale blue, a perfect cyclorama which would give our stage an apparent depth it did not have.

All these goings-on fall, through the curious conceit of literary composition, into ordered and logical progressions. Actually it was quite otherwise, transcending grammar and construction, hectic and tense—a veritable "typhoonaclone," to use a word we had coined long before for a fairy-tale wizard. The date for our opening was set, and approaching with dismaying speed. Reservations were coming in to the bookshop, and it seemed impossible that all could be in readiness by the appointed day. The last stitch was put in the last puppet costume just as the sun was coming up on the day of our opening. All that day we strung the marionettes, painted, rehearsed as best we could, trying to remember songs and cues our brains were too weary to retain. We reached the evening, needless to say, in a state of nervous tension, buoyed up by cigarettes and black coffee. Nobody had slept, really, for two days. The stain on the benches was barely dry, but, to all appearances, we were ready. For the few splendid moments while our first night audience arrived we could forget the pandemonium that reigned back-stage. The little street had its first glimpse of top-hats and evening wraps, and no opening, it seemed, could have been more auspicious.

But then began a series of events that in retrospect seem vastly amusing, but that then, weariness gnawing at our brains, seemed a tragic finale to our weeks of effort, rather than merely inevitable mishaps incidental to opening a new play in a new theater. A protruding nail began it. Then came the more-than-plump lady who had difficulty squeezing in between two rows of benches, and when once arrived at her destined place, sat down with a sigh of relief only to find that whenever she moved the two boards that made the seat of the bench pinched her in an anatomical region that was too embarrassing to mention, and too painful to ignore—a fact her sudden scream made very apparent. The last party to arrive had reserved one of the boxes at the rear of the theater. These were elevated some four feet and reached by narrow steps. The ladies of the party, suspicious but charmed, reached their perch successfully. The gentleman, a novelist inclined to pomposity in person as well as in literary style, reached the third step, and the step, with a sharp crack, gave way, precipitating the gentleman, unhurt but ruffled, on the floor, and attracting to him the eyes of the whole audience.

"Oh-h! Jimmie! Are you hurt, dear?" his wife, wringing her hands, cried out from above him.

"No I'm not hurt! Be Still!" hissed the novelist.

"Oh dear! He's hurt!"

"I'm *not* hurt, damn it! Shut up!"

"Well if you're not hurt we're marooned up here!" By this time the laughter held the small room, filling it to the last faded billow of velvet. But to us, attempting to appease our patron, apologizing for the step, cursing the carpenter, and hoisting the perspiring object of our solicitude to his seat, it was far from funny.

The performance got under way at last. It opened brightly with a "symphony orchestra." Sliding back the apron of the stage as the house-lights dimmed, by an intricate series of weights and pulleys that none but Harry could have conceived and none but he could manage, the platform containing twenty-four tousle-headed, dinner-jacketed musicians rose jerkily into view, in a waggish burlesque of Roxyism. There were too many puppets for individual performers to be virtuosi, but the bushy-haired conductor flailed the air with his baton, and his men, if they did not give a very good imitation of a musical performance, at least bounced and jiggled in ways that set the audience screaming with laughter. The recording we used was the well-worn Liszt Second Hungarian Rhapsody, and when the cross-eyed trumpeter brought his horn to his lips with a sweep that jerked his head back, or when the motionless drummer came suddenly to life to give one tremendous thump to the kettledrum, the laughter we hoped for rewarded us.

Our second number, too, was an unqualified success. We had made a puppet of Leatrice Joy, an actress then much in favor, and she had graciously consented to appear on opening night, sing for her puppet, and make a "personal appearance." She did both charmingly, and even wore the gown we had so carefully copied.

Next came the play, and it remained for us all, for a long time, a memory we had sooner forget. It seems incredible that so many things could have happened to defeat us. Broken strings, unfamiliar lines, a stage we were not yet acquainted with, effects that refused to work—a nightmare we were ill prepared to endure. Somehow we finished, and the audience, which must have felt our distress, was kind, and took the whole evening with laughing good humor. Next night "My Man Friday" was back on the boards, and for some days thereafter we rehearsed the new show before we once more ventured giving it a public performance.

17.

To enumerate in regular sequence the events of the next two years in the Olvera Street theater of our founding, would be tedious even if it were possible. For the entire period, with the exception of three months which we spent in Europe and on the New Hampshire farm, we performed five nights a week. In our minds the whole experience has become a memory of much hard work, much satisfaction, much happiness, many unusual contacts, and a few firm friends. For the first few months after our opening we literally lived in the street, taking over two of the rooms over the theater for living quarters, and we grew, in a very real sense, into its life. Proprietors of art shops, antique shops, craftsmen of all kinds—weavers, potters, metal workers, woodcarvers, came to investigate the street, and many finding it congenial, moved in, so we soon had much company. A photographer, setting up her studio in a north room above the theater, took over the long, drab corridor as gallery, and hung there each month a new collection of paintings or prints, some good, some bad, but all vastly more interesting than what had gone before. Visitors came in ever-increasing numbers, and our beginning schedule of three performances a week was soon extended to four and then five, with special showings, often, on "off nights."

Olvera Street rapidly became a sort of haven in the sprawling city for a group of congenial folk who found in its color and informality an oasis of leisurely living. It had its disadvantages. Locomotives chugged by its northern end day and night, switching freight cars and puffing clouds of soot into the air; the rumble of trucks never ceased; a nearby soap factory often provided it with an odor the candlemaker's perfume could not quench; outside its

Ballyhoo in front of the Olvera Street theater (1930).

boundaries were warehouses, grimy store buildings, and squalor. But all these were distant enough to be forgotten, and simply provided a deep pedal-point to the placid reality of the street itself.

It was a joy when one awoke in the morning to the swish of water on the tiles, and found the street clean and shining from its bath, the Mexican vendors arriving to open their small ramadas, setting out their pots, their huaraches, their knicknacks, building their charcoal fires for the preparation of their beans and tortillas, chattering in staccato Spanish to one another. In the heat of noon it was languorous and still, but perhaps friendliest of all at night, with lanterns swinging under every awning, guitars strumming, voices blending in the sugary melodies Mexicans adore. It was prodigal of picturesque characters—Margarita, black-shawled, chunky, smoking long black cigarettes, her two braids bobbing below her waist; of Juan, usually drunk, sleeping on a bench in the sun like a discarded bundle of old rags; José, dapper and handsome in his tight-fitting silver-buttoned trousers; Miguel, always singing; Catalina with her flowers and Calandria with her birds. It was, of course, artificial, but it managed to have about it a certain authentic charm lent it by the age of the buildings flanking it and by the genuineness of the Mexican life that it sustained, and that was so immediately and completely at home in it. And none were more at home than the shoe-shine boys— six of them, from husky Jesus to tiny Toribio. Frequently, in the early afternoon, they would congregate in the patio outside the theater, pool the nickels and pennies they had earned during the morning, and hand them to Alberto, who would then race off to one of the Mexican movie houses on Main Street. For Alberto was a born story teller, and two hours later, he would be back with his friends sitting on their shine-boxes in a circle around him while he told in detail and with gestures the adventure he had just witnessed. Thus all six, for the price of one ticket, could enjoy the film as much, I believe, as though they had actually seen it.

For our part we were too busy to mingle much in the outer life of the street. We only knew that, so far as one is ever able to determine, we were in the right place. Our task was not an easy one. We were attempting to make a commercial success of a project that, in the two or three previous attempts that had been made in America, had proved abortive, and while one or two lingered on under patronage or with volunteer workers, had dwindled and died. We were making our attempt in what was a notoriously poor show-town, a town so bestridden by the colossus of the Cinema that legitimate theater was overshadowed. We had, too, regarding our enterprise strictly from a common-sense angle, the disadvantage of being so small that the usual channels of paid publicity were almost entirely closed to us. In our favor was the wide interest in Olvera Street, and the fact that, except for the impromptu musicians and the cafes, we provided the only entertainment there was.

Our earliest performances were for a short time uncertainly attended. During the days we bent every effort toward building audiences—by mail, by talking about ourselves incessantly, and by keeping the theater open afternoons for the inspection of curious visitors. We had begun, on that first disastrous night, to acquire autographs. The wide expanse of wall-board forming the base of the wall made an ideal slate. We kept ever handy, tucked away beneath one of the boxes, a jar of white show-card paint and

The first autographed walls in the Olvera Street theater (1930).

a fine brush, and whenever a celebrity came to our theater he was seldom allowed to escape without signing our wall. Leatrice Joy had started it, and others were ready to follow. Olvera Street was an immediate attraction to the Hollywood colony, ever alert for something new, and before many weeks passed our walls were sprinkled with an amusing assortment of names. As time went on these grew until there was scarcely room for more, and the deciphering of these signatures became an interesting game for our patrons and an enticing come-on for the sightseers who wandered in during the day.

The names covered diverse fields of endeavor. Our requirement was only that the signer be a well-known personality. His artistic excellence might be questioned, but if he bore a name the world recognized, on the wall he went. Thus, side by side, one might find Harold Bell Wright and Norma Talmadge, Jane Cowl and Gilda Gray, Charlie Chaplin and Walter Hampden, Gloria Swanson and Albert Einstein, Mme. Matzenauer and the Duncan Sisters, Dolores del Rio and William Lyon Phelps. There were, at last, some two hundred. Nearly all were acquired easily, though there would occasionally be complications, as when a celebrity whose name we coveted would be a member of a large and convivial party, all of whom must "write on the blackboard."

If these insistent ones could not be tactfully side-tracked, they were allowed to sign, and, as soon as the house was empty, their names were carefully washed away, leaving only the signature we wanted for our wall's adornment. Sometimes, too, rather more often than we wished, proud patrons would whisper in our ear that their party included the Royal Left Eagle of the Bisons of America, the mayor of Paducah, or the first cousin of Gary Cooper. These had to be pacified or, if nothing else could be done, permitted to offer their esteemed guest the paint-pot, happily ignorant of the fact that a few moments later the esteemed guest's signature would be only a little whitened water in a scrubbing-pail.

Many of these highly diverse celebrities proved excellent patrons and interesting acquaintances who would linger over their after-theater coffee, charmed by the intimacy of the place, or by some phase of the theater or the performance that particularly pleased them. Chaplin, for example, talked fluently and intensely on pantomime. John Barrymore seemed entranced by the fact that it was real theater—"I can almost smell the grease paint!" he muttered, with a typically Barrymore gesture. John McCormack loved the opera singer; Leslie Howard, the animals; Klemperer, the orchestra; Adolph Ochs, a particular line about New York; Marie Dressler, the chorus of cotton-pickers. Don Herold arrived one night with his autograph already written out on a square of wallboard—one of his inimitable peak-nosed characters remarking to the world at large, "I always thought a puppet was the exhaust-pipe on a motorcycle."

It was not too long before we were playing to capacity houses, a condition that obtained with few exceptions until the close of our first year. We were proud of our success. Our small theater was becoming known as the most amusing spot in town, and its fame, we were continually surprised to hear, had spread far. "I heard of your theater in Vienna," or "Someone in Paris told us about your place," became increasingly familiar. Our patronage included the more alert Angelenos, winter residents, and the constant stream of interesting visitors that come and go in Hollywood.

Our success was in many respects phenomenal, for it was achieved almost entirely by word-of-mouth. Two or three of the local papers were kind in the matter of reviews, but others which found a full column scarcely enough space for reviewing the latest picture of Gloria Gush, ignored us, though our Topsy, we knew, was a much better actress. In the East the women's clubs had proved admirable allies, so when we began getting calls from various Los Angeles women's clubs to "just bring along a few puppets and give a short talk," we considered they were offering us a valuable wedge into a large potential audience, good publicity, and an opportunity to make advantageous contacts for our venture. We soon discovered, however, that these clubs had motives quite as selfish as our own, and with much less justification, for whereas our aim was frankly to entertain, theirs was professedly to sponsor by their influence the Better Things of the community. As it turned out, we were providing them with entertainment for nothing, and the much-touted advantages we were to derive from these ordeals never materialized.

Our first such experience was with a club whose palatial quarters were on Wilshire Boulevard. Today an impressive thoroughfare, Wilshire Boulevard in the early Thirties was a singular combination of the Rue de la Paix and a Midway at the amusement park, where, elbow to elbow, stood Elizabeth Arden and Buddy Squirrel's Nut Shoppe, Gothic churches and gas stations designed after the Taj Mahal, blue theaters and pink vegetable markets. The appearance of the club gave us to suppose that our fortunes would be made. We prepared extensively, took along armloads of marionettes, posters, photographs. We had requested an "orthophonic Victrola." This was a relatively new type of machine whose reproductive capacities would be laughable now, but were then so far superior to prior models that we always used them in our performances. We were greeted on our arrival at the club by a large and excited lady, dripping with lace and bristling with feathers, and in full evening dress in the middle of the afternoon, who assured us that all was in readiness except for the "Orthopaedic!" Later we realized that this one incident was perhaps payment enough for an otherwise wasted afternoon. There were perhaps fifty women present, most of whom seemed duplicates, in various sizes, of our excited hostess. All were, we were assured, Lovers of the Drama. They thought "the dolls were cute," and we were told that, though they rarely went out in the evening, and—dear me!—Olvera Street?—Isn't that down in that awful Plaza section?—they would, one and all, rally to our support. Fortunately we did not wait for them.

Meantime we were working continually on new productions. As our third bill we revived an old "Bluebeard" script, completely revised and rewritten. We inserted in it a chorus of seven wives who, at the climax of the piece, flocked merrily on stage announcing that they had been, after all, not murdered, but only anesthetized, and here they were to celebrate the unmasking of their misunderstood spouse, whose beard, a mere "fiction of string and glue" hid his bow legs, which he had acquired from riding horseback too assiduously in his days as a traveling salesman. All came to a happy conclusion, however, when Ariane, taking a genuine fancy to her husband's concavity, sang:

> O fascinating Bluebeard,
> I'll sit between your knees
> and be an exclamation point
> in their parentheses.

Later in the season a revival would not do. Business was flourishing, people were being turned away nightly, reservations were being made two weeks in advance, and in this amiable glow of success a new vehicle was needed. We found it in the story of Noah, and in my bookshop, in intervals between phone calls, attending possible purchasers and pacifying disappointed ticket-seekers, "Mister Noah" came into existence. It became our most popular piece, and rightly so, for it offered boundless opportunities for fun-poking. The animals, of course, were enormously amusing, as puppet animals always are, when they cavorted up the gangplank into the Ark, and later, on board, when they bickered and complained as passengers are wont to do. There were goggle-eyed camels, giraffes, skunks—a not too popular couple—rabbits, timid and a good deal disturbed at the teachings of one Margaret Sanger, lions, ducks—from the suburb of Downey, of course—zebras, and a pathetic pair of dodos whose present non-existence was accounted for by Noah's eagerness to sail, which led him to corral two dodos, but, alas, two males. There was, last of all, left weeping on the shore as the rains descended, a dinosaur whose sheer dimensions compelled his exclusion from the ship.

The cruise proceeded in a relatively orthodox fashion until the dove returned, not with an olive branch, but with a liquor bottle, and the Ark came to rest atop of Mt. Wilson, where it disturbed, though the flood unaccountably had not, Albert Einstein at his cosmic conjecturings, and where it was shortly greeted by Sid Grauman and a committee from the Los Angeles Chamber of Commerce.

It was all a bit of spoofing the Angelenos, or such of them as visited us, took in good part, and reservations soon came in floods, properly enough. It even resulted in an invitation to the unforgettable Breakfast Club, an amazing institution that attracted each Wednesday morning at the dreary hour of eight, some six or seven hundred seemingly sane men and women to a cavernous and draughty hall where they greeted each other as "Ham" and "Egg," sat at long tables for a large but tepid breakfast, put their arms around their neighbors' waists to bellow the "Seasick Song," listened to amplified speeches by visiting celebrities, most of whom looked sleepy and somewhat surprised, applauded movie-stars and aviators, editors and college presidents, laughed and shouted uproariously, and labeled the whole fantastic charade "The Shrine of Friendship."

We came to the spring and the end of a solid year's run, tired out, but eminently gratified at the outcome of our venture. After a good deal of discussion we decided we would close the theater for the summer and vote ourselves a vacation, and having made the decision, out went the sign—ONLY EIGHT MORE WEEKS! Then, miraculously, it became six, and there were wails and heart-rending entreaties for seats, and lines of the hopeful sitting nightly on steps and benches in hopes of a cancellation. The six became five, and four, and three, and we became calloused to the pleas of ticket seekers, and a little skeptical of the number of visiting aunts from Boston who would return there heartbroken if they could not spend their last night in California with the puppets. We reached closing week in a state of happy exhaustion, and when we had covered the last dangling marionette and turned the key in the workshop door it was with relief and yet with pleasant satisfaction.

18.

Eight o'clock on a September night in Olvera Street, the air soft and warm as spring. Late diners hurried along to cafes, early diners strolled and loitered. Somewhere to the right a guitar strummed monotonously and a wailing voice cut through the soft air in a folk-song, half complaint, half petulant sweetness. For us it was the time of preparation for the evening performance. The theater was lighted and open. In the small foyer candles flared and sputtered as they sucked up the first reluctant wax. The little fountain was filled with fresh flowers from the great basket Señor Banuelos bore on his shoulder. The shawl was flung over a corner of the wall, marionettes were brought into the patio and hung on hooks to entice the unwary. From upstairs came the basket of brightly colored coffee cups, in readiness for after-theater drinking. "It's past eight—you'd better get into costume!" admonished Roddy anxiously from the rear door of the bookshop. He was already dressed in corduroy trousers and a gaily colored silk shirt. Eight-fifteen. Tickets were going faster now, and Roddy appeared once more, this time to drag from its hidingplace under the stairs a collapsible stand, painted red and liberally decorated with gold—a stand nearly as tall as himself, behind which he stood on a chair, having added to the previous costume a red scarf and a high silk hat, and dispensed tickets to an ever-increasing crowd. From under the stairs too came the hurdy-gurdy, to be borne outside into the patio, placed atop the wall, and cranked relentlessly in spite of its age and asthma, until it screeched forth its master selection—an Irish jig so foreign to the atmosphere of the street, and yet so singularly in keeping with it. Harry mean-time put through their paces two or three of our portrait puppets.

Jetta Goudal would implore Heaven, and kneeling, sob until her shoulders shook, to the vast and unfeeling delight of the crowd. Douglas Fairbanks would strut and swagger, hand on hip. Charlie Chaplin, to murmers from the smiling Mexican fringe which always surrounded the white inner circle of "Ah, Carlito!" would trip and stumble, jauntily swing his cane and tilt his hat as the music wheezed and thundered. Nine o'clock, the theater filled and buzzing. The doors were closed, Roddy gave last-minute instructions to our hostess who guarded the door and seated late arrivals, and down the side aisle we marched, ducking through the narrow door at the right of the stage into the dim region of back-stage and positions we knew so well. The curtain of "the little bull" rolled up bumpily, its pulleys protesting with tiny mouse-like squeaks. At a signal from Harry the houselights dimmed, the gong sounded its four slow notes, the stage lights blazed into our faces, and the show had begun.

To this routine we returned in September, after a summer in New Hampshire for me, and a summer in Europe for Roddy and Harry, with an eagerness that quite belied our joy at leaving it in June. Our reopening was not exactly a resumption of our activity where we had dropped it. There were new obstacles to overcome, chief among them being one of our own making. During the summer, with an eye to economy, we had leased the theater to a student of Harry's who planned to do a puppet show depicting the history of Los Angeles. It sounded like most inept material for Mr. Punch and his nose-thumbing crew, but it was, after all, none of our affair. The performances were so different from ours that we found, when we returned, that many had been disappointed and permanently soured on puppets, and that many more had to be convinced all over again that the original company was once more back in its own theater.

We set to work at once on a new production and an idea which had been fermenting in all our minds since spring. This time we went to Rome for our inspiration, and starting with only a title, "Caesar Julius," we wove against a classical background of Roman bath, pagan temple and Colosseum, an absurd story involving Caesar Julius himself, Aphasia, his shrewish wife, Mark

Roman matron and chorus of gladiators from 1931 production of Caesar Julius.

Antony, and Cleopatra, who turned out to be a race horse from Cairo (Illinois). Into this strange mélange of gladiators, vestal virgins, bath attendants, and chariot races, wandered, somehow, Al Capone and Legs Diamond to angle in on the racing racket.

They were in togas, with derby hats and cigars. Supplying the final touch of absurdity, Hedda Hopper and Louella Parsons appeared as reporters covering the Rome beat.

The opening was auspicious, and amusing. Because it happened to coincide with the opening of a new Warner Brothers' picture palace on Wilshire Boulevard, an event which had filled the local papers for days, we had fewer of the movie crowd in attendance than at our previous first nights. We had, however, a full house of fans and even a few celebrities. Marie Dressler, who never missed a new show at our theater, was there, and Lady Ravensdale, and Jetta Goudal, and Irene Rich. The public relations staff of Warner Brothers had concocted for their opening a real novelty—the Bridge of Stars. It was an actual bridge spanning Wilshire Boulevard, a bridge which permitted stars and satellites to mount on the north side of the thoroughfare, cross it high above the heads of the gaping crowds below, and descend once more into the astonishing lobby of the theater itself, to smile their plastic smiles into curious cameras, and speak into the waiting microphone the magic words all the world was waiting to hear: "I'm sure tonight's picture is going to be a great success for Warner Brothers, and I wish you were here." Or, with a bit more originality: "I wish you were here, folks. I'm sure this picture is going to be a great success for Warner Brothers."

Not to be outdone, we constructed, from the level of the entrance up the one six-inch step into the foyer proper, a short gangplank which we labeled "The Bridge of Scars," installed a "baby-spot" with a red gelatine to swing over the heads of our customers, and a microphone, with the loud speaker inside the theater. All arrivals had to enter by way of the Bridge of Scars, and were invited to "speak a few words to the folks back home," to the chagrin of the arrival and the delight of those who were already inside.

"Caesar Julius" marked once more a return of prosperity to the theatre, and once more we were playing to packed houses, liberally sprinkled with celebrities more and more diverse. Cecil Beaton came to sketch the Haydn Trio for *Vogue*; Gustave Baumann came from Santa Fe and spent many hours sketching back-stage and in the theater itself; William Beebe, fresh from the Galapagos, came to sit in the front row and glean from "Mister Noah" new knowledge concerning the flora and fauna of the world; Marlene Dietrich came, and was not recognized; Garbo came, and the whole audience struggled to keep its mind on the play—as did, it must be admitted, the puppeteers.

One Sunday afternoon in January we gave a private performance of "Mister Noah" for Einstein. After one experience with Hollywood theaters, an opening at Grauman's Chinese in which the bewildered scientist was fairly torn to bits, he had foresworn theater-going entirely. But a puppet show was different. Furthermore he was persuaded by Galinka, a Dutch girl who was studying art in Los Angeles and was a good friend of the Einsteins. He arrived smiling, and bowing stiffly from the waist as he greeted each of us in turn. His gray suit was rumpled, and his broad-brimmed hat seemed to sit uncomfortably on his head. It was, indeed, a head that would have made the most regal of headgear seem mundane and out of place. With him came a few of his associates from Pasadena. He chuckled delightedly at the musicians, and at "Mister Noah" he roared in earnest. Straining our knowledge of German to the utmost we had managed to translate two or three of the verses sung by the animals as they boarded the Ark. The result must have been, to a native German, funnier than the originals, for they were syntactically fantastic, and mingled English and German with a blithe disregard of linguistic proprieties. When in the final scene his own puppet appeared—an entrance he had not expected—for a moment it was met with surprised silence, and then by a truly Olympian guffaw.

After the performance he stayed for some time, asking questions, nibbling cookies, examining the puppets, trying to work the small violinist, and chuckling at the blue-smocked replica of himself. He viewed it critically. "Gut!" he said. "Gut, gut! Aber zu schmächtig, zu schlank!" whereupon, fumbling in his pocket, he drew out a page of a letter, crumpled it carefully into a ball, and poked it up beneath the smock. He viewed the augmented embonpoint with approval, thanked us all, and smiling, took his way

Albert Einstein poses with his portrait puppet on the campus of Cal Tech (1931).

down the street, mingling with the Sunday throng, who, to his great satisfaction, paid him no notice. All save sharp-eyed Margarita, who ran after him, curtsying and spluttering in excited Spanish. Into his hand she thrust a fat yellow gourd, varnished and shining, around the neck of which was tied a huge bow of pink satin. Carrying it proudly, he disappeared.

And so the year sped by. Early in the spring we announced a new production, our last for the season, "The Pie-eyed Piper." "Caesar Julius" had been elaborate enough with its ballet of vestal virgins, its chariot race on a hand-propelled treadmill, its cheering spectators, but this new production eclipsed all the others. It was built, as our preceding ones had been, on a deliberate reversal of the familiar story. In our version an American mayor visiting the Hamelin Chamber of Commerce suggested to them the American method of ridding the town of rats—the passing of an ordinance. When the Piper and his little German band appeared, however, the contract that had been awarded to him went to Mayor Snorter. The piper's revenge took the form of luring all the women of the town to a near-by carnival, where, on carousel and Ferris wheel they turned blithely, forgetting their housewifely duties with a completeness that soon brought the male population to its knees. All this was complicated considerably by surviving rodents—the three blind mice who hadn't been able to read the ordinance, Elmer who was deaf and hadn't heard the music, and Gwendolyn, the sole surviving female rat who, so she informed the audience in a torrid torch song as she sat perched on top of a beer stein in a small pencil circle of spotlight, had fainted by the riverside at the sorry spectacle of her sisters and brothers, aunts and cousins, drowning wholesale, charmed by the music of the pie-eyed piper, the dyspeptic drummer, and the brute with the big bassoon.

Once more the workshop and stage became a madhouse of activity. Once more surprised clerks in various shops puzzled at the peculiar requests they received from impatient puppeteers. "A half yard of pink tulle, please. That ought to be enough for six ballet skirts, oughtn't it?" Friends volunteered to help, and whoever wandered in was soon put to work painting, sewing, tacking, winding hands, putting screw eyes in waiting scores of arms and legs.

When the new bill was safely in and running smoothly, we were relieved that we had another successful show, but vaguely discontented too. For nearly two years we had been in one spot. We had made a theater and a reputation. We had succeeded where everyone else had failed in running a true puppet theater in America as a strictly commercial venture, paying its way, relying only on itself. We were a little tired of Los Angeles, tired of routine, and were casting, as everyone involved in the theatre did cast, those days, interested eyes on New York, where a success such as we had enjoyed in Los Angeles would, we felt, mean something. We were told it was ridiculous to give up a profitable enterprise for an uncertianty, but that was precisely the argument to strengthen our resolve. Consequently when our last program appeared it carried our farewell to Los Angeles and the announcement of our plans for the summer: "Somewhere in the green vicinity of Franconia or Sugar Hill is an old barn that is due for a big surprise, for along about knee-deep in June, The Puppeteers will arive, and by the time fire-crackers are popping they'll be showing New Englanders what Cleopatra really looked like, and giving escaped Park Avenuers the low-down on Little Eva. Summer theaters have brightened the Eastern resort map in many places, but the White Mountains offer virgin territory, and a perfectly swell place to spend the summer." So on the twenty-eighth of May we gave our last performance in the Teatro Torito, locked its doors, packed the contents of the theater in a freight car, and started on a new adventure.

19.

We left in that fine frenzy of illogical joy in freedom that seems perennially, after so many months of stable living, to be a thing desired above all others, and to be attained at any cost. The green of things as we drove East and came once more into the precious, misprized land of seasons, showers, and green that after a year in the dry and dusty hills of California seemed to us this particular June an omen of green pastures ahead. Mr. Punch, it seemed, cocky with success, could not in so pleasant a land do aught but add more success, and New Hampshire greeted us with a smiling face.

The smile seemed a shade less cordial after a week of barn-hunting. We had thought it the easiest thing in the world find ourselves a barn, move in, hang out our sign, and start showing, but when it came to actually renting one, we found we had been much too optimistic. We scoured the countryside, we poked into cow-sheds and skirted straw-stacks, we interviewed farmers and summer tennants, meeting with varied reactions. Farmer Smith's barn would do, but what about the fence? Farmer Jackson's was ideal as to space, but too far from the main road. This one seemed perfection, but Farmer Stout couldn't very well move out his cows; that was ideally located, but so tumbledown that we dare not risk it. This was empty and well cared for and altogether perfect, but Squire Jones was damned if he was going to have his quiet summer disturbed by God knew what goings-on; that might do, but how would one light it?

One carload of freight was already sitting on a siding in Littleton when we settled on an enormous place at Maplewood. Physically it was perfect, and though its location was not what we had hoped, a little mutual optimism persuaded us that we had found the ideal spot for our summer activities. It had been in its prime a combination of coach-house and servant's quarters for the summer place of a retired and eccentric New England admiral. He had built his house more or less to resemble a ship, with glassed in deck that ran completely around the second story. This house fronted the main highway, but behind, down a lane several hundred yards long, stood the coach-house. The admiral, it seems, when he bade farewell to the sea, turned to land conveyances with an enthusiasm that resulted in his having a coach-house larger than his mansion. It was a huge structure. To the west was a large house of three stories and many rooms which had once housed the grooms and hostlers. Adjoining this on the east side was the barn, consisting of a spacious carriage room, low-ceilinged, but big as a barn itself. This room was paneled with beautifully finished pine, and it looked out, through its great door, on the birch-covered hills of New Hampshire. Overhead was a loft large as a skating rink, its slanted roof rising dimly. Beneath, in the rear (the whole structure was built on a gentle hillside which sloped down through a blackberry-tangled meadow to deep woods), were stables and tack rooms. The whole was strongly built, neatly painted, reasonably free from the usual impedimenta of old barns save in the back part, which held an amazing assortment of vehicles from phaetons and smart-looking gigs to pony carts and even a tally-ho. There were eleven in all, not counting an old Winton automobile, large as a freight car, which reposed in the midst of the carriages, inert and helpless as they, half full of corn cobs and covered with the gray webs of generations of spiders.

The loft, of course, would be the theater proper, and the carriage room would make a greenroom beyond our wildest imaginings. Furthermore, the house afforded the company (augmented for the summer by Roddy's sister, vacationing from college and acting as our hostess, and by a young friend from Ann Arbor, acting as general assistant, who must certainly have come for the lark, for surely the salary he received could have been no inducement)—afforded the company, I hasten to add before this sentence gets the best of me, shelter from storms seasonal and storms temperamental that upset, occasionally, the serenity of the summer.

We announced our opening for early July, and there remained an incredible amount of work to be done. We cleaned and painted and hammered and tacked, sweated and grunted through the long New Hampshire days, and by opening night we were, somehow, ready. We had reason to feel proud of the transformation we had wrought in the admiral's coach-house. Outside it was, to be sure, much the same, save for a broad stairway that led up to the theater proper on the east side of the building. But the greenroom was transformed indeed—spacious and charming, lighted only with candles mounted on three carriage wheels suspended from the ceiling. The carpenters had built for us a pine table, long and massive, with benches on either side, to hold scrapbooks and coffee-cups. The pine walls were lined with photographs and sketches, posters and puppets, and the general effect was both hospitable and charming. Upstairs we had done little more than build in our stage, masking it with velvet we had brought from the Coast, construct benches, and set up an artificial wall of our autographs to hide the sloping angle of the barn roof. For the rest, the rafters slanting up into the dim shadows overhead were decorative enough.

As car after car came up the long lane, as our patrons enjoyed the hospitality of the greenroom, as they laughed and shouted at the antics of the Pie-Eyed Piper and his eccentric crew, as they finally departed, the red tail-lights of their cars swaying through the elm trees and out of sight, it seemed we had made another auspicious beginning. There was just one thing we had overlooked—The Depression. This was 1931. In California it had been talked about and even felt in a premonitory way, but not by us. The dollars came in so eagerly that the much publicized Depression had never been brought to us in any way that mattered. It was only a thing of headlines and hearsay.

But here, though the hills were as green as ever, the air as fresh, the clouds compounded of the same blown cotton they had always been, the superficial aspect of the land failed to tell the grim story. For white house after white house was shuttered, lawn after lawn grown to a tangled wilderness, hotels we had always found bustling with vacationers were either not open at all, or haunted by a pathetic few who seemed to skulk in the shadows, ashamed to flaunt their prosperity in the face of an impoverished society.

And so began a summer that enriched us mightily in sky and cloud, in green fields and white birches, in walks through quiet woods, in blueberries for breakfast, in baths in mountain streams, in talks by firelight and rides by moonlight, but that chastened us in spirit and shrunk our purses to proportions much more familiar and much more in keeping with the modest state of the puppet showman than they had been on leaving California. We had been spoiled by two years of unrivaled popularity. It seemed a little unfair that we should have to dig for business after one period of exalted success. But dig we did, by every means open to us—by stories in the local papers, by posters tacked everywhere, by personal visits to hotel managers and hostesses, by dressing Harry as a clown and driving over the hills and through the valleys, hurdy-gurdy wheezing, tossing out handbills to gaping children and amused or suspicious adults. But the prevailing economic apathy was too much for us. Business at Tally-Ho Theater was so unpredictable that, after a time, without relaxing our efforts in the slightest, we were able to take our audiences philosophically as they came, or as they failed to come.

Evening would descend, with an apple-green sky as clear as spring water, and we would "set the show," wash the dinner dishes, array ourselves in costume, and sit, in the four high-backed rockers that graced the veranda, calmed by the peacefulness of the dusk, and only a bit curious as to the possible patrons who might be showing up for the performance. It would grow darker, time, in fact, for early arrivals, if there were to be any. Along the highway cars would pass, motors humming faintly, headlights making moving planes of sudden white in the gathering darkness.

"Bet that car's going to turn in." "What'll you bet?" "It's slowing up!" "Reading the sign, probably." "They're turning in!" An eager moment, that. "Turning around! In our driveway! Wouldn't you know it!" Faint disgust in the tone, this time, and a hint of amusement. Then at last, when it seemed no-one might be coming, a car would turn in, and another—perhaps several, perhaps only two or three.

But many or few, at the first pair of lights that were seen to be definitely coming down the lane, top-hats went on, chairs were left rocking, empty and telltale, candles were lighted, lights snapped on, and soon the show under way again, with seven spectators or seventy. Their reactions, however, were familiar whatever their number, and we soon found that we had here, as we had had in the West, a small group of enthusiastic patrons who came again and again, bringing week-end guests and such neighbors as they might have in that sparse season, with a persistence that must have been annoying to their friends, but was certainly gratifying to us. Park Avenue was represented by a large and shiny lady, well corseted, glittering with jet and gentility; suburban New Jersey by a Unitarian minister who found something in the puppets to delight his soul; Boston by several trim ladies in velvet chokers who found the plays a little shocking in parts, but clever, you know, clever; New Hampshire itself by a village postmaster and his family, who spent, I know, much more than their modest means warranted on Mr. Punch and his impertinent friends. There was an informality about it all that was even greater than in our other theaters. There was more room to loaf, for one thing, to sit and chat, coffee-cup and cigarette forgotten in chatting. It was all impractical, erratic, and yet very pleasant.

Not all evenings, of course, were water-clear. Rains fell that summer with dismaying and energetic frequency, their falling accompanied, generally by cannonades of thunder rolling among the hills, by miracles of lightning that turned skies to a billowing canvas ceiling, lurid and sooty, and by winds that whipped trees until they seemed to writhe in a struggle to tear themselves from the soil, and that wailed gustily and damply through the eaves and angles of the barn and house. The rains always seemed to be particularly torrential on the nights "Mister Noah" was to be on the boards. There was poetic justice in that, to be sure, but a justice we could not always appreciate. Furthermore the roof leaked, and the rains, delaying usually until a scant hour before show time, neccessitated our rushing upstairs with all available pans, pots, kettles and rags, and sitting, huddled drearily in the draughty loft as the rain thundered on the roof and dropped with flat tinny persistence—ping-ping-ping-ping—into the pans. If the rain stopped, or promised to stop, and a car hove in view, we hastily removed the offending receptacles, and greeted our arriving guests with smiles that belied our trepidation, guiding them to seats we hoped were under no undiscovered chink in the shingles that might suddenly let fall a lurking raindrop on an unsuspecting cheek or chin. Twice on such occasions we had to stop the show, our voices being no competition for the roar of water overhead and the bombardment of thunder that echoed and rumbled among the mountains. Then too there was a skunk who lived under the barn and took frequent promenades across the entranceway with his family in tow. He too seemed always to appear on the nights of "Mister Noah," and although he proved himself a perfect gentleman, he worried us a good deal.

There is something about a small audience, if it is made up of Nice People that is friendly and in a way reassuring. Perhaps it is that they are gratified because performers have given their best for so modest a reward. At any rate, the whole summer, now that it is only a memory, synthesizes itself into a pleasant whole, one which from a purely matter-of-fact standpoint we should have been happy to see come to a close, but whose ending we actually viewed with real regret. In September Bev, our young friend from Ann Arbor, returned to his home, Priscilla to the library, and the Puppeteers to The Plantation for plans and plottings.

20.

Manhattan provided Mr. Punch with buffetings such as he had never had to parry before. It was as though the great gods of Economic Stress, of Law, of Politics, of Real Estate Values, of Misunderstanding, of sheer and overpowering Metropolitanism conspired to harry him and crush his poor wooden head. We came to New York late enough in September to have reveled once more in the glory of a New Hampsire autumn. But peace and quiet demand a longer immersion if they are to provide real immunity from the strain of such a life as we found ourselves plunged into. The evils of the Big City, laugh at them as we will, are very real, if less glamorous and of a different sort from those depicted in the barber-shop ballads and the lurid fiction of another day.

We left New Hampshire in the optimistic expectation of returning there within a week or so to get our puppets and paraphernalia and carry them off to the location we should so easily find for them in New York. We knew what we wanted—a vacant stable or store building, preferably in the East Fifties, which we could without too great a financial outlay convert to a theater, just as we had done in Los Angeles. We took our separate ways from the hotel every morning, walked and peered and interviewed and followed innumerable leads which led only up blind alleys. There was no shortage of places. We found old stables which had been empty for years, and which fairly begged to be used for some such purpose as we proposed. We would, on making such a discovery, unearth from some subterranean retreat a grumbling janitor who would let us in through a complaining door to the dim interior, which we would then appraise as coolly as we were able with a view to its adaptability to our needs. So many of them would have been ideal, and there were, in our minds at least, stable-puppet theaters scattered all over the East Side. But only in our minds, for when the vision confronted the actual hard details, it crumpled and faded and vanished weakly into limbo. For janitors were not landlords, and landlords were not inspectors, and inspectors were, very definitely, not officials bending conscientious efforts toward the establishment of an honest enterprise.

The landlords themselves were a little pathetic. Some were eager to have us as tenants, some were openly dubious, some frankly discouraging. There was, for example, the velvet-gowned, frizzly haired old lady, living in the back room of a decaying brownstone house in a crazy clutter of Japanese parasols suspended from the ceiling, Coney Island dolls, painted shells, enamelled coconuts hanging from velvet ribbons, frilled floor-lamps standing on tables, taffeta cushions on a Steinway grand piano, and a general air of illogical accumulation. She would rent, but what about inspectors? There was another lady living in tarnished elegance amid heavy Victorian furniture, eager, yet unable to make the changes that would have made her property readily acceptable to the inspectors. And so it went. Night after night we came back to the hotel, limp with the drugged weariness that comes from fruitless and disappointing search.

Always it was the inspectors who stood, a horrid multiheaded monster, blocking the way. Rents, to be sure, were appalling, but we were willing to chance them so great was our faith in our show and its attractiveness to New Yorkers. But the inspectors we could not satisfy. They held the key, and they would not release it without the tribute money they considered their due. I recall them with so intense a loathing that they become synthesized in my mind into one overweight, pig-eyed individual whose morals one despised, but whose approval one must, nevertheless, have. It did not matter to him that we were three young men eager to make an independent and honest living in a time when subways and parks and waterfronts were littered with young men who would have given their hands for something to do, and who yet had no such opportunity as we had. It was a sickening experience. In our naïvete we assumed that inspectors, being public officials on the city payroll, would do their duty conscientiously but honestly. We found instead that their approval was dependent wholly on the amount of bribe they were offered, or the political pull of the property owner or his agent. We offered no bribes, we had no pull, and in consequence we got nowhere. On more than a half-dozen properties we came to amicable agreements with the owners. But when the inspectors descended, buildings that were fireproof were declared hazardous, exits that were ample were declared insufficient, wiring that had been approved a few months previously was found antiquated. Had it been a matter of one inspector we would not have been so shocked, but in each case there were four whose approval had to be secured—four who moved with snail-like indifference to our eagerness and our diminishing capital, involving us in delays that were not only expensive, but heartbreaking as well. In one building, apparently a perfect "risk," the objection was that a former tenant, by cutting a door in a partition without sanction of the Building Department had committed a violation which stood as a black mark against the building which could only be wiped away by having the door blocked up again before the partition could once more be torn out by us, with official sanction! Once we found a solidly built two-story garage to which it seemed no possible exception could be taken, since the second floor was already occupied by an elegantly brocaded speakeasy. But a puppet show? That would require the written consent of every property owner on the block. We undertook even that, but when we found that three were abroad, one recently passed on to a region, we trust, untroubled by inspectors, and one ready only to suggest that we move in with the flea-circus on Forty-second Street, we bowed to the inevitable and left the field to the speakeasy, whose bribes, of course, were commensurate with the greed of the inspectors. We found at last, on East Fortieth Street, what seemed an ideal spot. It was the former home of an exclusive club which had obeyed the tendency of the times and moved to more modern quarters uptown. Its concert hall was admirably suited to our purposes, and since it had been used for years by singers, lecturers, and recitalists of all sorts, since it was amply provided with exits, and completely fireproof, there seemed no possible excuse for its rejection by The Enemy. Furthermore, the owner was delighted with the idea. She saw at once our problem and how perfectly it could be solved by her property. The inspectors were duly informed of our intentions, and after the usual harrowing delay they appeared, grunted, peered, and left, assuring us their report would be forthcoming. But it was not, and we made one more hated trip to City Hall where, after the usual hour of sitting on a bench watching twelve or fourteen public officials across the dividing wooden fence sitting on one another's desks matching pennies, or reading the latest news, we were admitted to the office of the "chief," where we learned that, under a recent zoning ordinance, our prospective theater was bisected by an imaginary line running from end to end, which made fourteen feet of it available for our purposes and eighteen feet irrevocably unavailable. The patent absurdity of the situation did not, apparently, appear to the inspector. What would he advise us to do, then? Well, we might construct a fire wall longitudinally down the hall. That this would destroy not only the proportions of the room but its usefulness as well meant nothing to him. He dismissed us with the airy suggestion that we "try to find something else."

The depths we sank to after this intelligent pronouncement were abysmal, for they combined discouragement and a growing but wholly impotent rage at the obtuseness of all officialdom. We were tempted to throw over the whole idea. And yet, here we were, possessors of an entertainment that had been acclaimed, that had weathered the vicissitudes of nearly ten years, and that we knew was worth struggling for. After a few hours of glumly staring at each other in the dormitory-like room we had, for economy's sake, moved to, we decided to put ourselves in the hands of a realtor. Guile it seemed was the only weapon against guile. The simple way, the obvious and aboveboard way of establishing a business in Manhattan had, it further seemed, been sloughed off long ago and forgotten. It had become instead a

rather unpleasant Machiavellian game of outwitting or circum-
venting the law.

Our realtor proved to be all that a Manhattan realtor should
be. Yet, clever as he was, he was no magician, and the palms of
the inspectors still greedily insisted. Could we line them? We
could not. What capital we had left must go into the equipping of
the theater. Well, perhaps the landlord, if he were genuinely
eager to have us as tenants, could manage the inspectors. And
then occurred one of those singular happenings that cannot be
explained by any logic we know. In looking through a guest book
where former patrons of our shows had, if they wished, signed
their names, I came to a halt at the signature of a Mrs. McCooey.
McCooey. Could it by any chance be *the* Mrs. McCooey, whose
husband's voice made the Tammany tiger cower? The address
was Brooklyn, the initials were right, the telephone directory
confirmed the fact. If she had signed her name she had done so of
her own free will, and that would seem to indicate that she had
thought our performance worthy of some slight effort on her part.
Or would she, perhaps, be simply one-of-those-persons-who-
sign-guest-books? It was a slender chance, so slender in fact that I
dared not tell my partners about it. In all secrecy I wrote to the
unknown lady a letter so persuasive that it could hardly, I
thought, be overlooked, even if she had forgotten a summer
evening's diversion and an autograph in the Puppeteers' guest
book.

Days passed, and I had relegated the whole incident to the
limbo that was so rapidly filling these days with disappointments,
when suddenly a letter arrived from the "Democratic Committee
of Kings County, Office of John H. McCooey." "Dear Mr.
Brown," it read, "Mrs. McCooey has requested me to acknowl-
edge your letter addressed to her. I would suggest that you call
upon Mr. David J. Hogan at the above address at your conve-
nience. Mr. Hogan will take the matter up and do everything
possible to have your request granted."

To Brooklyn the subway express was scarcely fast enough, the
dingy stairs and trembling elevator of Number Four Court
Square wholly inadequate to carry me to the office of the miracu-

lous Mr. Hogan. I arrived in a state of nervousness that would have done my cause little good had I been compelled then and there to plead it. Mr. Hogan, however, speaking around his cigar in perfect Brooklynese that was heaven to my ears, required no pleading. He was there to do the will of McCooey. He extracted from his scarred desk a visiting card bearing his master's embossed name, and across its back, in a flowing Spencerian hand, wrote "This will introduce Mr. Forman Brown. Do what you can for him. John H. McCooey."

"Take this to Gallagher," he said, and waved me away. Buttoning the card in my pocket as carefully as though it had been a pardon from a sentence of death, I reached Manhattan in a daze. For Gallagher was the "chief," the man we could never see, the man behind the door whose opening was the signal for papers to be put away, feet taken off desks, and expressions fixed into some semblance of mental activity.

Our realtor had meantime found us a building not by any means ideal as to location, since it was in a strictly commercial street little traversed at night, but which did offer us sufficient space, a landlord who was agreeable to our enterprise and willing to install for us a new front in place of the conventional plate glass that had always marked the place as a store. With the magic card of Hogan and the somewhat institutional smile of Gallagher, with the cooperation of the landlord, the persuasiveness of the realtor, and the insistence of our attorney, the lease was signed and the approval of the inspectors given, though grudgingly, as they felt that the fifty dollars offered them by the landlord was totally inadequate. "Take it back an' keep it till it grows up! Dis job's woit two hunnerd bucks!" growled one of them in disgust. But there was the shadow of McCooey, and he gave, at last, his reluctant signature, pocketed the proffered bill, and we were launched, for better or for worse, on what seemed very murky waters indeed. We had planned to open in October at the latest. It was now nearly Thanksgiving time, and there was a dismaying amount of work to be done. We set December 6th as opening date and plunged in, and, as always seemed to be the case, were somehow ready when that night arrived.

Interior of The Puppet Show, the Yale Puppeteers' New York theater (1932).

This New York opening was one we might well have worried over, for it was serving to launch us on a venture for which we had the highest hopes and toward which we had long aspired. Our situation was quite different from what it had been in the West. There we had the advantage of a ridiculously low rental in a location that was in itself an attraction, a constant stream of visitors passing our doors, and the eager cooperation of all the people who made up the small community of Olvera Street. Here, on the contrary, we were paying an excessive rental for a location that was utterly without atmosphere, and, indeed, in spite of its proximity to Fifth Avenue and Times Square, almost deserted at night, save for a few diners visiting the three or four restaurants in the block, or by casually strolling theater-goers bound for the brighter lights of Broadway. We were opening, furthermore, in a city that presented us with more competition in the field of entertainment than any other we might have chosen—in a city, too, that had still to be convinced that a puppet show could be of any interest to an adult and sophisticated theater-goer.

Our theater was undeniably arresting. In a street of small conventional shop-fronts it attracted immediate attention. We had
removed the plate glass and built in a front of white stucco with a
central entrance, deeply recessed, giving access to the theater
itself by way of two blue doors. On either side the facade was
pierced by a small grilled window with a perkily striped awning
cut from tin and painted blue and white. Inside the long bare
expanse had been transformed into a theater much like the
Teatro Torito, with the autographed walls (which we had removed and brought east with us), gaily striped canopy for a ceiling, and proscenium in red and gold that always seemed appropriate to the antics of Mr. Punch. But here, with much more
space at our disposal, we were able to devote more than half the
length of the room to purposes of display. Here we hung our
pictures, our foreign posters, our precious Goldonis, and, on the
pine table we had brought down from New Hampshire with the
rest of the equipment, there was ample room for our scrapbooks,
coffee cups and guest book—as had been recently proved, a most
important adjunct of our enterprise.

But the first plunge was difficult. We wanted a truly impressive
opening such as we had had in the West, with celebrities and
excitement. A reservation from Otis Skinner, whom we had met
the previous summer, delighted us, but we were avaricious. And
then, about a week before our opening, we learned that Marie
Dressler was in town. We knew she was not well, and called her
hotel not without foreboding. She was, however, as we knew she
would be, delighted to know we were in town and eager to hear
our plans. So that very afternoon found us chatting with her in
her suite at the Savoy Plaza. She was in New York for treatment,
and was going out almost not at all, but—an opening of the Yale
Puppeteers?—that was something she could not miss, and she
began laying plans immediately for a party of twenty—twenty
who would "do you boys some good." For a half-hour she kept
us, talking and planning, and putting a rather discouraged trio
into a much brighter state of mind.

So, thanks to that great lady, our opening in New York was a
gala one. In her party were Anne Morgan, Mrs. W. K. Vander-

bilt, Mr. and Mrs. Fritz Kreisler, James Forbes, and a dozen others, all Manhattanites of importance, whose enthusiasm was so genuine and whose laughter so hearty that we were, it seemed, amply repaid for the weeks of frustration.

But after the excitement of the first night had worn off Mr. Punch found his days exceedingly drab and his small theater, which suited his needs and his temperament so admirably, a rather lonely place. There was little money left for advertising, and advertising, in consequence, suddenly assumed an importance it had never had before. Never had so small a theatrical venture received better notices, and it was gratifying to have recognized critics, seasoned through years of Broadway play-going, find in "The Pie-Eyed Piper" and "Mister Noah" something genuinely fresh and unpretentious and worthy of their critical approval. But laudatory reviews, particularly in the blackest of theatrical seasons, 1932, were not enough, and Mister Punch found himself existing very precariously.

By every means we could think of we tried to bolster our venture, for, having gambled on it everything we had built up through the years, we were determined it must succeed. It was a discouraging matter and many a night found us plodding to our apartment, tired and silent, and wondering to ourselves whether we would not be wiser to desert the show and find ourselves where remuneration, small though it might be, would be certain. And then, with the unpredictability that seems to be a rule of the theater, would come a performance so well attended, so enthusiastic, that it would give us courage to face ensuing audiences too small and too shy, in the prevailing emptiness, to make their pleasure known. And so the season progressed, and somehow from week to week we hung on until, as spring came round, with that indefinable airy tingling that even in the canyons of concrete that are Manhattan insinuates itself into every breath one takes, we did seem to be making some progress. It was encouraging, too, every Sunday morning when we opened the theatrical pages of the *Times* to find ourselves creeping slowly toward the top of the box listing "long run attractions." More people were finding their way to us, and the novelty of what we had to offer, something small and intimate in a city of superlatives, came to be better and better known.

Bright moments often illumined our run. There were celebrities, not so many as in Hollywood, to be sure, but perhaps more interesting. I. A. R. Wylie and her white bullterrier became frequent visitors. Zona Gale, adding her small neat autograph to our wall surveyed it from a distance with a critical eye and murmured, not unpleased, "It's like calico." William Lyon Phelps, en route to a lecture for the Brooklyn ladies, amused us by finding "Mister Noah" slightly blasphemous. Muriel Draper, surprisingly turbaned, found our likeness of Gary Cooper so appealing that she invited, for a special midnight performance, a hundred "Garyflappers." The party included a movie star or two, some Broadway actresses, a few Park Avenue types, and a heterogeneous and astonishing assortment of poets, Harlem habitues, prizefighters, and eccentrics, all come to pay their jaded respects to a small wooden figure who, fortunately, could not laugh. Strange characters wandered into the theater during the day as well—slightly inebriated ladies who always thought they were in a speakeasy, and where was the bar?; curious idlers, people with promotional ideas, collectors of toy theaters, retired actors who seemed always a little envious of the eternal youthfulness that was Punch.

Just across the street from us was the welfare department of the Stage Relief Society, an organization that gathered costumes and garments from all possible sources, and, refurbishing them, outfitted down-and-out vaudevillians, made hopeful but indigent juveniles presentable for try-outs, and dispensed such cheer as they might to a profession doubly smitten by the depression and the mechanical competition of radio and films. The workers, also jobless actors, were at once interested in our theater, and every week we supplied them with twenty or thirty passes. Those who used them were always appreciative, and we were glad to have them in our audiences. One afternoon while the Players Club revival of "Uncle Tom's Cabin" was in progress, we invited the whole cast to the theater, and played for them our own less authentic version of the piece, to their unbounded delight.

Katherine Warren, whom we had known in New England, and who was now playing Roxane to Walter Hampden's Cyrano, arranged a party for the Cyrano company, and they came one Sunday night, filling our small playhouse to capacity. For the occasion Harry had made a portrait puppet of Mr. Hampden as Cyrano de Bergerac, and I had written for him a special number. It came as an utter surprise, and his emotion was deep and genuine. Seated near him was a delightfully young old lady who had visited our theater many times, but concerning whom we knew very little. After the performance she whispered to me that long ago she had played opposite Richard Mansfield, and did I think Mr. Hampden would be interested? He was, needless to say, and the result of their meeting was a conversation of genuine pleasure for them both. She was Rillie Deaves, and as one of the earliest Belasco stars, known as "the willowy Miss Deaves," had been the toast of the town. That small incident gave us the friendship of a charming woman, a friendship that became a highlight of our season.

June brought with it heat and the inevitable slacking off of trade that all theaters expect. So, early in the month we locked our doors, put up a sign announcing our reopening in the fall, sublet our apartment, loaded ourselves into our car that had been stored all winter in the Bronx, and started for The Plantation.

21.

June had never seemed more alluring. The tracks of the road that led in along the bank of the loquacious little river were almost concealed beneath the rank growth of grass and weeds. The house seemed smaller than ever, buried almost to the windows in the green inundation of the new growth. And once more we experienced the age-old benediction of Place. There were worries galore, worries we knew we should have to face before the fall opening, but in this lovely and quiet land proportions seemed to adjust themselves unobtrusively to a healthy and just arrangement that kept future worries in the future, and distant eventualities comfortingly distant. Each day was a day to enjoy, a day prodigal of happiness that was there for the grasping.

June changed imperceptibly into July, with warmer days, briefer and lustier showers, and the weeds of the roadway flattened by the passing over them of our car and the scuffling of our village-bound feet. And out of this restful procession of days emerged one with a surprise. It came in the form of a telegram which reached us, two days late, by a leisurely and roundabout process that spoke well for our seclusion. It came from the New York story editor of one of the Hollywood studios, whom I recalled as having been a patron of our theater during our Olvera Street days. Would I call him at once? As usual, the calling devolved on me. I waited long enough in the local telephone exchange to hear a memorable conversation between the local operator and a talkative friend before my call was completed. When it finally was, I learned that a picture was brewing in Hollywood which involved puppets, and would I come to New York at once, at the company's expense, to talk things over?

Next day I left. There was, it seemed, a picture going into production soon the story of which centered around a Parisian puppet theater and the family which owned it. In a burst of zeal of the distinctly Hollywood sort, a famous troupe of European marionettes, the same Teatro dei Piccoli Harry had vainly pursued in Italy, had been signed for the job. When the director of the film, however, had talked to the director of the marionettes, he had received a liberal education in the field of his immediate interest. For, if puppets were to be an integral part of the film, as he wished, special puppets would have to be built and special routines worked out. The Europeans could manage this, of course? *Mais oui!* But it would involve, of course, a trip to Europe, sculptors, costumers, six months, a year—who knows? And on the rock of Latin tradition split the wave of Hollywood impetuosity, with the resultant telegram that had so surprisingly dropped into the middle of a blue New Hampshire day. Could WE make puppets to order, in wholesale lots, and without undue temperamental displays? We could. What would be our price? I swallowed, hesitated and stated a figure we had, with some trepidation, agreed on. It was calmly received. I was given a check to cover my expenses, and assured that we should soon hear their decision.

The news I brought back to The Plantation was more upsetting than the telegram had been, for now there was a definite objective to fasten our conjectures to, and every sentence was soon prefaced with an "if." It was all highly tentative, to be sure, but who, in our circumstances, could have regarded the possibility of a Hollywood contract as other than the kind and well-timed manifestation of a beneficent Fate? I came back from New York as a mundane sort of guardian angel bearing tidings of good things to follow. The coming, however, was slow, and as days passed and there was no further word, we became increasingly certain that our price had been too high, that our foreign competitors had been converted to an American view of things, that the whole idea had been scrapped and, most of all, as former residents of Hollywood we were most egregious fools indeed to expect any logical conclusion to all these preliminaries. And so, while we still hoped, we did so individually and secretly. We had planned a trek to Michigan for early August, and so early one morning we locked the door and started for Montreal. Something kept whispering to me that New York should be notified of our move, so from a small hamlet in Ontario, about noon, I put in a call, using all the nickels the bemused French barmaid could collect. New York came through at last. "Where the devil are you guys? I've been trying all morning to reach you! Can you go to Hollywood right away—a four week contract—if not all of you, at least Burnett?" I stumblingly said we could. "Call me at noon tomorrow, from wherever you are, and we'll have the details worked out."

The customary joys of the motor tourist were, I must admit, somewhat denatured for us during the next twenty-four hours. In the little town on the banks of the St. Lawrence where we stopped for the night, a stifling night which made sitting on the river bank much pleasanter than going to bed, we had difficulty waiting for the next day. The next day, from the outskirts of Toronto, with no nickels to be concerned with, and "Reverse the charges, please" slipping easily off the tongue, we learned that the contract was definitely ours. Harry was to proceed at once to the Coast, with a fourth puppeteer. Roddy and I were to return to New York, pack all available marionettes, and follow as soon as we could. Harry elected to drive, so in Michigan he picked up Bev, our helper of the previous summer, a generous check for expenses, and was off. Roddy and I, almost as soon as we arrived, set off again for the East. Some of our belongings had to be collected from The Plantation, which must then be closed for the winter. The rest had to be packed in New York and sent off to their strange address, and to what strange adventures, in the cinema city.

Arriving once more in Hollywood, not this time as vagabond puppet showmen, unknown and with a reputation to make, but as recognized artists in our field, fresh from a New York season, and with the added benison of a movie contract to shed its aura about our happy heads, was a new and pleasant experience. There were scores of friends to call on and acquaintances to greet, and the prospect of an interesting four weeks at the studio. Mister Punch at first seemed strangely out of place on the movie lot, an insignificant intruder in this world of superlatives. To him was assigned a generous corner in the paint shop, flanked by the art department and the enormous lofts where back-drops were so meticulously painted that they never quite fool you into regarding them as real. Here was the workshop Harry must have dreamed of, and soon our puppets were unpacked and hung on hastily built racks, holding court for the interested crew of studio mechanics, extras and office people that came straggling in to view this modest wonder. So, even in this alien place, Mister Punch established himself and made friends with his customary ease and nonchalance.

Plans for the picture on which we were to work seemed to us very hazy. The director, Rowland V. Lee, a man of great enthusiasm and considerable temperament, outlined the story to us and gave us a vague idea of what was to be our share in it. But specifically, whether we were to create puppets of seraphim or blackamoors, no one seemed to know. The script was not finished, and day by day some new idea of the director or of the playwright who had been called in to work on it, gave the plot a new twist. The insidious virus of The Puppet seemed to have taken its toll here too. Not even the inoculation of Hollywood immunized these people, and plans flourished with a blithe disregard for the conventional limits of what a puppet can do as determined for him by his wooden anatomy. In the face of this bewildering uncertainty Harry marshalled his forces and began turning out parts wholesale—legs, arms, hands, bodies, controllers, in factory quantities.

While my three partners were concentrating on this effort, my lot was somewhat different. At the instigation of the story editor who had first approached us on the subject of the contract, I was at once assigned the unexpected job of writing lyrics for the film. The music was entrusted to a young German composer, Frederick Hollander, who had been brought to the studio some three months before my arrival, and in the classic Hollywood tradition, been given nothing to do. He occupied a "bungalow" next to that of the director—a small brown-shingled house of three rooms, comfortable and pleasant, with a fine piano, wide windows, vine-shaded, that opened to the cool breezes of the Pacific, and a capacious—and empty—desk.

The story being in the fluid state in which it seemed day after day to continue, there was very little for me to do. My composer-collaborator, already disillusioned, spent little time in the bungalow. He was a small man of great personal charm and great talent. In Germany he had written the songs that helped make Marlene Dietrich famous, and his cabaret, "Tingel-Tangel," which I later had the pleasure of translating into English, had been a sensation in pre-war Berlin. His particular talent made an excellent complement for my own, it seemed, for while my German was much too sketchy to permit me any very well defined appreciation of the songs he showed me, I could easily recognize in them the same slightly satiric humorous quality that had characterized my puppet plays and sketches. It seemed, indeed, a happy chance that had brought us together. Since his appearing at the studio at all, save to collect his weekly pay check, was almost an impertinence, he satisfied himself with an hour or so a day in his bungalow, generally around lunch time, for the table at the studio cafe was notably good. For the rest of the time the quarters were mine. I tried valiantly for a few days to be busy, and to pretend to be busy when I was not. However, the August days were long and somnolent, and I soon began floor-pacing, always a bad sign. In one of these restless moods the director found me one day. "What's the matter?" he asked, regarding me with an amused and knowing eye. "Haven't you got anything to read, or anything of your own to work on?" I answered, taken somewhat by surprise, that I had been mulling over an idea for a book. "Work on it, then. If you don't you'll go nuts." Taking this as an order from my superior, that is what I did, while my partners, no doubt, sawing, whittling, painting, envied my leisurely existence.

Our contract called for four weeks. Three of these had already slipped away, and there was not yet even a date announced for the shooting to start. Puppet parts were accumulating in the workshop, and rather definite and not too complimentary ideas of studio efficiency were accumulating in our heads—but nothing seemed to happen. The sun poured down, the days passed by in golden procession. In the director's bungalow next door story conferences were in progress, those fantastic Hollywood substitutes for the editorial function, in which the author's story (unified, one may suppose, by something of his skill or personality) is torn to bits, added to, subtracted from, patched, padded, and cut finally into something impersonal and nondescript because it is everybody's and nobody's. One day, hotter than the rest, I overtook the playwright en route to the studio cafe, and he volunteered, with a singular admixture, I thought, of relief and regret, that his work was done. "Of course," he added resignedly, "they'll cut all the best parts, and when it finally gets to the screen it won't be mine. But that's Hollywood. It's wonderful. They hire an expensive writer—and I am an expensive writer—in order to tell him how to write."

"You've been around Hollywood a long time, haven't you?" I asked, remembering his Broadway successes of ten or more years back.

"Too damn long!" was his comment. "A writer, you see, however bad he is and however much he takes all this as a racket and a matter of course, couldn't write a whole script without having somewhere, in a few places, some good spots—spots he really felt—fresh and original; but those are bound to be the spots they first cut. It's a gift. I don't know how they manage to pick them so flawlessly. Hell, let's have lunch!"

We had been on the lot six weeks before a scene was shot, long enough to make us feel quite at home in the fantastic city of Chinese pagodas, Norman towers, dry-land ocean liners, western ranchos, eighteenth century gardens and Irish villages, so realistic to look at, yet so flimsy that a strong gale might send them crashing—a deserted city that might be the dream of a madman. Long enough, too, to know the various personalities that make up the intricate life of the place, and to be acquainted with some of the intrigue that motivated and at the same time delayed its work.

And then, on a day when there seemed to be no more reason

Gene Raymond and Lilian Harvey puppets used in the Fox film, I Am Suzanne
(1933).

for activity than on any of those that had preceded it, word
suddenly came that we were to start shooting. We were plunged
at once into the actual business of film-making, and while our
opinion of the general inefficiency of studio methods remained
unchanged, our attitude became more tolerant, and our respect
for the director who could bring any order out of such chaos
grew. For the mass of detail, mechanical, artistic, personal, and
temperamental that must be dealt with and somehow subordi-
nated and synthesized in a motion-picture studio is dismaying.
And into the midst of this hubbub strode Mister Punch. Some of
his nonchalance, to be sure, was missing, but in a few days it
returned and stood him in increasingly good stead during the
grueling days that followed.

Our task was not of equal difficulty. Some sequences of the

film were ours alone, and on these we worked feverishly, and put
in hours no union would ever sanction. But in many sequences
we did not appear at all, or were called in merely to operate one
marionette, probably one of the portrait figures Harry had made
of the two principals of the film, Lilian Harvey and Gene
Raymond. On these occasions our most arduous task was waiting. Waiting, waiting, waiting for a call that might come at any
moment, or that might not come until another day, or two days,
or three, depending on the plan or whim of the director. He
became at once, when the actual shooting started, and for reasons
that soon became apparent, a complete dictator whom one approached with fear and trembling, and whose every wish was
signal for someone to jump to attention. We had no way of
knowing what would be wanted next, for the logic of the shooting
schedule was apparent only to the director and his aides, having
no relation whatever to the order of events in the story. And the
story, indeed, underwent daily, almost hourly transmutations as
the director's idea imposed itself more and more.

And then the Teatro dei Piccoli arrived, in a flurry of baggage
and staccato Italian. We looked forward to meeting Mr. Podrecca
and his company, but as a day, two days, three days passed, we
finally realized that our presence on the lot was resented by these
performers, and that even stronger than their resentment was the
fear on the part of the producer that, if we met, dead puppeteers
would strew the studio floors and litter the beautifully symmetri-
cal geranium beds. It was an absurd situation, and one we finally
met, wearied of circling like fighting cocks, by the simple expe-
dient of introducing ourselves. The hostility, so far as outward
manifestations went, vanished. During the two weeks they were
at work we stayed tactfully in the background, content in the
knowledge that our share in the film was the more important, and
our contract, being of so much longer duration, the more profitable.

While my partners, with such assistance as they had never
remotely dreamed of—miniature department, costume de-
signers, a whole staff of seamstresses—turned out puppets to the
number of two hundred or more, I had my interludes with the

music department. From the first it became apparent that the
director had made a tactical blunder in setting to work on the film
a composer who was new to the scene and a foreigner, and a
lyric-writer who was not only new, but not even a member of the
large music staff. The obstacles to our work would have been
laughable if they had not been so childish. Three songs were
required. Hollander and I were both facile writers, and we could
easily have performed the assignment in as many days, but
change after paltry change was required, each one bringing the
songs down from the Continental sophistication that had been
theirs to the level of the commercial popular song, above which
level the mental processes of the musical director did not rise. A
love song was required, a song that was to be sung first by two
marionettes and later by the boy and girl who were supposedly
their manipulators. "Wooden Woman" was the title of the song I
submitted, a title which fitted the situation and was, I thought,
not bad. "No sex appeal," was the verdict, "Don't mean a damn
thing. Now if it was 'Wooden Shoes'. . . ." Again I submitted a
lyric which rhymed "often" and "soften." "What the hell is this?"
asked the music director, shifting his cigar to the other side of his
mouth and his feet to the corner of his desk. " 'Soften' and 'often'?" (He prounced "often" with unmistakable emphasis on the
"t"). "Hell, that ain't a rhyme! Soften and of-ten! Jeez! You gotta
make things rhyme, you know, June and moon!"

And with such diversions passed day after aggravating day.
They were long and varied, for each morning at seven-thirty the
film that had been made the previous day was run off in a small
projection room, and at these rushes we had to be present to
catch any errors in action and check any idiosyncracies in puppet
costume or make-up. Since cameras ground very often until
seven in the evening or later, and there was often work still to be
done in the shop, night found us quite ready for bed.

The picture was far behind schedule. The director, since he
was also co-author of the story, made more and more frequent
revisions in the script, and the film spun out to surprising,
frightening lengths. Can after can was carried off to the
laboratories and locked in the heavy steel vaults until it seemed

Ribbon Ballet from 1933 film, I Am Suzanne.

impossible that from this mass of disjointed sequences it would ever be possible to piece together a unified whole. We had been on the lot fourteen weeks, and we expected daily to be finished, and yet so chaotic seemed the whole affair that we had no way of knowing what we would be asked to do next. And then suddenly, after a day unprecedented in grueling work, in temperamental outbursts, in frayed nerves, and in general confusion of actors, technicians, valets, electricians and extras we were, definitely, finished.

Into their trunks went our puppets and into the somewhat surprised hands of the studio prop department went the two hundred or more figures we had made and that were now the property of the studio, to be wrapped in paper and laid along the shelves, never, it was likely, to be used again. And in stacks of flat shiny cans lay the closely coiled film that represented, in its thousands of slippery feet, their life work. What happened to them, who knows. Some, I suppose, may have been sneaked out as acceptable gifts for children of the property men, but most have no doubt gone the sorry route of the clanking endless belt that carries studio refuse to a fiery and certain end.

But by Christmas time their shadows were dancing around the world. I AM SUZANNE, flashed the marquee of the Radio City Music Hall. I AM SUZANNE, read the posters in London and Sydney; SUZANNE, C'EST MOI, they flaunted in Paris; ICH BIN SUZANNE, they acclaimed in Berlin.

"I believe," wrote Anatole France, "in the immortal soul of the marionette," and his sentence seemed never more true than when we, a little breathless, first saw these creatures of our making leap into shadow-life on a thousand screens in a dozen countries. This was for Mister Punch and his rowdy crew a new venture, but not by any means, the last. He would go on and on. Irving and Booth, Coquelin and Grimaldi—these were names and memories, but Mister Punch, eternally youthful, eternally raucous, would live forever, thumbing his nose at a thousand hangmen and at Death himself.

Part II

Turnabout Theatre

22.

The weeks of hard work were over and we were tired. Most of our puppets and equipment were now in Hollywood, and the thought of launching another season in New York in our own small theater, with all the problems we had met before, many of which we knew we would never be able to solve, became less and less attractive. Our old theater in Olvera Street was standing empty, and after much discussion we decided to chance another season. We made the necessary arrangements and moved back to the Teatro Torito for a "gala return engagement." It was somewhat less than gala. Though we played for several months, the old magic was gone. The street had changed. Some of the fine shops were gone. Adrian, the celebrated costume designer at Metro-Goldwyn-Mayer had been our nearest neighbor with a charming small boutique, but now his doors were closed. So were those of the decorator, Bertram Grassby. The atmosphere was now more like that of a carnival, noisy and crowded. Also, during our absence, a few doors south of our theater, another puppet troupe had moved in. Their performances were loud and mindless, but colorful and popular with the new breed of visitors who would have been little amused by our verbal gymnastics. The novelty of the street had worn off, and while its popularity steadily increased, its character, to us, at least, was a disappointment.

When we finally closed, we packed our gear—much more prudently this time—and returned to New York. Not, this time to the theater on West Forty-sixth Street—we had given up our lease there—but to the building we had so coveted before, and been denied by the Building Department's ridiculous demand that it be bisected down the middle for zoning purposes. The building was still there, and we fell in love with it all over again.

Just east of Lexington Avenue on East Fortieth Street, it had once been a church. The story goes that Mrs. Tonetti, who owned it, had gone out shopping one fine afternoon and when she came home said to her sculptor husband, "Dear, I've just bought a church." One entered the building through tall iron gates into an entryway, tiled and vaulted, that might have come straight out of Florence. A few broad steps led down to the basement, and it was this basement that we wanted for our New York headquarters. It consisted of one huge room and a kitchen. But the room was incredible. Its walls had been decorated by Palmer Cox, the artist whose creation of the Brownies had made him famous with children the country over. But here he had gone classical, and his murals in tones of faded browns and pastels might have come from some wealthy Roman's house. There were even, at intervals around the walls, painted caryatids so skillfully painted they seemed really to be holding up the ceiling. There was a scattering of Persian rugs, several large Italianate pieces of furniture—chairs, sofas, chests—a Steinway grand piano, and best of all a workable Franklin stove, which cheered us on many a chilly night.

We knew we could not operate here as a theater. The inspectors had made that quite plain. We could, though, operate as a club, so we sent out announcements for week-end performances, meanwhile booking as many dates as possible during the week in nearby towns in Connecticut, New Jersey, Pennsylvania, Long Island and the environs of the city. The Bel Geddes show had been so complicated and cumbersome that, though artistically it was a success, practically it was a disaster. The musical plays we had done in our own theaters here in New York and on the Coast were elaborate and impossible to tour. Furthermore they required a minimum of four puppeteers, and we were only three, and three who were weary of packing and unpacking heavy trunks and cartons, and of spending more time setting up and tearing down shows than in actually performing them. We knew we must simplify, so we made a bold innovation: we discarded the proscenium arch and the curtains that had for centuries hidden the operation of the puppets. This has been done many times since, but not before, I believe, by a professional company.

Under the new plan, the marionettes performed on a bare platform covered with black velvet and against a black velvet back-drop. There were spotlights on standards at either side of the stage, and behind it a single rack where the figures were hung in readiness for their entrances. When props were needed they were openly set in place by one of the puppeteers. At one side, hidden in shadow, was the piano. We were dressed alike in unobtrusive dark dinner clothes, so although from the waist up we were visible to the audience, since the lights were focused only on the playing area of the stage, we found that the viewer within a very few minutes had become so absorbed with the marionettes and their antics that we who pulled the strings were quite forgotten. While it is true that a few people told us they felt that the illusion one always gets with a well-designed puppet show was lost, our

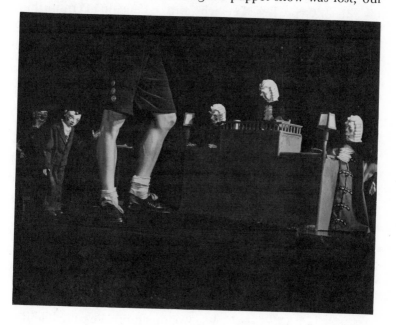

Oliver J. Gullible in court with his son (Harry). Gullible's Travels (1931).

audiences seemed to find these simplified performances immensely entertaining, and the unexpected opportunity of watching the hands of the manipulators of the marionettes in the shadows above the puppet stage, fascinating.

In our new quarters our expenses were much less, and our enjoyment much greater. When we were gone during the week on out-of-town engagements, we could be assured of a congenial place to return to. Those of our old patrons who came to our club fell in love with it, as we did. There were no regular rows of seats. Our guests arranged themselves as they pleased on individual chairs in front of the stage, which, built into only one corner of the room left the rest of it open and inviting for coffee and conversation. The informality of the place was its charm.

It was during our tenancy here that I began writing special material that attracted the attention of Leonard Sillman, who was preparing a second edition of *New Faces*. The room was perfect for auditions, and a few memorable ones took place there, notably one for Gypsy Rose Lee, who arrived done up in ermine from head to toe, and created a great to-do when she discovered her diamonds were missing. They were found in the ladies' room, but that particular episode did not create the most propitious atmosphere for listening to my songs.

During this time, too, we made a brief foray onto the Broadway scene. We were booked, with the old show—the heavy one—into the Nora Bayes Theater for a week. The Nora Bayes was a small theater set on top of another—the Forty-Sixth Street, and it should have been ideal for a puppet production. I am sure this is what the promotor had in mind in booking us there. But the sad fact was that the Bayes had been lighted so seldom in the past seasons that New Yorkers had forgotten it existed. Also the problem of getting two- or three-hundred people through the lobby of one theater and up to another by elevator, some found a little forbidding. We were glad, at the week's end, to get back to our cozy quarters.

Meantime, we had developed the new and more simplified show into a true musical revue in miniature. We called it "It's a Small World."

Harry as Miss Lily Putia poses with Oliver J. Gullible (1931).

"It's a Small World" had its official opening at the Lyceum Theater in New York during the Christmas season, and the reviews were flattering indeed. Even the thorniest critics succumbed to the charm of the marionettes and sprinkled their notices with such welcome adjectives as "clever," "amusing," "adroit," "literate," "fresh," "witty," and "original."

The puppet cast of "It's a Small World" consisted of portrait marionettes: skilled miniatures of characters in the news, amazingly like their models. There was Helen Hayes as Victoria Regina, singing "We Are Not Amused." There were Lunt and Fontaine as they appeared in *Amphytrion 38*. There was John L. Lewis entering heaven, complete with eyebrows, halo and wings. F. D. R. was fishing from a rowboat, and Eleanor sang, "My Day." Hitler and Mussolini appeared in "Sister Act," and Alex Woollcott, in a rocking chair, sang "Sitting in Sutton Place Knitting." There was even an undersea sketch, with a pair of domestic fishes singing "Beebe Is Coming to Tea, to Tea," with William himself arriving on cue in his bathysphere. It was a revue in miniature, with enough wit and sophistication to convert the most stubborn nonbeliever, even the distinguished old Britisher who, after a performance one night for the English-Speaking Union in New York, stood examining the portrait puppet of Mrs. Roosevelt and murmuring to himself, "Fancy anyone doing that to Queen Mary!"

But it did not, unfortunately, convert the public. Christmas matinees, traditionally, are shows for the kiddies. Ours was not. Michael Myerberg, who had persuaded us into the venture, had not, apparently, persuaded himself that an adequate share of his budget should be spent on publicity. And there were other problems we had not foreseen. When we drove smartly up to the Lyceum loading dock with our new Packard and our trim trailer carrying the show, we were confronted with a bulky gentleman blocking the doorway.

"This a union truck?"

We thought that a pretty funny question. He did not.

"Nuthin' unloaded on this stage that ain't on a union truck. I'll call one."

He did. The truck arrived—a truck big enough to carry a

dozen shows the size of ours. As its driver and the bulky gentleman discussed the weather, the three of us unloaded our show
from our trailer and loaded it into the truck.

"Now what?" we asked.

"Just wait here."

We waited. The truck drove around the block and returned to
the same spot.

"That'll be forty bucks."

We paid, and loaded our equipment onto the stage, as our
stagehand friend stood picking his teeth.

Our show was completely self-contained. It required no scenery, there were no props to be handled by any but ourselves, and
no curtain to be raised. The only task the stage crew had to
perform was to lower and raise the asbestos curtain before each
performance, to demonstrate to the public that the sanctity of the
New York fire laws was being protected. The stage crew consisted
of four ponderous men who spent the entire two weeks of our
engagement playing poker in some subterranean retreat, collecting their salaries of ninety dollars per week—in the middle Thirties rather a splendid sum. They collected. We did not. We
closed on a Saturday and were told to come back early Monday to
clear the stage and pack the show. When we arrived the loading
door was locked, and the caretaker, an old man who might well
have been cast as the Ancient Mariner, handed us a notice in-
forming us that since Mr. Myerberg had failed to pay the theater
rental, nothing was to be removed from the theater, or dire consequences were predicted.

We couldn't believe it. Our show—our entire stock-in-trade
was being held for ransom! "Call Rebecca!" someone had sense
enough to demand. Rebecca Brownstein, though officially the
attorney for Actor's Equity, we considered our attorney as well.
She was, still better, a valued friend whose advice had often
helped us avoid the follies show-folk seem especially prone to.
We called. When she heard what had happened she said, "Don't
wait a minute! Get everything out, however you have to do it! If
the stage doors are locked, carry it out through the lobby. If you
can't get a truck, get taxis—and get busy!"

Someone, meantime, had also called our manager, Catherine

Bamman. She arrived, and she was a formidable woman. So the three of us and Miss Bamman frantically started tossing things into boxes as best we could, props, lights, marionettes, and all the dozens of uncataloguable odds and ends that somehow, put together, make a puppet show. As soon as a box was filled it was shoved across the stage apron and toted down the aisle to the lobby, where, despite the protests of the Ancient Mariner, it was stacked in a pile that was beyond description.

The entire front of the Lyceum Theater consisted of a series of doors, open when performances were scheduled, latched on the inside, save for the one door nearest the box office, when the theater was dark. The poor old caretaker was beside himself. As soon as one of us would open one door, he would hurry to close it, only to find that behind him, another of us was opening another door and carrying out another piece of equipment to the sidewalk of Forty-fourth Street. Mumbling protests, he would totter back across the lobby, only to find another door disgorging assorted junk onto the street, or, still more frustrating, Miss Bamman, who, aroused, could have intimidated Atilla the Hun, blocking his way. He did his doddering best, but four agile puppeteers and an irate manager were too much for him. It was an unequal battle.

We began calling taxis, and soon had four of them lined up in front of the theater. Into them we stuffed our show, while pedestrians stood in the snow and tried to figure out what was going on. The New York theatrical district is accustomed to peculiar sights, but by the time our cabs skidded off we had acquired quite a gallery. We were in a state of collapse, but we still had our show, our glowing notices, and some valuable, if bitter, show-biz experience. Rebecca prepared the necessary papers, and I remember standing in the shadows on Central Park South waiting to serve them on the probably insolvent Mr. Myerberg.

Despite all this, "It's a Small World" became the basis of the show we toured coast-to-coast with never again such unhappy results. On this tour, the reaction of the club women was often appreciative and always polite. It was the college audiences, however, that were the most rewarding. Our small entertainment came as a complete contrast to the lectures and concerts they

The Haydn Trio. "Sunday Nights at Nine" at the Barbizon Plaza (1934).

were used to. It brought a bit of Broadway to these eager youngsters. It was sheer fun; it was humor, it was satire, and they loved
it. Gone were the days of the Model T's. Now we traveled in style
in a sleek blue Packard convertible, with a small trailer, painted
to match, to carry the show.

Our winters we spent in New York. We had acquired a manager who was at the same time in charge of the small theater in the Barbizon-Plaze Hotel, on Central Park South. It was a pleasant theater, comfortable and intimate, though the backstage facilities were miserable. The theater, so many blocks from the Times Square theatrical district, was something of a problem, but Catherine Bamman (that was the lady's name) had a Bright Idea. New York was a dead city Sunday nights, so, said she, why not an intimate sort of revue to be called "Sunday Nights at Nine?" Young performers who were starting careers in the theater, in radio or in supper clubs, were certainly free on Sundays, and when the hotel management offered them free rooms with breakfast thrown in, (literally, through a slot in the door), they jumped at the chance. Here was suddenly security for the winter with a warm, comfortable room and a good address—all this for a few hours work on Sunday night.

As a revue, "Sunday Nights at Nine" was something of a hodge-podge, but it did have about it a fine careless air of informality, and a cast of engaging young performers. Among them were Shirley Booth, playing during the week in her first Broadway hit *Three Men on a Horse*, Van Heflin, not yet in films, Helen Howe, Vandy Cape, assorted singers and dancers—and—The Yale Puppeteers. Most of the performers brought their own material—Shirley Booth, for example, was brilliant in some Dorothy Parker monologues. We did, to begin with, a rhymed comment on the news of the day, called "The March of Rhyme," and a two-piano number, Knipp and Tuchk. In the second season, however, I began to write a few songs and sketches, and Harry began doubling as actor and by the third winter we felt ourselves an important part of the show. When the project finally collapsed, the indefatigable Miss Bamman decided we were to be her star attraction, so for three years under her efficient management, we did the club and college circuit from Maine to California. But it was those three seasons at the Barbizon-Plaza that had made us impatient with the limitations of puppets, and eager to seek Broader Horizons. After all, during those years I had written special material for Shirley Booth and others, had worked in radio writing special material for Joe Cook and his guests, and

The club and college circuit (1939).

had performed my "March of Rhymes" for several weeks on a CBS feature called "Club Columbia" where I also provided for each broadcast, with Raymond Scott as composer, an original song.

My debut on the Joe Cook show was a memorable one. It was to be my stint each week to write a short sketch in which Joe would interview someone with an unusual occupation. My first assignment was with a gentleman in a Penny Arcade on Forty-second Street who ate glass; his specialties being tumblers and light bulbs. He turned out to be a large and rather formidable man who was very proud of his work. A few minutes conversation with him gave me all the material I needed. And I did produce a funny few minutes of dialogue which pleased the producers and delighted Joe. I was riding high.

The show was broadcast in the evening and rehearsed just before it went on the air. In those days, learning one's lines was not necessary. One simply read them. My glass-eater arrived late, was handed his script and shoved up to the microphone. He looked worried. "It's simple," I told him. "Joe will read the question and you read the answers, and that's all there is to it. Be sure and wait for the laughs." He looked more worried still, but not half so worried as the rest of us when it turned out that he couldn't read. So Joe ad-libbed the spot, and my carefully carpentered dialogue went down the drain. Everyone was very nice about it, and thought the whole episode pretty hilarious, but I'm afraid my laughter was a little forced.

On the west coast I had translated, with some acclaim, two of Frederick Hollander's intimate revues for his Tingle Tangel Theater. My interest in the stage expanded with every assignment. Harry, too, had smelled grease paint both in "Sunday Nights at Nine" and near the farm in Franconia where we spent our summers—a theater staffed principally by Yale drama students. And Roddy—Roddy was always ready for any project that held promise of some connection with a box office.

23.

I am sure it did not happen suddenly, but those tantalizing whiffs of the more rarefied air of The Theater made the world of the marionette seem too confining for our newly developed interests. Why, we thought, might it not be possible to combine puppets and people in a completely new sort of theater, with Harry making the marionettes and directing the puppet shows, me providing the plays, songs and sketches, and Roddy managing the whole affair? With puppets we were at home. We had proved on a hundred stages that with them we could draw laughter and applause from even the most sophisticated audiences. In the realm of live theater, however, we were novices. Still we felt such a theater was possible, though what form it eventually might take we hadn't a notion. Our marionette productions were fairly elaborate miniature musical comedies, really, with dozens of figures, scenery, lights and all the complicated paraphernalia such a show requires. The problem would be to dispose of all this equipment quickly enough to make room for the live actors. The questions of how this was to be done was discussed endlessly. Before too long, we realized an ingredient was lacking: we needed a fourth partner with more knowledge of such things than the three of us had or could muster. There was never a question in our minds as to where such a theater should be. It must of course be in Hollywood, a town that had welcomed us so warmly before and where, we hoped, we would still be pleasantly remembered.

The problem of the fourth member solved itself very neatly when we met Dorothy Neumann. Our first actual encounter with Dottie might, I guess, be described as unconventional. Harry had that summer agreed to play the part of a butler in one

of the plays at the Whitefield Playhouse, where Dottie was doubling as actress and costumer. The Franconia farm where we were
spending our summer was some six miles from the Playhouse,
and it was without a phone. In spite of our frequent visits there,
somehow our paths had never crossed. Dottie had never been
able to get the necessary measurements for the butler's uniform,
and time was getting short. One morning we dropped by the
theater to chat with friends, and as Harry came walking across the
field, Dottie spotted him. When she learned he was the missing
butler, she grabbed her tape-measure, dashed up to him, dropped
to her knees, thrust one end of the tape into his crotch, rose, said
"Thanks!" and took off, leaving an astonished young man staring
after her. Before the summer was over, we were all laughing at
the episode and becoming good friends.

Dottie was a few years younger than we. She combined technical knowledge of the stage from her studies at Carnegie Tech
and at Yale with practical experience in the Broadway Theater.
We had first seen her at Whitefield playing character roles with
great sensitivity and skill, and we knew she had directed and—
most certainly!—done costume work. But would she take a
chance on a venture as nebulous as ours? She would indeed, and
her immediate enthusiasm enforced our belief in our idea. When
we learned that she had seen us in action at the Barbizon-Plaza,
and had approved of what she saw, we were even more pleased. It
was decided that she would stay in New York until we had found
a location on the coast, and really needed her advice and help.

So one wintry morning the three of us drove off once again,
California bound. There were a few good bookings en route
which we cheerfully accepted because, if our plans were to come
to anything, we needed every penny we could garner. Our performances were by now fairly routine, so we could focus all our
energies on The Great Project.

It was while we were spinning across the endless monotony of
Texas that the idea hit us. Which one actually came up with it
first none of us remembers, but we knew in a flash we had found
the solution. If it was too difficult in a small theater—and ours
must be an intimate one—to strike the marionette stage in prepa-

ration for the live revue, why not two stages, one for puppets and one for people? Why not, indeed? And what better name for such a playhouse than Turnabout Theater? It had a nice alliterative ring to it, and it told the story. It must be, then, a theater with a stage at either end of the auditorium, with seats that could some-how be reversed. But what kind of seats? Individual chairs that the patrons would turn around themselves? Pandemonium! And certain to evoke instant hysteria in any scrupulous fire inspector. Swivel seats? Too much space. Suggestions, some of outrageous absurdity, burgeoned, but from it all emerged the perfect solution: streetcar seats. In 1940 there were still streetcars with double seats, the backs of which, when he came to the end of the line, the motorman flung over with a crashing series of bangs until all the seats faced in the opposite direction and the car was ready for the return trip.

We knew now how the theater must work, but where were we to find a building we could adapt to our own peculiar needs? Obviously no existing theater would do. We inspected the empty ones, though, and dozens of other buildings as well, but even when we found one that seemed remotely possible, our interest failed to ignite any similar feelings in the owner we approached. Most of them, I am afraid, regarded the whole project as crazy, and us, its promoters, even crazier. Dottie, fortunately for her, was spared the weeks of frustration we endured since she was still safe at home in New York.

On the far west side of Hollywood was a street called La Cienega Boulevard. It was a broad street that ran straight south from the Hollywood hills across the spreading town. Near its intersection with Wilshire Boulevard a few restaurants had been built, and midway between Wilshire Boulevard and the hills was the one feature that made the street memorable—an oil well in the exact middle of the street, a well that pumped steadily, day and night. But near the north end, towards the hills, it was relatively undeveloped, mostly vacant lots with a few not very substantial-looking wood or stucco buildings scattered along it, buildings occupied principally by decorators and dealers in antiques. In one of these rather impermanent looking buildings a good friend had started a shop, and it was at his suggestion that we approached its owner. This gentleman owned much property along the street and rumors had it that he was planning further developments. And a gentleman he was. He listened to our plans and neither laughed nor brushed us off. He remembered, it seems, that during our Olvera Street days, his wife had brought a party to our theater and had been unable to get in. The house was sold out.

Perhaps that incident of some ten years before made him more receptive to our new project. At any rate he listened. And the rumor was true. He was planning a new building on La Cienega. It was to have two wings with a patio between, opening at the rear on an alley. When he finally agreed to accept us as tenants, he entered into our scheme with an eagerness unusual and unexpected in a landlord. With his architect, his plan for the building was altered so that the theater—*our* theater—would be at the back of the lot, paralleling the alley, away from the street noises, with the two wings, now considerably shortened, extending to the street from either end of the theater, thus creating in the center a large patio enclosed on three sides. We did have some qualms about the location. It was not quite Hollywood and not quite Beverly Hills, in fact, to some of our friends it seemed a remote and questionable spot for a theater. But the enthusiasm of our new landlord seemed to compensate for any failings the site might have. And, after all, what else was there?

I think we all wondered how a supposedly perspicacious business man could have accepted us so readily. Our financial status was certainly not impressive. The long weeks of searching for a theater had depleted our small nest egg dramatically, and the cost of the venture we were embarking on seemed ever more formidable. Perhaps it was our "front" that made us so acceptable. The Packard was new and shiny and obviously expensive, and Roddy, always the showman, insisted that we appear prosperous even when our situation was the most precarious. So we had rented a large house in the Hollywood hills overlooking the Sunset Strip and the whole city, a house that stood out from its stucco and redwood neighbors like a somewhat surprised visitor from Connecticut or Pennsylvania. For it was strictly colonial in style, sheathed in white clapboards, with spacious rooms, decently furnished, even to a Steinway grand piano, and with a wing at the back to accommodate two maids. Maids we didn't have, but since we were all busy from dawn 'till dusk running about the city on a multitude of errands, Roddy also decided we needed a cook and house boy chauffeur. The cook, Joseph, was black, and a gem. Dinner every night was an event we could look forward to even after the most exhausting and discouraging day. He watched over us like a mother, and his ministrations were an enormous spur to our morale, though the grocery bills, when they came in, were frightening. So was the rent, and so were all the other bills that mounted day by day. We invented some non-existent backers in the east, I'm afraid, in addition to some legitimate ones who bailed us out when things got too hairy. And some way, thanks to the help of these good friends and Roddy's remarkable ability to stall our creditors, we managed.

24.

Meanwhile the building was progressing, the stages were being built, and the problem of the seats had been solved. Los Angeles once had an excellent transportation service—the Pacific Electric Company's Big Red Cars which criss-crossed the sprawling and ever-expanding city and its scattered suburbs. They were fast, quiet and pollution free, and those who remember them fervently wish they were back again. A call to the main office revealed the fact that several old cars were being dismantled, and were, at that moment, reposing at the harbor waiting to be broken up for scrap and shipped to Japan—this in 1940! A trip to this inter-urban Gehenna was all that was needed. The seats were there, and available at $3.50 each. We planned on having eleven rows in the new theater, each row accommodating fourteen patrons, giving us, on the main floor, a seating capacity of 154 persons. This meant, since each of these sturdy discoveries was intended for two, that we needed seventy-seven of the Pacific Electric's best at a total cost of $269.50. Some of the seats were upholstered in leather, some in heavy straw matting, and with new covers they would be both attractive and practical.

Although spring in California is not too different from the other seasons of the year, in those smog-free days it did somehow put a new feel in the air. It was March, and now we needed Dottie, so a wire was sent off and she was on her way.

The building was up now and the theater really beginning to take shape. The auditorium stretched across the back of the structure, paralleling the street and the alley. At the south end was the revue stage with, on the alley side, a narrow dressing room for the men, and on the other side of the stage, extending into the south wing, a larger dressing room for the ladies and a spacious—or so it seemed at the time—workshop for scenery, props and costumes. At stage right, entered through a small door from the men's dressing room was a platform lower than the stage level, designed to hold the piano. At the north end of the theater was the puppet stage, and behind this the workshop where the marionettes were made and costumed and the sets and miniature props designed and constructed. On a series of pulley-operated battens the casts of the various shows could be suspended and pulled up to the high ceiling out of harm's way—rows, ultimately, of gaily clad small figures that never failed to intrigue the backstage visitors. Adjoining the puppet stage, with entrances from both the auditorium and the patio was a large Green Room, and beyond this, occupying a considerable part of the north wing, a complete suite of living rooms—for we planned, as soon as it

The patio and entrance to Turnabout Theatre.

was feasible, to live at the theater. On the west, or street side of the auditorium was a balcony wide enough for only one row of eighteen swivel chairs, entered through a series of five doors from an outside balcony flanked by stairways at either end leading down to the patio, and built against the walls of the two wings of the building. An architect friend, Allen Siple, volunteered the design for this outer balcony and the stairs, and planned the color scheme for the entire building, inside and out. The effect delighted us. The building itself was painted white, but the front wall of the theater was a deep shade of russet red. The stair rails and the balcony railing were white, and the double doors beneath, providing the main entrance to the theater, and the five doors of the balcony were a deep marine blue. The patio was still a wasteland, but the façade of the theater with its simple white railings against the dull red walls and blue doors was charming.

We worried about that patio. Now it was simply raw earth heaped with sand, cement and the usual rubble of any construction site. We knew something must be done with it since through it must come our audiences, but our budget certainly admitted of no elaborate landscaping. We needn't have worried. The owner, who had cheerfully—and surprisingly—concurred in all our suggestions, was obviously proud of the results, and not about to have the effect ruined by a meager and unprepossessing approach. "How about some trees?" he asked. We agreed eagerly, envisioning a few spindly saplings which might, if fate smiled on our venture, in time be "as high as an elephant's eye." We had not considered that wonderful California miracle, instant landscaping, and we had underestimated the enthusiasm of our landlord. So conceive our delight when one morning four olive trees, each some twenty feet high, were hauled in with much difficulty and set in the ground, two on either side of the patio, over which their branches met in a leafy canopy. The next step was clearing and leveling the patio, and the arrival of a new crew of workmen who paved the entire surface with warm red brick which curved gracefully around the gnarled trunks of the olives, leaving room for the fully grown plants that followed the paving. In the space of a few days the new theater looked as though it might have existed for decades. One impressionable lady, shortly after we opened, was overheard telling an eastern visitor that this passage between the olive trees was actually a small remaining section of the original road built by the Franciscan friars to connect their missions.

25.

The days were rushing by, and the busier we became the more there seemed to be to do. The seats had arrived. Since they could not be fastened to concrete, a wooden floor had to be built over it, and each of the seventy-seven seats screwed firmly in place. The worn brown leather and soiled straw matting were not handsome, to be sure, but there they were, and they did appear to be practical. And, since we had decided to use the same colors inside the theater and out, we felt, with the russet walls, blue covers for the seats would be quite perfect, as they proved eventually to be. The proscenium arches of each stage had been plastered, but they looked dismayingly blank and uninteresting. So did the balcony with its four supporting posts. Allen Siple once more came to the rescue, studied the place, lighted his pipe, scratched his ear, and muttered "Staff." We looked blank, and in case the reader is as uninformed as we were, I refer him to Mr. Webster, who says, "Staff: a kind of plaster combined with fibrous material used for temporary ornamental buildings. Orig. Unknown." We soon discovered that in Hollywood, at least, it was used not only for "temporary buildings," but for movie sets, banks, restaurants, Bel Air mansions, ice-cream parlors and Forest Lawn; in fact, almost any place where the extravagant and the rococo, even if fake, seemed appropriate to the builder.

We were conducted by our friend to an enormous lot halfway downtown where every square inch, in sheds and in the open, was bursting with staff: pillars, pedestals, peristyles and pilasters; friezes and dados, lunettes and medallions, cornices, capitols and cornucopias. We couldn't believe such a prodigal wealth of theatrical stuff—or staff—existed. We finally chose to frame the two

proscenium arches with wide borders of a reasonably classic design, copied, probably, from some Roman temple and, to occupy
the center space over the stage, appropriately dramatic bas-reliefs.
To sheath the balcony, we found several large panels, also in
bas-relief, cast, the proud proprietor told us from a marble piece
which, mounted above his cavernous fireplace, had adorned the
mansion of some movie mogul with an unfortunate fondness for
the more exuberant features of the Italian baroque. Wherever the
original might have come from, these copies, set side by side,
made a frieze covering the entire length of the balcony. A frieze
rampant with curlicues, twining vines, and a profusion of cupids
in peculiar positions.

As soon as all this glaringly white decoration was in place, we
knew it would have to be painted, and we knew too that the
expanse of wall opposite the balcony would never do. It demanded a matching balcony, but since such a structure could
have no practical purpose, there being no access to it and no
sufficient room for supporting posts, we decided to make a false
balcony—a very narrow one—similarly decorated, where we
would install a row of life-size dummies—a sort of permanent
audience. Perhaps they would give us courage if flesh-and-blood
customers should fail to turn up. So another series of panels was
bought and installed, and we were unanimously delighted with
the effect.

I should explain the balcony—the real one—and why it had
five doors to accommodate only eighteen people. We had thought
originally of dividing it into five boxes, to be labeled Hat Box,
Powder Box, Jewel Box, Match Box and Music Box, but we
found they would be much too small for the four chairs we had
planned for each of them. So the partitions were discarded and
the single row of swivel seats installed. But the doors remained,
and they, too, seemed to call for some ornamentation. But all
that must come later. Now there were more pressing concerns,
for we had not only the theater to prepare and equip—the lights,
the switchboards, the rigging, the hundred details one only
thought of when something was suddenly needed that wasn't
there—but the show as well, or rather shows, for with two stages

our problems were doubled. We had at least decided on the proper puppet show to open the theater. It was to be a revival of what, ten years before, had been our most popular production, "Mr. Noah," brought up to date with a few changes and a new third act. This would be preceded by the Haydn Trio and "The March of Rhyme," both of which had become trademarks of The Yale Puppeteers.

The Haydn Trio consisted of white-wigged gentlemen in white satin knee breeches and scarlet coats grouped around a miniature gold piano. It had been much photographed, and even sketched, by Cecil Beaton, for an article in *Vogue*. The "March of Rhyme" was performed by a Commedia dell'Arte figure in long black robe and shovel hat who, with notebook and plumed pen in hand, commented in rhyme on the goings-on in the world.

> *Ladies and gentlemen, the March of Rhyme,*
> *presenting the latest events of the time*
> *in a manner that suits the affairs I rehearse:*
> *my recital, in short, goes from verse to verse.*

Then followed six or eight satirical quatrains which could be changed, eliminated or added to (as they often were) at a moment's notice, so the comment was always fresh. "Mr Noah" was, of course, our own musical version of the famous story. In Act I a chorus of sinners taunted Noah, who warned them of the dire consequences of their behavior. It introduced Mrs. Noah, the three sons and their wives (who weren't too keen on the old man's idea), and came to a grand climax with the entrance of the animals and their boarding the Ark. Act II was set on board, and concerned itself with the domestic problems that arose, such as that of the two dodo birds who turned out to be both male, and the single mosquito who, just as Noah is congratulating himself on having neglected to provide her with a mate and thus having freed the world from *that* particular pest, informs him that

Left, view from revue stage of Turnabout Theatre on closing night (1956).

> *. . . this morning at five, before you were alive*
> *to my Mephistophelian laughter*
> *I laid six thousand eggs on the porcupine's legs*
> *and eight thousand more on the rafter!*

The act closed with Mr. and Mrs. Rabbit proudly hopping in, followed by a stageful of tiny bunnies. In previous versions, on Olvera Street and in New York, Act III had found the Ark landing on Mount Wilson, to be greeted by Albert Einstein, who was then working at Cal Tech in Pasadena, and had been much amused to see himself as a puppet, and at Ellis Island, where the welcoming committee consisted of a chorus of customs men.

This time the setting was Los Angeles' Miracle Mile, a new shopping area adjoining the La Brea tar pits, that was being much publicized, and was blossoming nearly every evening with tremendous colored searchlights that swept across the night skies to advertise the opening of a new gas station, or florist shop, or haberdashery. The man who supplied these lights was one Otto K. Olsen, so of course, we had a rousing chorus of his white-jacketed minions singing, "Let there be light, said Otto K. Olsen," and continuing

> *. . . Jupiter and Venus twinkle down,*   -
> *to extinguish them is our motto.*
> *Though God lights the sky over every other town,*
> *In Hollywood it's done by Otto.*

We heard later that Mr. Olsen, like Queen Victoria, was not amused, but the audiences were, vastly.

So much for the puppets. No, not quite, for we still would need two boys who must be trained as puppeteers and who could double in the revue. These we found in a Gilbert and Sullivan production at the Hollywood High School—two senior students with good singing voices and acceptable stage presence. Here too, we recruited a "team"—a blond girl and boy who danced together and were young and attractive. The principals, of course, would be Dottie Neumann and Harry, with me at the piano to accompany and announce the numbers.

Harry's forte was the frustrated little man and the wistful clown. In such interpretations he had developed into a fine comedian. Dottie's character parts, either comic or serious, were always finely conceived. We did need a comedienne, and we found one in Frances Osborne. One especially hot day she came trudging up the long hill to our house. She looked an unlikely candidate. She was tired, perspiring and disheveled, and we listened to her more out of politeness than from any notion she might prove to be a possibility. Then, without accompaniment, she launched into "She Was Only a Bird in a Gilded Cage" in a soprano that could shatter not only crystal, but bulletproof glass. Her whole personality seemed to change. Suddenly she sparkled. We knew we had found our singing comedienne; I knew she was someone I could write for. She was engaged on the spot.

26.

We had settled on July tenth for our opening, so we were soon in the throes of rehearsals. The frustrations and discouragements of rehearsals. The uncertainties, the fatigue were lightened all too infrequently by the small triumphs when things go right for a change. At the same time Harry was working with the new assistants, and the decoration of the theater never stopped.

A painter friend, a shy and wispy little woman, volunteered to do the doors. She adored horses, and since carousels, too, seemed akin to the turnabout idea (after all, didn't the British call them roundabouts?) a wonderful pair of prancing steeds, lavishly caparisoned, soon adorned the main entrance doors. On the five doors above, she painted charmingly appropriate designs: a frivolous hat emerging atop a powder-box, etc. Later, this particular designation caused some confusion when some lady would open the door and find not the privacy she hoped for, but a balcony full of people. Our painter was meticulous, and time was growing short. We were sure, when she at last mounted the ladder to start work on that long expanse of bas-relief sheathing the two balconies, that she could never complete the job. After spending an entire morning on one small cupid, she realized this herself and with her relieved permission, we called on our friend down the street. He was not only quick, he was witty, and soon the cavorting cupids were pink of cheek and rosy of bottom, with golden curls and pastel wings. He even added a few details the sculptor had never envisioned. One cupid, I'm sure, though his position certainly suggested it, must have been surprised to find himself sitting on a cupid-sized potty. Soon the prosceniums, too, were shining with gold, as were the two spreading chandeliers which an ingenious artisan had fashioned for us from assorted brass tubing, glass lampshades and bangles. The effect was theatrical, and exactly right. The blue carpets were installed in the aisles, and seats reupholstered in blue, with matching blue seat covers fitted over their backs.

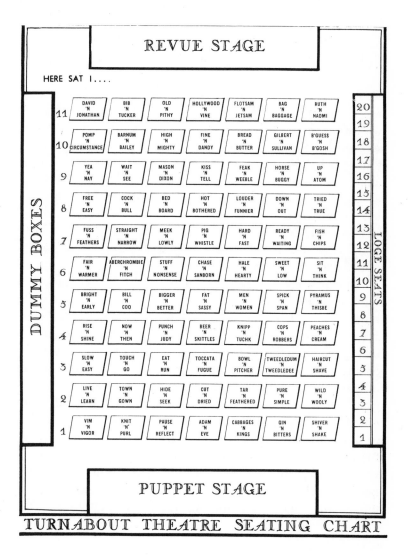

REVUE STAGE

HERE SAT I....

11	DAVID 'N JONATHAN	BIB 'N TUCKER	OLD 'N PITHY	HOLLYWOOD 'N VINE	FLOTSAM 'N JETSAM	BAG 'N BAGGAGE	RUTH 'N NAOMI	20
								19
10	POMP 'N CIRCUMSTANCE	BARNUM 'N BAILEY	HIGH 'N MIGHTY	FINE 'N DANDY	BREAD 'N BUTTER	GILBERT 'N SULLIVAN	B'GUESS 'N B'GOSH	18
								17
9	YEA 'N NAY	WAIT 'N SEE	MASON 'N DIXON	KISS 'N TELL	FEAK 'N WEEBLE	HORSE 'N BUGGY	UP 'N ATOM	16
								15
8	FREE 'N EASY	COCK 'N BULL	BED 'N BOARD	HOT 'N BOTHERED	LOUDER 'N FUNNIER	DOWN 'N OUT	TRIED 'N TRUE	14
								13
7	FUSS 'N FEATHERS	STRAIGHT 'N NARROW	MEEK 'N LOWLY	PIG 'N WHISTLE	HARD 'N FAST	READY 'N WAITING	FISH 'N CHIPS	12
6	FAIR 'N WARMER	ABERCHROMBIE 'N FITCH	STUFF 'N NONSENSE	CHASE 'N SANBORN	HALE 'N HEARTY	SWEET 'N LOW	SIT 'N THINK	11
								10
5	BRIGHT 'N EARLY	BILL 'N COO	BIGGER 'N BETTER	FAT 'N SASSY	MEN 'N WOMEN	SPICK 'N SPAN	PYRAMUS 'N THISBE	9
								8
4	RISE 'N SHINE	NOW 'N THEN	PUNCH 'N JUDY	BEER 'N SKITTLES	KNIPP 'N TUCHK	COPS 'N ROBBERS	PEACHES 'N CREAM	7
								6
3	SLOW 'N EASY	TOUCH 'N GO	EAT 'N RUN	TOCCATA 'N FUGUE	BOWL 'N PITCHER	TWEEDLEDUM 'N TWEEDLEDEE	HAIRCUT 'N SHAVE	5
								4
2	LIVE 'N LEARN	TOWN 'N GOWN	HIDE 'N SEEK	CUT 'N DRIED	TAR 'N FEATHERED	PURE 'N SIMPLE	WILD 'N WOOLY	3
								2
1	VIM 'N VIGOR	KNIT 'N' PURL	PAUSE 'N REFLECT	ADAM 'N EVE	CABBAGES 'N KINGS	GIN 'N BITTERS	SHIVER 'N SHAKE	1

DUMMY BOXES

LOGE SEATS

PUPPET STAGE

TURNABOUT THEATRE SEATING CHART

Those seats, I think, deserve a paragraph to themselves. Since they were in pairs, we decided to give them names instead of numbers and for days our labors would be interrupted by someone shouting out a new combination—after all, we needed seventy-seven of them! So there were Free and Easy, Knipp and Tuchk, Adam and Eve, Fat and Sassy, Down and Out, Up and Atom—and seventy-one others plus, I might add, a good many that we reluctantly rejected. These names we had a seamstress stitch in white script on both front and back of each seat cover.

Then there was the problem of the rows. We decided to number them from the puppet stage, so Row 1, facing the puppets, became, when the seats were reversed, the back, or eleventh row for the revue. That meant, of course, that the choicest seats were in the center of the house, only five or six rows distance from either stage, but many patrons wanted to be close to the puppets, and just as many, unfortunately, preferred the revue. It was only when someone demanded front row seats for *both* shows that we were in trouble. When the whole setup of the theater had been carefully explained to one bewildered lady she said, "Goodness! I hope my husband can stand it! He always gets carsick riding backwards!"

So the new theater had somehow been born, and in the Green Room we occasionally found a few moments to relax and discuss things. It was a large, low-ceilinged room, painted a restful gray-green, with built-in benches along three sides upholstered in bright yellow fabric. For the north wall, with a large window looking out into our neighbor's patio, we had bought wallpaper of the same shade as the walls, with a design of white plumes connected by swags of simulated fishnet—very stylized and handsome, we thought. When the paperhanger had completed his work, we discovered he had done the entire thing upside down. The plumes that were supposed to stand proudly erect, drooped, while the swags that were *supposed* to droop, billowed pointlessly upward. Well, perhaps the Turnabout idea had infected even him, so we laughed at a time we needed laughter, and for the entire existence of the theater the paper remained, cheerfully topsy-turvey.

Two or three weeks before our opening, we were invited to a party given by two young film producers, and there we were happy to meet a friend from New York, Helen Deutsch. Too busy to have followed the gossip columns as to who was where, and why, we had not known she was on the coast. We had met her when she was doing publicity for a number of Broadway stars, and she had arranged interviews with some of them and obtained photographs to assist Harry in making puppet portraits. Helen Hayes, Katharine Cornell, and the Lunts, as I recall it, were in her stable. It was a pleasant party with much talk of the new theater, and shortly thereafter, one afternoon when we were all more or less in a state of collapse, we were happily interrupted by a visit from Miss Deutsch. The question she put to us as soon as greetings were over was an astonishing one.

"How would you like," she asked, "to have Elsa Lanchester in your show?"

The four Turnabout partners in front of their theater (1941).

This was greeted by what I believe is commonly called a stunned silence, but the looks on our respective faces must have told her we were quite sure our hearing must be impaired. Elsa Lanchester? We knew very little of her background as a performer in London cabarets. We did know she was the wife of Charles Laughton, that she had created memorable portraits in the movies, *Henry VIII* and *Rembrandt* and on the Broadway stage, and that among the acting fraternity she was regarded with genuine awe as an actress of rare and special talent. So how could it be that she was offering to appear in a new and untested theater with people she had never met and probably had only casually heard of? And yet, Helen assured us, the offer was genuine and sincere. Elsa, it seems, was between films, was ambitious and eager to have an opportunity to display facets of her talent with which Hollywood was quite as unfamiliar as we were.

It sounded logical enough, but we still could not credit such good fortune until, next day, our friend actually arrived with Miss Lanchester in tow. Having only seen her on the screen in character parts, we were not prepared for the vibrancy of this woman with the tangle of flaming hair. We had all been concerned ever since Helen's visit of the day before with questions raised by this surprising new element she had injected into our plans. Elsa would come in, we were told, for two weeks on a trial basis. Her name alone, we knew, would probably fill the house and give us publicity a new venture like ours would need so badly. But we all wondered, I think, what would happen when the two weeks were up and the star (for she would be the only well-known name in the company) departed. That worry was eliminated almost at once when she suggested it might be wise if we opened without her, and let her make her debut with us after our first two weeks of operation. Charles, she said, felt that by this arrangement the theater would gain a second flurry of publicity just when it might be most needed—one when the theater opened and another, two weeks later, when Elsa appeared. We naturally agreed. So we arranged another meeting, shook hands, and away went Elsa, leaving us in a fine state of euphoria to get on with our urgent business of putting the show in shape for the opening.

Though we had yet to meet him, we were already grateful to
Charles Laughton (as we later had so many occasions to be) for
understanding our problems so sympathetically. We knew from
our New York experience the difficulties of getting adequate publicity, and the importance of having it. Advertising rates for the
small theater, unfortunately, are proportionally even greater than
for the large, for the more space one buys the lower the rate. This
time we were more foresighted. We had hired a team of publicity
persons, a he and a she, and a strange pair they were. She was the
front for the team, or perhaps she should more properly have
been called the façade, for she really could only be described in
architectural terms. She was built four-square, like Solomon's
temple: as wide as she was high. She had a short haircut, and she
wore tailored tweed suits, unadorned, with a man's shirt and tie
and, apparently, men's shoes. Her nickname was Cupid. Her
partner was a nondescript little man, half her size, but perhaps,
for our uses, twice as important. Cupid was something of a Hollywood character. She knew everyone, and shamelessly traded on
that knowledge. Eddie moved in quite different circles, but he
was on a first-name basis with every entertainment editor in
town. The two almost never appeared together. Indeed, I doubt if
Cupid's acquaintances even knew of Eddie's existence.

At the time, Cupid's principal interest was Lady Mendl, for
whom she was trying to put together a radio show to rival a
similar one in New York. If there could be "Luncheon at the
Waldorf with Ilka Chase," why not "Breakfast at the Beverly
Hills" with Lady Mendl? We were all invited to attend the
first—and last—broadcast, and since we felt one of us should put
in an appearance, I was elected. The ballroom was buzzing with
celebrities and would-be celebrities some of whom I recognized,
but none of whom I knew. I sat alone at a table in the back. Two
youngsters joined me—the children, they told me, of Richard
Barthelmess. They were nice children, but not brilliant conver-
sationalists. There appeared to be no breakfast, and whatever
might have been happening on the platform was completely inaudible to me. I was eventually rescued by two gentlemen who
asked me if I wasn't starving. I was. Wasn't I bored? I was.

Wouldn't I like to get the hell out of there and get something to eat? I would. One of my rescuers proved to be the adopted son of Sir Charles and Lady M., and his companion, Mainbocher, the dressmaker. We all three wound up at a drive-in on the Sunset Strip for bacon and eggs, and when they admired my suit and asked the name of my tailor, I'm ashamed to say I evaded the question, thinking it, just then, inexpedient to say it came from a rack in Wanamaker's basement, on sale at $19.50.

Though our opening was announced for July tenth, we had booked the ninth for a preview performance, selling out the entire house to Collier Young for a private party. This preview audience, so far as celebrities went, quite outshone the actual official opening. Collier, an ex-New Yorker, had many friends from the stage as well as from the films, and both media were well represented: the stage by Burgess Meredith, Miriam Hopkins,

Edna Best, Mary Martin and Richard Halliday; the Hollywood colony by Janet Gaynor and Adrian, Jack Warner, Alfred Hitchcock, Eddie Sutherland and Sir Cedric and Lady Hardwicke. As in our previous theaters they were asked to sign the walls, so even before opening night we had an impressive start on what came to be the most distinguished autograph collection in Hollywood.

The new theater delighted everyone. They loved the decor, the seat names, the small cupid that hung over the box office window with a "No Refunds" sign suspended from an unexpected part of his anatomy, the patio, and the whole idea of the two stages and the reversible seats. "Great idea," one man was heard to say. "I've always wanted to go to the theater where, if I didn't like the show, I could turn my back on it." Fortunately, no one ever did. They loved, too, the small sign that was thrust through the curtain as the houselights dimmed. "Mary, Mary quite contrary, Please remove your millinery," it read. Though the stages were high, the floor was level, and in the early forties, some ladies still wore pretty formidable hats.

"Mr. Noah" was well received, as it had always been, and at its conclusion, when Harry dropped down on the puppet stage, seeming twelve feet tall, the audience gasped as they always did at the illusion. By that time I had been able to mop my face and present myself in front of the act curtain to invite the audience to have coffee in the patio, to reverse their seats, and, when they came back in, to be sure to occupy their own locations. "If you've been sitting in PURE AND SIMPLE, don't try to get in HOT AND BOTHERED: I know that may seem a little tough on those of you in front to find yourselves in the back, but after all Turnabout is fair play—so turnabout!" Thereupon ensued the usual confusion and laughter, and soon the theater was emptied and the seats facing the opposite way.

The revue always began with my entrance through the act curtain for an announcement which was only an excuse for stopping in mid-sentence, fixing my eye on the box where the dummy figures were still seated, heads still turned toward the puppet stage and saying, "I beg your pardon. I wonder if you people in the boxes understood that the performance will continue at this end of the theater?"—whereupon a stagehand pulled a rope backstage, and all the heads turned with a jerk to face me. The laugh that always followed gave me time to duck back through the curtains, through the men's dressing room, and make a proper entrance at the piano to begin the opening. This was always bright, well-costumed, and got the show off to a good start. As to what followed, the response on these two nights was polite, but far from overwhelming. The high spots were the singles of Harry, Dotty and Frances Osborne. Harry, in this first revue (which was called, properly enough, "No Strings") did a number about the percussionist in the orchestra who sits through the entire symphony waiting to play one "ping" on his triangle. Dottie did a number I had written in New York for Shirley Booth, and did it very well indeed. In Franny, we knew at once we had a real find. The young performers did their best, espe-

Opening number, Turnabout Theatre. From left, Frances Osborne, Dorothy Neumann, Bill Buck, Forman Brown, Harry Burnett.

cially in a gentle spoof of *Our Town*, but they were amateurs. We were feeling our way, and we knew there was much work to be done.

For the official opening Cupid had captured Lady Mendl, Bette Davis—who became one of our most consistent fans—and a few lesser celebrities, as well as some names from the social register. With both audiences we felt the stellar attraction was really the theater itself, and it was now up to us to create performances to match the charm of their setting.

We started making changes at once. One boy was dropped and another hired. I think we must all have been hypnotized by his audition, for this tall, gangling youth had a bass-baritone voice so sonorous we were certain we had made a great discovery. Unwittingly, we had. But when he cut loose on our small stage with the rest of us, the rest of us became practically inaudible. So after two or three performances he ended his brief career with us by sitting on a park bench, pantomiming Abe Lincoln while I read the lines I had written. We were not too surprised, a very few years later, when the young man hypnotized the operatic world from New York to Moscow with his Boris and his Don Giovanni. He was now known as George London.

27.

Meantime, we were awaiting the introduction of Elsa into the show with a good deal of anticipation, and some anxiety. I remember with what trepidation, I came to the Laughton's house for the first time to discuss her numbers. It was a beautiful house atop the Pacific Palisades with a great expanse of lawn and towering shade trees between it and the bougainvillaea-covered wall at the edge of the cliffs. Beyond this there was nothing but the blue Pacific. In the house itself, I remember dark shining floors, white rugs, lovely old pieces of furniture, and open windows where sheer white curtains were always stirring in the breeze from the ocean. Since she was to be with us so short a time, there was no thought of new material for her. The songs she had done in London seemed right for us, as they proved to be. It was agreed she would have three spots in the show. So she came, and she conquered.

As a singing actress, I have always found Elsa hard to describe. Charles insisted always that she be considered not a singer, but a diseuse in the manner of Yvette Guilbert. She was not, indeed, a trained singer, but her way with a song was unforgettable and her versatility constantly amazed us and delighted our audiences. She could, in the course of an hour, be an obnoxious brat, a Cockney charwoman, and a beautifully gowned creature of astonishing beauty. Her magnetism was unfailing, and when she became part of the show suddenly everyone else in the cast seemed, not as sometimes happens, to suffer, but to glow the more brightly.

We felt we really had a show. The notices were surprisingly good, and the audiences started building. It was gratifying to find people who had already seen the show coming back with friends

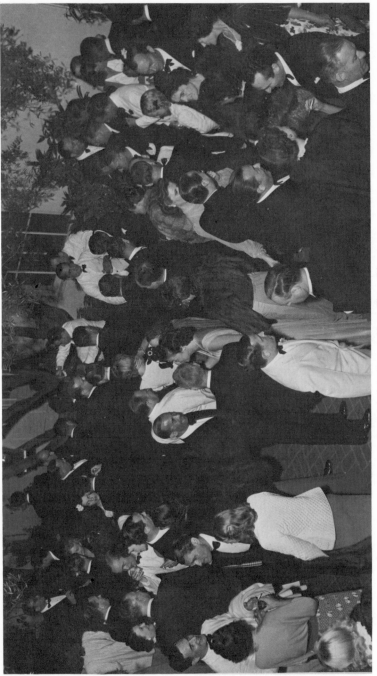

Intermission time at Turnabout Theatre

and out-of-town visitors. Our principal worry was what would happen when Elsa left. We needn't have worried, for she stayed, and the two weeks lengthened to seven, when a previous film commitment terminated her engagement. We were fortunate in having, as a replacement, Brenda Forbes, who had just arrived from New York. She was an extremely funny woman, but she was not Elsa, and attendance slackened.

The recession, fortunately, was a short one, for when Brenda departed, Elsa came back, to begin an engagement that lasted nearly twelve years. Nothing was said at the time, as I recall, about how long she would stay. We were only delighted that she was back. It was obvious that she would need new material, and surely she must have wondered whether I could write the kind of songs her peculiar talents demanded. I'm sure I wondered and worried. It was a challenge, and an opportunity. The first song I wrote for her was something called, "If You Can't Get in the Corners." The line originated with a cleaning woman working for the Laughtons who expressed her aversion to vacuum cleaners by explaining that "if you can't get in the corners you may as well give up." It was a funny song, and Elsa, as she always did, made it much funnier than I ever imagined it might be. In a sleazy cotton dress, hair skinned back in a knot, feet encased in a disreputable pair of Charles' bedroom slippers, mop in hand, she was so fearfully earnest in her denunciation of all mechanical devices that she might well have made new converts to the broom and dust rag.

Elsa's way with a song was a revelation to me, and I think to all of us. When I would submit a new number to her she would read the lyrics, often humming quietly and tunelessly, and without comment. She would tuck it in her bag, and nothing more would be heard of it for several days. When it next appeared, the whole number would have been choreographed to the smallest detail. Every lift of an eyebrow, every smallest gesture would be so meticulously worked out that, once the song was done on the stage, it never changed. Many performers "try out" numbers, changing this or that night after night. But Elsa knew the effects she wanted and how to produce them, so accompanying her at

Elsa Lanchester performing
  "Since Mr. Badger-Butts Gave Me His Hyphen," and ...

"When a Lady Has a Piazza."

Elsa and Forman discussing a new number.

the piano I could know with absolute certainty what to expect. Of course, there were sometimes lines that she thought ineffective, or wrong for her, and these I would change and rewrite until she was satisfied the new line would "play," but this was always done before the number was ever presented. With an artistry that cannot be explained, she somehow managed to fill an empty stage and make of every number a production.

I remember two instances that illustrate how completely the magic could work. We were breaking in a new stagehand. He had watched the show from the front for two nights, and now he was to take over curtains and props. Before Elsa's middle number, "If

You Peek in My Gazebo," he came dashing to Dottie's dressing table wanting to know where the trellis was. "What trellis?" Dottie asked. "The one for Miss Lanchester's number, the one with the roses on it!" It took some persuasion to convince him there had been no trellis—only an empty stage. On another occasion, a visitor from the east who had attended the theater some weeks earlier, asked at the box office if Miss Lanchester was by any chance going to do the number where she sat in a rocking chair on a vine covered veranda of a house—he had forgotten the title of the song. The number he thought he remembered so vividly was "When a Lady Has a Piazza," which was done with a straight chair, no rocker, no veranda, no vines, and yet Elsa had managed to create for him an entire stage setting.

With the new songs, there began a long and rewarding collaboration. Elsa was always eager for new numbers, and I only later realized how fortunate I was as a writer to have a performer of her talent to make my songs come to life. With the rest of the company, too, I was lucky, for Dottie, Franny and Harry, each one so different, presented different problems and I marvel now at how busy I must have been keeping them all supplied.

28.

By the time Elsa came back to the theater after her brief departure, we had acquired two more performers that made our small company a truly professional one. Gita Perl had come to this country with the Trudi Schoop Ballet, for which her husband Lothar was accompanist. Gita was a charming dancer, and Lothar accompanied her brilliantly. He, too, was given a spot in the show in which he improvised on some simple melody, playing it in the style of any composer members of the audience might request. Bach, Beethoven, Mozart, Johann Strauss—these were the names most frequently asked for, though one night when someone shouted "Offenbach!" Lothar, startled, got a fine laugh by commenting, "Bach I often get, but not often Offenbach." Together these new recruits provided just the proper relief from too many songs and sketches.

So now business began to build, with many sold-out houses on weekends, and quite respectable attendance at the other performances. I am afraid that to many people in show business the box office is the most important part of the theater. If that were true, ours would scarcely have qualified, not in size, at least. Tucked under the balcony, the window through which ticket sales were made was topped by a red-and-white striped awning and the aforementioned cupid. Inside was a shelf, breast high, with a money drawer beneath it and the ticket rack at one's left. Behind was a built-in desk, and between, room for one person only, though with careful maneuvering a second could, if necessary, be squeezed in. The whole thing was about the size of a very modest clothes closet. Since we were now officially licensed and launched upon the business of selling tickets to the public, and since the government was rather fussy about admission taxes, it very soon became evident that we needed an accountant; so we hired Lina. Lina was a no-nonsense sort of lady in her sixties, and it became evident all too soon that she had a very suspicious nature. The only entrance to this important cubbyhole was from the auditorium, just next to the door leading to the dressing rooms, and during the early days of the theater not an hour passed without one of us needing something: a paper of pins, a box of tacks, a bottle of glue, a spool of thread. Since the door was a Dutch door and the money drawer not a foot away from it, it seemed only logical to take out the needed fifty cents or so, and hardly worthwhile making out the slip one was supposed to make out. The result of this was, of course, that the books would never balance. Lina scolded, Lina threatened, and we did truly pity her in her anguished attempts to account for the missing pennies. Finally she rebelled, and ordered a cash register installed. Although none of us had ever heard of such a device in a theater box office, out of respect for Lina, or from sheer intimidation, we agreed to try it. It arrived, and it was indeed impressive, but certainly never intended for use in a broom closet. Awed as we were by this shining behemoth, we tried earnestly, for a day, to use it. But we found that when one of us would ring up a sale, and the money drawer would fly open, it would hit us in the stomach, and if we failed to dodge, we were likely to find ourselves catapulted through the Dutch door and into the aisle of the theater. The cash register went back next day, and Lina moved to Oregon to recover.

Meantime, our walls were beginning to blossom with autographs of the famous—film and stage stars, writers, musicians. The signing was by invitation, generally at intermission time, and to the best of my recollection only one, Ann Harding, ever refused. The signatures were written in chalk, and then, after the performance, Harry would carefully trace them in white paint and they would become permanent parts of the decoration. The chalk had the additional advantage that, as sometimes happened, if the mayor of Tuscaloosa, or the second cousin of Gary Cooper insisted on adding his signature, we could accede graciously, and an hour later erase his brief moment of fame. And he would never be the wiser unless, of course, he sent some emissary to confirm it. The first signature (though it was actually a simple caricature of his famous profile) was that of Alfred Hitchcock. Emil Ludwig came one night and was so impressed by the Turnabout idea that he sent us a short essay in German about it. Translated, we used it, with his approval, as forward to the souvenir program we soon had printed. Theodore Dreiser signed, and Sinclair Lewis, and Thomas Mann; Bruno Walter and Otto Klemperer; Renoir, the director, and Rene Clair. There were, too, some surprising combinations to be picked from our "album" and at least one of our more frivolous patrons amused himself, he told us, by teaming up Lauritz Melchior and Rudy Vallee, Jose Iturbi and Liberace, Galli-Curci and Ethel Waters, Blanche Yurka and Patsy Kelly, Raymond Massey and Groucho Marx, Nazimova and Mae West.

Every week showed improvement, and then came December

Mary Pickford signs the Turnabout wall,
observed by Buddy Rogers and Roland Young.

7, 1941. We had been invited, all four of us, to lunch with Charles and Elsa that Sunday. We drove up to their house to find both of them on the doorstep, and we knew at once that something dreadful had happened. It was not, needless to say, the pleasant luncheon we always anticipated at the Laughtons'. The uninvited guest to whom we all listened with increasing shock was the radio, and the news of Pearl Harbor was increasingly grim. None of us knew what war might do to our plans. We knew we must carry on from sheer financial necessity, and Charles and Elsa, who remembered how the theater had flourished in London during the first world war, encouraged us. We three were all past draft age, and Turnabout Theater was the culmination of everything we had worked for.

Those first few nights after the 7th were not encouraging. In Los Angeles, a blackout was immediately put into effect, and on Tuesday night (we were dark on Mondays) six lone souls showed up at the box office, flashlights in hand. We showed them the theater, introduced the cast, gave them coffee, returned their money, and sent them off into the dark. Elsa, afraid the drive in from the Palisades might prove impossible, arrived on Wednesday before dark with blankets and thermos, prepared to spend the night at the theater. That proved unnecessary, and on subsequent nights audiences began trickling back until by the beginning of summer, we were doing nearly capacity business.

Perhaps a word should be said about this "business." We were determined to operate Turnabout as a professional theater, so everyone in the company was on a salary. Salaries were, necessarily small, but to ambitious young actors any salary in the Hollywood of the Forties was a welcome surprise. There were a dozen small theaters in the Los Angeles area where actors worked in the hope that some agent or producer might see them and sign them to a film contract. Often they paid for this dubious privilege. Sometimes they did receive token salaries, but these they were expected on payday to kick back to the management. If they proved uncooperative, there were a dozen hopefuls waiting to fill their roles.

Fortunately for us, business improved steadily, and within a

Harry Burnett with some of the members of his cast (1946).

year, the house was filled to capacity every night, and, during the summer months, when southern California was swarming with vacationers, we were often booked solidly as much as six weeks in advance. Turnabout Theater had become a major tourist attraction. Along with the Farmers' Market and Forest Lawn, it was now a "must see," and many were the sad tales we in the box office listened to from those who "must have tickets," and for whom no tickets were available. Audiences not only loved the show, they loved the theater with all its tricks and gimmicks. The named seats intrigued them, and occasionally and quite accidentally, amusing pairings occurred, as on the night Greer Garson and her new husband, Richard Ney, found themselves seated in "Yea and Nay." Mr. Ney was amused. Miss Garson was not. Nor was a very old gentleman, who was accompanied by a girl who was obviously not his granddaughter, amused at being ushered to "Hot and Bothered."

So began fifteen remarkable years of fun and hard, hard work. The boredom that sometimes becomes a danger to the performer in a long-run was never ours at Turnabout. We were too busy constantly writing, rehearsing and producing new marionette shows and new revue numbers. Ours was a completely self-contained operation. Harry created all the puppets, directed the puppet plays and was in complete command of that end of the theater. Roddy was forever busy with box office, planning and publicity, Dottie with costuming, directing and rehearsing, and I with writing. I doubt whether there has ever been another theater in this country devoted exclusively to the work of one writer, and being that writer was both a challenge and a responsibility. A list of the puppet productions and the revue numbers produced between 1941 and 1956 gives, I think, an idea of the effort involving us all. We produced, during those years, *ten* complete marionette plays, and *ten* "live" revues. After the first few weeks when Miss Lanchester used her own material, the only revue numbers that did not involve all of us creatively were those of our dancers: Gita Perl during the two years she was with us, and Lotte Goslar during her twelve year "run." A complete catalogue of the plays and revue numbers will be found at the end of this book.

29.

Lotte Goslar, at least on the west coast, was our discovery. During our last years in New York, Lotte had arrived in town with Erica Mann, Thomas Mann's daughter, in "The Peppermill Revue." The show was very European, and it was unmercifully belabored by the New York critics, who, apparently, were totally unfamiliar with that type of cabaret. It played in a small theater atop the Chanin Building, and we three were among the lucky few who saw it, and who fell completely in love with Lotte. Her clowning was hilarious, her miming superb, and we knew if ever we should be lucky enough to find ourselves in the role of producer, Lotte we must have. So, when Gita and Lothar Perl heard the siren call of New York, we got in touch with Lotte, who in the meantime had found a berth in a Broadway show. But the show had closed, and Lotte agreed to join us. I shan't soon forget our meeting at the railway station in Los Angeles. I had never seen her without a bulbous red nose, or a pair of over-sized feet, and she had never seen me. But she was unmistakable, and that meeting began a long and happy collaboration. Her unique brand of humor was exactly right for what we were doing, and since audiences needed only to watch her, she provided just the contrast and relief from the attentive listening the rest of the show demanded.

There were, of course, in addition to the numbers already mentioned, a good many others that didn't work. It very often happened that a song or a sketch that we thought hilarious would be met, in performance either with complete puzzlement or the stony silence that turns an actor's heart to lead. Sometimes we tried to lay this lack of approval to an unresponsive audience, but

222

Lotte Goslar in "Grandma Always Danced."

since our audiences were almost always responsive, that excuse seldom served after a second try. So in the files is a reasonably fat folder of numbers marked, regretfully, "Didn't Work"—a file retained only because somebody in the company once liked it, learned it, and suffered from its demise.

In the theater, things soon began to settle into a fairly predictable routine. At nine every morning, Roddy opened the box office and unlocked the doors for Flora, who saw to keeping the theater spic and span. Flora was a very small black woman with unbounded energy who quickly became an essential member of the Turnabout troupe. She thought we were funny people, and her giggle was infectious. My partners she soon was calling by their first names, but for some strange reason I was always Mr. Brown to her, and I still am.

At ten, Ethelyn arrived. Ethelyn Bassett was a maiden lady of charm, intelligence, and infinite patience, such a rarity among box office personnel that we knew we had discovered a jewel, indeed. A life-long resident of Los Angeles, she knew many of our regular customers, and whether she knew them or not, never did we have a complaint about rudeness. And so, until four in the afternoon, she explained, consoled, and soothed the frustrated, all with such ladylike aplomb that she could appease the most disgruntled. At four Roddy took over, and at seven I came on and took charge until curtain time. The ushers and puppeteers had arrived by eight, and Dottie would be in the dressing room checking costumes, props and lights. At eight-thirty the doors opened, and our audience, many of whom had been sitting under the olive trees enjoying the evening, began coming in to their assigned seats. Promptly at nine, Roddy and Harry, who had been greeting our customers at the door, closed the big central doors, I emerged from the box office as Dottie entered it, and the three of us, Harry, Roddy and I paraded across the back of the theater (the audience was facing the puppet stage), down the far aisle, and through the small arched doorway that led backstage, to the strain of "Gaité Parisien." As soon as we were in place, the houselights dimmed, the stage lights went on, the red velvet curtain swished open and the show was on.

Forman Brown.

Except for the opening number, all the other music for the marionettes was performed "live" on a small four–octave piano—the only kind that would fit in the very limited space alongside the proscenium arch. Here, at the keyboard, with very little elbow-room, I could play, sing, and, while not busy on the bridge operating one of the puppets, keep watch of what was happening on stage. This was important, for in any marionette production there always seems to be inevitable accidents, which necessitated, in our case, a bit of musical ad-libbing.

After the pianist came the play of the evening. These plays, like the previous ones in Olvera Street and in our New York theater, were done "live." Tape had not yet been invented, and performers were still able to make themselves heard without the aid of microphones and amplification. This was particularly hard for the puppeteer, and standing as he was behind curtains, with only the aperture of the stage opening through which to direct his voice, but I am sure performances were smoother in those days than they are today, when almost without exception, the entire show is recorded on tape, and if, as must sometimes happen, strings tangle, or for some other reason action stops for a moment, the tape goes blindly on, and the action completely loses syncronization with the sound.

Which of the miniature musicals proved to be most popular with our audiences, it would be hard to say. "Mister Noah" was infallible, but each of the others had its own fervent and loyal admirers, and during all the years since Turnabout Theater has been closed, we have been running into strangers in unexpected places, both here and abroad, who, learning who we were, have begun quoting their favorite lines or singing snatches of remembered songs. I recall an evening in the lounge of a pensione in Taoramina when an English gentleman gleefully recited a verse from "Bearding Bluebeard" in which one of the wives addresses her bow-legged husband:

> O fascinating Bluebeard,
> I'll sit between your knees
> and be an exclamation point
> in their parentheses.

When the play of the evening, whatever it might be, came to an end, and Harry had dropped down from the back bridge onto the stage, seemingly a gigantic Gulliver arriving in Lilliputia, I

made my little Turnabout speech, and during the clatter and
confusion of the turning of the seats, made my way down the
aisle to the box office to relieve Dottie so she could get backstage

Lotte Goslar and Harry Burnett in "The Polka."

to dress for the opening number. Roddy went to the patio and the coffee urn, and Harry, always dripping with perspiration from his chores on the puppet stage, grabbed his dinner jacket and a thermos of coffee and hurried down the back alley and through the stage door to his dressing room. It was on one of these nights that he was caught in the headlights of a cruising police car, whose officers were extremely suspicious of this disheveled character running down a dark alley clutching a tuxedo and a thermos jug. He had to stand, shivering, and explain the entire operation of the theater before he was released, and once in the safety of his dressing room, a quicker make-up job was never accomplished.

Actors and actresses are notorious for temperament. Turn-about Theater, I think, was on the whole singularly blessed in this regard, for temperament really gave us very little trouble. The men's dressing room could hardly have such problems since it was generally occupied only by Harry Burnett, and, fleetingly, by one of the puppeteers who had been commandeered to appear in a revue number. But the women's dressing room always had four occupants: Dorothy Neumann, Frances Osborne, either Gita Perl or Lotte Goslar, and Elsa, or, if she were away, some other guest performer. Dottie, fortunately, as director of the revues, was even tempered, or seemed so. Franny was either on the heights or in the depths. Lotte was always having costume problems, and her reliance on pins alarmed us all. Her costumes, of course, for the most part were rags and tatters: enormous shoes, red noses, fright wigs and various bits and pieces of cloth. But things were always coming detached, or getting lost, and backstage could be thrown into a panic at some part of her costume that was misplaced, or so tentatively in place that we prayed it might stay intact 'till her number ended. Lotte, too, in the matter of billing, had demands that were sometimes hard to satisfy. Roddy, into whose lap these problems eventually would fall, could be adamant, and at the first hint of trouble could instill awe into the heart of the miscreant, and such minor flurries as occurred, he would manage to subdue.

Elsa, though she never played the leading lady, was of course

recognized by all of us as the star attraction. She is a witty woman, and her wit could sometimes be sharp. But in spite of these
four very different personalities in the confines of a crowded
room, there was seldom any serious friction. And Lotte loved
fun, though during her first few months with us she must have
been bewildered by the verbal insanity that sometimes affected
us. The sound "w" was a mystery to her, and on her first Christmas in California, Elsa and Dottie presented her with a doormat
on which the "w" of "Welcome" had been carefully whittled
down to a "v." And there were other encounters with the English
language that we found pretty hilarious, as when, planning to
equip her kitchen, she asked where she might go to buy "a set of
bowel covers."

Elsa did not endure fools lightly. I recall the night when such a
one, visiting Rotarian, wearing a plastic red bow tie, sat in the
center of the front row. As soon as Elsa appeared, the tie lit up
with a bright red light which continued blinking on and off
during all of her numbers. I could see the temper heating up, and
was surprised that nothing happened while she was on stage. The
moment the curtains closed on the finale, however, out through
the dressing room and into the auditorium she stormed, and
before the offending visitor even had time to retrieve his hat, she
was confronting him with a lecture on proper deportment in a
theater which I dare say he still remembers. I have heard of
people "slinking out" of a bad situation, but seldom seen it happen. This one, however, slunk the definitive slink and disappeared into the night.

Elsa and Charles guarded their privacy jealously, although
Charles was always much more at ease with strangers than Elsa.
Both of them shunned the Hollywood social round-about, and it
was during the Forties that they bought a cabin at Idyllwild, a
mountain community some hundred miles from Los Angeles.
The cabin was of logs, with a great stone fireplace and a large,
unroofed verandah looking out across the evergreen tree tops to
the jagged upthrust of Mt. Taquitz. The theater's dark night was
Monday, so every month or so the six of us—Elsa, Charles,
Dottie, Harry, Roddy and I would take off after the show, drive to

Backstage at the Turnabout Theatre.

the cabin where we would arrive about two in the morning, open our jugs of coffee, and eat our sandwiches sitting on cushions around the fire. Next day there was generally a hike up some mountain path. Laden with picnic baskets we would find some great flat rock beside a stream where we could picnic, and loaf, or, sometimes, splash about in the chilly water before lying in the sun on the warm slab of granite to dry ourselves. They were relaxing times of good talk and welcome respite from the responsibilities of the week. Tuesday morning we would drive back to the city. Charles was always the perfect host, and Elsa was more at ease with us, and we with her, during these brief interludes than at any other time.

Charles came to the theater nearly every night. Arriving after the intermission, he would stand in the patio, talking, often, with a close friend of all of us, Gordon Amende. Gordon was an American who made his home in Paris. After barely eluding the Nazi invasion, he came to California by devious ways through Portugal and Canada, and for many months stayed with us at the theater. He was a man slightly older than we, an expert in antiques, and a gentleman of great understanding. It was through Gordon that we learned the tragedy of this superlative actor's life. Charles felt himself to be fat, ugly, and unattractive, and yet he was drawn to young men who *were* attractive, and he could not believe that any favors these young men granted him could be given other than because of his fame or his money. No one, he was sure, could ever give him true and unselfish affection.

He was an amazingly complex man. His taste in music, in literature, in painting, in furniture was impeccable, yet he looked, as someone unkindly wrote of him, "like an unmade bed." I think he was the unhappiest man I have ever known, and yet he could be the most affable creature alive, as he proved repeatedly. He loved my mother, whom he called "Petunia," and teased her unmercifully. On one Mother's Day, he even recorded an impromptu version of "M Is for the Million Things She Gave Me," and it is a hilarious record which I still cherish.

There was only one occasion when he actually performed on our stage, and that was due to a domestic accident in which Elsa, in a struggle with a recalcitrant cupboard door, emerged with a black eye which the most careful makeup failed to disguise. So Charles, to the delight of the audience, went on—and on—and on. He told stories, he quoted Shakespeare, he read from the Bible and Thomas Wolfe, he recited limericks and delayed the finale by a good half hour. No one minded except Elsa, who stood in the wings muttering to herself, the principal audible sentence being "What a ham!" Charles would have been happy to appear the following night, or for the entire week, and was greatly disappointed at Elsa's firm veto of the idea. Elsa, her shiner much less colorful, and now nicely camouflaged, went on, leaving Charles to do the muttering.

During the Forties and Fifties, Hollywood's two rival gossip columnists, Hedda Hopper and Louella Parsons, were at their vulturine zenith, and few stars, however respectable, escaped their pryings and peerings, not even Charles and Elsa, who lived lives as private and quiet as any couple in town. But Charles, one time, contracted to make a film at Universal Studios. The studios were in the San Fernando Valley, some twenty miles from the Laughtons' home in the Pacific Palisades. Since Charles's role, one of his famous ones—Quasimodo—in *The Hunchback of Notre Dame*, required extensive make-up, he found he must be at the studio by six in the morning to endure two hours of reconstruction work on his face and head before facing a gruelling day in front of the cameras. The drive from home to the studio and the return trip each day seemed just too much, so for the duration of the shooting, he took a small apartment near the studio. Almost at once, rival columnists were hinting that the Laughtons had separated and that a divorce was imminent. They were furious at these reports and when spies from the Hopper and Parsons camp began coming to the theater and questioning anyone they could corner, they got no answers from us. Finally, when a reservation was made for Miss Hopper herself one evening, we alerted Charles, and weary as he was, he came to the theater that night, and when Elsa emerged from the dressing room and many of the audience still lingered in the aisles, Charles embraced and kissed her, and arm in arm the two walked to their waiting car. The rumors subsided as quickly as they had surfaced.

Dottie, meanwhile, was proving herself invaluable as actress, as director of the revues, and as costumer. It was perhaps the latter department that gave her the most trouble. Her costume budget was meager, and the used clothing departments of the

Good Will and Salvation Army stores provided unexpected riches. There came a day, though, when the costume racks bulged with unusable items of clothing—old dresses, shoes, jackets, aprons—so she bundled them all in her car and deposited

Dorothy Neumann in "The Ballad of Annie Mae Ford," from "About Face."

them at a nearby Good Will store. That afternoon Harry entered the backstage room bearing a huge bundle of clothing. "See what I got up at the Good Will for fifty cents!" he announced proudly. He had bought back everything she had discarded.

There was another memorable episode that had to do with the costume department. I had written a number for three gossiping ladies sitting under hair dryers in a beauty salon. Since no one could hear what the others were saying, the number developed into a surrealist conversation that was completely pointless, and very funny. Dottie and Franny were two of the women, and Harry, in a shapeless house dress and a dreadful wig, was the third. The problem was the hair dryers. Such props are expensive to rent, and difficult to fake. Dottie, as usual, came up with the solution: three inverted plastic wastebaskets suspended from a batten. So off she went to the nearest Woolworth's, where she

"At the Beauty Shoppe"—Frances Osborne, Harry Burnett, and Dorothy Neumann.

stood surveying a row of baskets of various sizes neatly arranged on a high shelf. "May I see that one?" she asked the girl. It was lifted down and handed to Dottie, who promptly turned it over and put it on her head, which it completely covered. "This will do nicely," came a cultured though rather hollow voice from the interior of the basket. "I'll take three, please." To this day, I dare say that salesgirl relates the story as proof of the fact that Hollywood is inhabited by lunatics, and perhaps she is right.

There were other ladies involved with Turnabout Theater from time to time. I have mentioned Flora, but not her daughter, Odetta, who occasionally came to help her mother with the cleaning. I should have mentioned that the theater was often filled with music. Harry loved opera, and strains of Puccini, Verdi, and Wagner were often heard above the grumbling of Flora's vacuum cleaner. At such times, Odetta would simply sit down in one of the theater seats and listen, entranced. She was sixteen, and had, we discovered, a lovely natural singing voice. Her absolute enchantment with singing led Harry to take her to Janet Spencer, perhaps the best vocal coach in the city, and to arrange for her lessons. She developed a soprano voice that was clear and young and of fine quality. We cast her in a children's show we were readying for Saturday afternoons, and she sang in it for many performances. Physically, she was developing into a statuesque young woman of great beauty, with a head that could have modeled for a fine piece of African bronze. And her mind developed too, to the point where she realized that as an operatic soprano she stood little chance without years of arduous work. So she studied guitar, and became—just how I'll never know—the amazing contralto she is today, with a voice that can fill the Hollywood Bowl, and that has thrilled thousands from Israel to Japan.

There were replacements in the revue company, too, from time to time. Franny became pregnant, and we were fortunate in finding Leota Lane, the one of the four Lane sisters who had concentrated on the stage rather than films. She was big and blonde and quite perfect for Brunhilde. Her singing, too, was much more authentically Wagnerian than Franny's, but Fran-

Front: Forman, Elsa, and Lotte; rear: Dorothy, Leota Lane, and Harry.

ny's sense of comedy and her outrageous exaggerations of operatic mannerisms left no doubt as to whom the number really belonged. Leota, however, was a fine performer, and her portraits of a bird-watcher, of various folk singers, and of a story teller on a morning television show for the kiddies, were memorable.

There were times, too, during the Fifties when Elsa took off for a few weeks of touring the supper club circuit, playing choice engagements with her Turnabout songs in New York, Montreal, Boston and other cities. When this happened, our problem as producers was more serious, but on the whole, the replacements we found, none of whom remotely resembled Elsa, were satisfying, and challenging to work with. The most approved by our audiences were probably Marais and Miranda. They had, of course, appeared in concert all over the world, and their repertory of folk songs was enormous. In recitals, they had always appeared in the conventional clothes recitalists generally wear, but now, for the first time, they were able to appear in costume, and this proved rewarding both to them and to our audiences.

The only other "team" that performed for us was the Duncan Sisters. Reviving some of their old vaudeville routines, and singing again songs from *Topsy and Eva*, their warmth and showmanship, different as this material was from anything else in the revue, made them popular with everyone. On another occasion, Virginia O'Brien, who had done so many musicals at M.G.M., came in with her dead-pan renditions of tired old ballads that she turned into something very new and very funny. Another Virginia, Virginia Sale, appeared, doing her mid-western monologues.

Other replacements deserve mention. Corinna Mura had been featured on Broadway in Cole Porter's *Mexican Hayride*. She was a brilliant performer. A stunning woman, who might have stepped straight out of a Goya, she was actually Irish, her true name being Wall, which translated neatly into Mura. But her temperament was assuredly Spanish. She could make her guitar sound like a full orchestra, and when she stepped through the curtains playing the opening chords of "Granada," it was as exciting a moment of theater as one could ever hope to enjoy.

Then there were Elizabeth Talbot-Martin, tall and beautiful, with her clever impressions of Eleanor Roosevelt and Hildegarde, and John Carter, the young tenor who had won the Metropolitan Opera auditions. The delightful comedienne, Queenie Leonard, was with us briefly, as was El Brendel, doing his dialect stories and one of his old vaudeville routines which involved, for some reason I can't recall, a great number of beans, many of which ended up on the stage floor, to the considerable irritation of Lotte, who followed him on stage. And there was—unforgettably—Gilda Gray. Gilda Gray, the shimmy queen of the 20's, star of the Ziegfeld Follies, had run through two or three husbands and, it was claimed, three million dollars. She came to our attention through Ralph Edwards, who wanted to present her on his television show, "This Is Your Life," and wanted us, as a part of the surprise gifts she would receive, to book her into Turnabout Theater as the star attraction for two weeks. The small salary we could pay her was in addition to the $1000 check she would be given on the show.

This happened at a time in the mid-Fifties, when Elsa had finally left, and business was suffering from the excitement over network television that, for the first time, was coming from New York. So we agreed, figuring the publicity given the theater on that popular TV show would compensate for whatever concessions we might have to make to accommodate Miss Gray to Turnabout Theater. We had only the foggiest of ideas as to what she looked like (thirty-year-old publicity pictures were little help) or what she could do as a performer. It was a rash gamble. I met the famous lady for the first time on the night of the broadcast when I presented her with the offer of the booking, and found her to be a blonde woman in her mid-fifties, though looking much younger. She had kept her figure, and except for the tell-tale signs that are, unfortunately, inevitable, she promised to present a good appearance on the stage. She had been living in the small guest house of a friend, and the money she got from "This Is Your Life" and the booking at our theater meant more to her than she cared to admit. As to what she might do on our stage, she had but one idea: to revive her famous shimmy number in which she sang, "The St. Louis Blues," which, she always insisted, had been written for her by W.C. Handy to perform in a Chicago night club. She still had her original costume, which consisted principally of twenty-five pounds of crystal beads. Our enthusiasm for this presentation wasn't excessive, but we felt, as a closing number it might work, if only for its nostalgic value, provided she had previously been properly introduced. So I wrote for her two numbers. The first was inspired by a gold charm bracelet with several bangles, each commemorating some highlight of her career. The bracelet was also one of the gifts she had received on the TV show, and "This Is My Life" was an obvious title for the number. Seven hundred dollars of the thousand she had been given she had spent on two evening gowns, so she made a rather splendid appearance. For her second number I concocted a sort of Sadie Thompson song, "Life Is Just a String of Islands," and complete with high button shoes, extravagant hat, and parasol, she managed very well. The climax of her appearance was, of course, the shimmy, and shimmy she did, to the tinkle of beads, some of which, unfortunately, she shed nightly, making footing in the finale a bit risky.

Her two weeks were a sell-out, thanks to the publicity and to loyal, or curious, patrons who had seen her in her hey-day. It was at the end of the two-week engagement, that our troubles began. Gilda would not leave. It was a singular situation. Audiences began to dwindle, and there were no other numbers she could do, or that we were able to create for her. After several weeks, feeling brutal and heartless, we had to insist that she leave, which she did after a stormy session. We liked Gilda very much. Embarrassingly generous, she gave all of us expensive gifts when we knew she had no money except the small salary we were paying her. But she could not forget her days of lavish spending, and she played the great lady to the end. I would frequently drive her home after the show, and listen to her tales of the Rolls she had in storage, and the magnificent furniture. There was no Rolls and no furniture, but I pretended to be impressed, and that was all the answer she required. We were all sorry to learn of her death not too many months after the closing of the theater.

It was thanks to Gilda that I attended my first—and last—Hollywood party. It was a party in the grand tradition, given by Sonja Henie in the garden of her Bel Air home. Gilda wore one of her new gowns, and we arrived, of course, late. The pool was filled with large pink wax lilies, in each of which a candle burned. Supper was served in a huge pink tent on round tables covered with pink linen. They were scattered between small trees, each in its white tub, and each decorated with hundreds of pink camellia blossoms. Gilda and I were directed to a table where, already seated, we joined Joan Crawford, Ethel Merman and June Allison. There was a strange tenseness at first. Miss Crawford, it seemed, had been a chorus girl in a Broadway show starring Gilda Gray. Joan, of course, was now one of the reigning queens of Hollywood, and Gilda an aging and nearly forgotten name. I found it an unpleasant evening, and was glad when the party broke up and we could leave. I thought the whole thing, quite apart from this minor embarrassment, a very dull affair.

After the first tentative months, Turnabout Theater rarely needed to hold auditions, but we had them anyway. Any successful theater such as ours in a city where actors are plentiful and productions few is bound to attract those who must have exposure or fail in their chosen and precarious field. And some fields did seem particularly precarious, as that of the young man who offered us a trained squirrel who could wave an American flag. One hopeful animal imitator phoned while I was in the box office, and before I could even say "Sorry, but . . ." he launched into his entire repertory of crowings, squealings, barkings, neighings, gobblings, mooings and roarings with a verve that left me speechless.

Then there were less exotic auditions which we agreed to because some patron felt they had discovered a talent that would be exactly right for our revue. It almost never was. One such was the sister of a famous western star of the silent days. We had not pictured her as an *older* sister, but older she was—much older— and she sang horrendously off key. There was a young divorcée whose ex-husband was one of the world's richest men. She fancied for herself a new career as a night club singer, and who were we to refuse her a hearing? She was, actually, not bad, but a night club singer we did not need. Introduced to us by the wife of a famous British film producer was a handsome young man who, why I shall never know, did for us a "dramatic reading." Our reaction pleased neither him nor the lady, and the audition concluded in our patio with the two of them screaming at each other so loudly that we had to ask them to continue their argument on the street—which they did. The young man, happily, grew older and wiser, became a successful producer himself and the husband of an Oscar-winning actress. He also changed his name to Paul Gregory, and although we met him frequently years later, neither he nor we ever mentioned that appalling afternoon.

30.

Aside from sold-out houses and enthusiastic audiences, one of the most gratifying aspects of our work to all of us was the number of patrons who returned to the theater again and again, bringing friends and visitors from as far away as Europe and India. In fact, quite early in our run we bought a quantity of blue pottery cups and metal holders, into which they fitted; each inscribed "Old Timer." A special glassed-in case was built in the Green Room, and everyone who had attended the theater ten times or more was given one of these mugs, and a special key for unlocking the cabinet. During the war years when sugar was rationed, everyone in the company saved his sugar coupons so there was also on a shelf of the cabinet, as a special treat for these loyal supporters, a bowl of sugar. Others had to drink their intermission coffee black. One couple, the Orrs, who lived in Costa Mesa, a good forty miles away, drove in regularly every Saturday night for over three hundred times, until they knew our shows so well that, I truly believe, one of its attractions for them was the hope that someone would fluff a line, miss a cue, or that something would go wrong on stage, which, actors and stagehands being human, it sometimes did.

And there were a few disconcerting moments for which the actors could not be blamed. Our stage manager was Jack Beardsley, and there seemed nothing he could not do in the way of producing needed props cheaply and almost magically. He was enormously efficient, and particularly important in a theater like ours, with a necessarily small staff. His efficiency was amply illustrated when he was drafted one week to pose on stage as Abe Lincoln. He sat in profile against a deep blue cyclorama, complete with stove-pipe hat, shawl and whiskers. It was only some nights later we discovered that these whiskers which looked so authentic to the audience, covered only the right side of his face—the side they could see.

Jack was not to blame for what happened to a Christmas finale one year. In it, the whole company, dressed in cloaks and stocking caps and muffled to the ears, sang carols, culminating in a special "Song of the Bells" which I had written. We had rented a set of chimes which were set up off stage, and Jack had contrived and built a large net arrangement which was filled with bushels of artificial snow and rigged above the acting area. When the chimes began, the snow would start sifting down, the voices would sing, the lanterns glow, and we would present to our audience a truly Pickwickian Christmas picture. The boy who was to control the fall of snow must this night have been carried away by the spirit of the season, for instead of giving the rope the gentle pulls as he had been taught, he gave such a terrific tug that the entire contents of the contraption descended in a blizzard of Alaskan proportions. Since the singers' faces were beatifically upturned, and their mouths open, "The Song of the Bells" came to a spluttering end, and a very quick curtain. I'm sure the Orrs loved it, but Dottie was in tears and the rest of us in hysterics.

We also endured one other catastrophic finale, worse than the other, really, because it happened on the opening night of a new revue, with local critics in the house. I had written a new finale number called "There's Magic in the Air Tonight." The idea for staging the number was that Harry would first appear as a magician, in elaborate oriental garb. When he clapped his hands, Jack and his assistant, also properly clad, would carry in a large box, set it down center stage and walk off. Harry would go into his song, and one by one, on their proper cues, the girls would enter, and as Harry raised the lid of the box, step inside, and when all four of them had disappeared, the boys would re-enter and carry off the box. End of number. Since the box could obviously not comfortably hold more than one adult at most, the trick was that the box had no bottom, but was to be set down over a trap door in the stage floor which would be opened from below by the assistant as soon as he could make it, whereupon the girls could descend one by one and return to the dressing room. On this unfortunate evening, the boys, probably more nervous than the performers, failed to make proper connection with the trap door. Harry, of course, was blissfully ignorant of this, as were the girls, until the moment came for opening the lid for Gita to step inside. Instead of the open trap and the descending steps below stage, there was the stage floor itself, solid and intact. Gita, with a gasp, stepped in. Harry closed the lid, still unconscious of what was going on. However, when he opened the box a second time for Dottie, there was Gita, who should have disappeared, somehow folded into one corner of the box, crying softly. Dottie, pretending

Harry in "I've Always Been the Hind End
Instead of the Refined End of the Horse."

nothing was amiss, stepped in—and the box was bursting with two weeping women. On went the number. When her turn came, Fanny, always a little blurry eyed without her glasses, peered in the box, did a double-take, and hurried off stage, as did Elsa, and the curtains closed on a shaken company and an utterly baffled audience.

One more contretemps of which, this time, fortunately, the audience was not aware, took place backstage between numbers as Harry was getting ready to go on for what was probably his most popular spot, "I've Always Been the Hind End Instead of the Refined End of the Horse." In this number, he played a tired old vaudevillian who, never able to make it to the Big Time, winds up playing the rear end of a comedy horse in a three-a-day variety show. The scene was a grubby dressing room into which, as fast exit music was heard off stage, the horse, Claribel, came clomping on. Separating immediately into two halves, Bill Buck (of whom more anon) would get quickly out of the front end, slick his hair, don his jacket, bid his partner a jaunty goodbye, and fly off for a fast date with one of the girls, leaving Harry, hot and rumpled, collapsing on a stool, the rear end of Claribel encircling him like an unlikely sort of picture frame with a tail.

Getting into this contraption was quite a feat. As I was announcing the number, both Bill and Harry would be scrambling into their respective parts of the equine anatomy; preparing to position themselves so Dottie could hook the two parts together and fling a frowsy satin blanket over the place where front and back joined. On this particular night, Bill was safely installed in the front end when there was a terrific commotion behind him, and Harry's hoarse whisper "My God, there's a cat in here!" Sure enough, at some time when the alley door was open, a stray cat had decided this strange construction of cotton padding would make a pleasant bed. The cat, as startled as Harry, made a hasty exit, and the entrance music that night went on a bit longer than usual.

This number, for some reason, appealed to actors, and to actors of very diverse talents. During the first few weeks of our run, we had offers to buy the number from Teddy Hart, Rudy

Vallee, Eddie Bracken, and Henry Fonda—but it stayed in our repertory for the entire fifteen years of the theater's existence.

Bill Buck came to us late in our run—much too late—for he proved himself invaluable: he was talented as puppeteer, stagehand, extra actor in many revue numbers, and dance partner with Lotte Goslar in some of her most hilarious inventions. A graduate of Northwestern and U.C.L.A., he has since been successful as teacher, director, and author of several novels for teenagers.

31.

I think all of us who worked at Turnabout have our own particular memories of audiences. We played 4,535 of them, and I can recall only one that was unruly and difficult—one that was attended by a considerable group of salesmen from, of all places, Forest Lawn. They had imbibed much too freely, and they seemed determined to out-talk and out-sing the performers. None of us had ever encountered quite such crudity in a theater, and I am sure the rest of our audience that night suffered as much as we did.

There was the night when Lauritz Melchior, sitting in one of the balcony seats, laughed so hard at Franny's rendition of "Brunhilde Rides Again" that he upset his chair and landed on the floor. Hilarity was occasioned on another night during Harry's number, "Look at the Book That I Took" by a young man, again in the balcony, who roared so loudly and infectiously that everyone in the house joined in, and tried to spot the producer of this Homeric laughter. The number answered the old question: If I were to be marooned on a desert island and could take only one book with me, what would it be? Harry, in tattered trousers, was discovered on a raft. Shipwrecked in the dark of night, he had seized the first book at hand—a very large book—which turned out to be the Telephone Directory, and his reading of it and comments on it were greeted unfailingly by laughter, but rarely by such bursts of merriment as it occasioned that night. After the show, the young man, still wiping his eyes, apologized for his laughter. (Imagine apologizing to a comedian for laughter!) It seems he had recently been torpedoed in the Pacific and had spent three days and nights on a raft. "I never thought it was an experience I could laugh at," he told Harry, "but I'll never think of it again *without* laughing."

There was an earthquake one night. It was not a severe one, but bad enough to jolt the theater and set the chandeliers swinging. There were gasps, and a few started to rise from their seats. It happened just as Harry was finishing his "Hind End of the Horse" number. I am not noted for ad-libs, but that night when I

Frances Osborne in "Brunhilde Rides Again."

Harry in "Look at the Book That I Took."

said "Now you can all go home and tell your grandchildren you were in the theater the night Harry Burnett nearly brought the house down," the tension dissipated in nervous laughter, everyone settled back, and the show continued.

Another memorable evening was that on which Mae West arrived in a long, black limousine, escorted by two extremely determined looking gentlemen who didn't seem at ease in the dinner clothes they were wearing. Miss West was dressed in white satin, and sparkled with what certainly seemed to be dozens of diamonds. Ours was an informal sort of theater, and when this formidable trio swept in through the patio it was like a royal procession. The pink and white enameled face under the hive of blonde hair never indicated an emotion. Nor did it during the entire evening. We were happy that a few nights later she came back, alone, dressed in slacks, and unrecognized, had apparently a fine time.

There was, in the early days of the theater, a lady on the Los Angeles Times, Catherine von Blon, who occasionally covered theatrical events. She could hardly be called a critic, since she

Forman, Frances, Harry, Lotte, Elsa, and Dorothy celebrate the 6th anniversary of the theater (1947).

liked everything and wrote with an effulgence that dazzled, but failed to inform. She generally would show up at the theater with a bevy of young men, though she was entitled to only two seats. One night, however, she arrived unannounced with her mother. There was only one single seat left in the house, in the first row for the revue, and directly in front of the piano. We expressed our regret to Miss von Blon, but she blithely said "Fine! Mama can sit on my lap," which mama did, and I spent an uncomfortable hour at the piano trying to pretend it hadn't happened. Elsa did a song of mine, "I Didn't Know Where to Look," and that night I am sure the lyric applied much more to me than to the lady in the song.

And there were special evenings—two, indeed, that became traditional and were celebrated every year—July tenth, the birthday of the theater, and New Year's Eve. On birthday nights, at the conclusion of the marionette show, everyone in the audience was given a slice of birthday cake with a small candle on it. Also on the plate was a book of matches, and at a signal, all the candles were lighted, the lights extinguished, and the darkened house would glow with 180 small flames for the few moments it took to sing "Happy Birthday."

Our New Year's Eve performance became the most popular of the year. On these nights, we would follow our regular two hour program with a second intermission, and a new stage revue which we would time as best we could to end just before the stroke of twelve. Then, at the piano, I would don a long white beard and wig, generally askew, and recite a few lines of doggere, ending, as I remember, with

> Some greet the New Year with a tear,
> and some, alas, get plastered.
> But all will hail the bright New Year—
> Where is the little . . . fellow?

At this point Harry, in diapers, and a ribbon across his chest bearing the new date, would pop through the curtains, followed by the rest of the company. Everyone would join in "Auld Lang

Syne," and adjourn to the Green Room for a supper of cold chicken, salad, and dessert. The only beverage was coffee, and there seemed to be a good many people in the city who managed to celebrate quite happily without any alcoholic stimulation. At any rate, we invariably, before they left the theater that night, took a few reservations for the next New Year's Eve party a year later.

32.

Turnabout Theater ended its run of nearly fifteen years on March 31, 1956. There had been a noticeable drop in attendance in the early Fifties, when live television was first beamed from New York to the west coast. As the novelty wore off, attendance slowly increased, but, except for week-ends, never quite returned to the capacity audiences we had previously played to. At the end of July in 1954, Elsa, after several brief absences for supper club appearances in the east, finally left the company. She had been so much a part of the whole Turnabout venture that her departure was a serious blow to us. She had been with us for nearly twelve years, and I had written for her during these years fifty or more songs. She had never received a salary, or wanted one, for I had turned over to her the copyrights to all her numbers, and since these had supplied most of the material for her club appearances, her one-woman shows, and her two record albums, "Songs from a Smoke-filled Room" and "Songs from a Shuttered Parlor," she felt amply recompensed. I think, too, at this time, she believed that our productions had perhaps lost some of their pristine freshness and spontaneity, and that not enough new songs were forthcoming. I never was conscious of any drying up of my "inspiration," if that is what it is called, but I suppose it is inevitable that after so many years and so many songs one can become a little tired. At any rate, Elsa left, certainly with regret on our part and, I believe, genuine regret on hers. The replacements we were able to book were all good performers, but Elsa had come to seem so vital a part of our operation that attendance began to decline, and nothing we could do seemed to reverse the trend.

We had geared our operation to capacity business. Now we

could not increase prices or decrease salaries and expenses. These, in fact, increased because of the need for more and more publicity. When we finally realized we were fighting a hopeless battle, we settled on March 31, 1956, as our closing date. I made an appointment with a very influential lady who had frequently attended our theater, Mrs. Dorothy Chandler, told her of our decision, and that we disliked very much the idea of closing our venture on an inglorious note. The result was a two column feature in the Los Angeles Times, and two final weeks of sold-out houses, with old patrons clamoring for seats and bemoaning our resolve. So, on the last night, as many of our former guest performers as were available came for a grand finale, and Turnabout Theater ended not with a whimper and not with a bang, but with a splendidly warm and gratifying farewell.

It had been a busy and happy fifteen years. Perhaps busyness and happiness go together. The theater itself would have seemed challenge enough for all of us. For Roddy it was, though even he found time to produce, in "Tommy Turnabout's Circus," the most beautiful children's show the city had ever seen. Harry learned to fly. Elsa made a number of films, insisting always that her evenings be free for Turnabout, and refusing to go on location. Dottie also appeared in several notable films, among them *The Snake Pit* and *Gigi*, making a fine reputation in Hollywood as a character actress. And I somehow managed to write lyrics for a Broadway musical, working with Rudolph Friml, Erich Korngold, and, though they were not present to give suggestions, the Strausses, Johann and Oscar, and Franz Lehar.

Roddy, foolishly protecting the box office one New Year's Eve, was shot through the chest by a burglar, and his life hung in the balance for days, but the show went on. Harry survived an emergency operation, and the show went on. I spent a week in the hospital in traction for a slipped disc, taxi-ing to and from the theater each night for the performance, and the show went on. There were bouts of influenza, laryngitis and sundry other ailments, but the show went on, and at the end I was the only one who had not missed one of the 4,535 performances, and now here we were at closing night.

We could all be proud of our accomplishment. In a city not

known for its sophistication, we had managed to build and maintain a place of literate entertainment that is still lovingly remembered by a host of theater-goers. There were genuine tears on both sides of the footlights that Spring night in 1956 when we joined hands to sing the last bars of the finale:

> *This world we build every night's a play world,*
> *one shining hour in an all too gray world.*
> *Tomorrow, then we build it all again,*
> *so for tonight, goodnight again!*

Closing night, 1956. Many of the performers who had made guest appearances during the theater's fifteen-year run came back for a final appearance. At the piano, Forman Brown. From left, Frances Osborne, Odetta, Leota Lane, Marian Bell, Lotte Goslar, Vivian Duncan, Harry Burnett, Rosetta Duncan, Virginia O'Brien, Corinna Mura, Queenie Leonard, Elizabeth Talbot-Martin, Inesita, and Dorothy Neumann. View from puppet stage.

Songs and Sketches

for the Turnabout Theatre,

1941–1956

Words and Music by

Forman Brown

The Puppet Productions

Bearding Bluebeard
The Brash Monkey
Caesar Julius
Gullible's Travels

It's a Small World
Mr. Noah
The Pie-Eyed Piper
Tom and Jerry

Uncle Tom's Heb'bn

The Revues

Opening Numbers

Gilbert and Sullivan
Good Morning
It's a Great Life
I Love to Play on My Kazoo
Openings Bore Us to Piece
Southern Exposure
There's Something Grand About
  a Band

The Things I Hate in This World
  Are Many
When You Find the World Is
  Full of Things
Why Must They Always Have
  These Openings
You've Got to Have an Opening
Turnabout

For Elsa Lanchester

Aloha
Amelia Out Strolling
At the Laundromat
The Ballad of the Oysterman
  (words by Oliver Wendell
  Holmes)
The Bells of Galway
The Bud, the Bloom, the Fading
  Rose
Catalogue Woman
The Chichivache
Cyril the Squirrel
Delphina

Every Thursday Night
Faith, Hope, and Charity
Fiji Fanny
4F Joe
The Frangi-Pani Tree
Georgianna Washington
How Nice of Mr. Mack
Glory Winters
I Shouldn't Have Gone to That
  Matinee
It's Nice to See You're Back
Lackadaisy Maissie
Lady-in-Waiting to the Queen

Linda and Her Londonderry Air
Look What Come Back in the
    Laundry
Melinda Mame
The Maharanee of Swat
Millie Lou Had Two of
    Everything
Miss Thompson of Cork
Why Mrs. Trotter?
Mona Lisa
My Man's Riding in the
    Moonlight
My New York Slip
The Night of the Butlers' Ball
Oahu Annie

On My Haircloth Sofa
Pretty Is as Pretty Does
Quicksilver Sam
The Ruined Maid (words by
    Thomas Hardy)
Since Mr. Badger-Butts Gave
    Me His Hyphen
Spying Is Trying
Three Light Ladies
Titania, Come Out of Your
    Cabaña
When a Lady Has a Piazza
The Widow's Walk
If You Peek Behind My
    Yashmak

Zelda the Welder

For Dorothy Neumann

The Ballad of Annie Mae Ford
Coach of the Piddlecomb High
    Eleven
Goodbye, Knob Creek
Graduation Day
If You Don't Like My
    Persimmons
Kitty, the Queen of Croquet
The Librarian
The Mail Box
Manhattan Portraits
Maps! Nuts!

Molly the Jolly Jaywalker
Mrs. Muggins Is the Name
The Victory Garden
Popkin's Popovers
The Quality of Mercy
Incident in Arch Street
The Swan Song of Myrtle P.
    Jones
When I Posed in That Grotto for
    Watteau
What the President Said to the
    Dean

For Harry Burnett

Alone in the Crowd
Goodbye, Joe
Here I Am, A Tree

The Hind End of the Horse
I'm Happy
The Lion Tamer

The Little Black Dress
The Lightning Bug
Love Song
Lullabye in Duplicate
The Man on the Pole
The Modest Nudist
My Fiddle and Me

Nothin' in My Pocket
One-Two, One-Two
Outside Lookin' In
The Paper Hanger
Strings
Here I Sit in the Symphony
The Village Smithy

For Frances Osborne

Across the Sands of Magogagog
Arbor Day
Birds
The Bell Song
Brunhilde Rides Again
Folk Songs of Tuscany
The Grasshopper
I Met Him at a Pastry Shop in
  Montmartre
I Sit and Shell My Peas
Lysandre

I Contribute to the Delinquency
  of Miners
Mon Chou Chou
My Uncle Ben
Palm Springs on Saturday Night
The Recitalist
The Prince of Minsk
The Rain
School Crossing—Stop!
The Sing-Song Lady
Sonia McGonigle Tettrazini
  Flynn
Riddlecum-Fa-La-La

For Forman Brown

Abernathy, Fothergill,
  Stoningham and Klump
April Night in Springfield
The Elevator Girl
The Zither Song
It's I Who Measure Ladies at
  Lane Bryant's
Look on the Sunny Side
Maman Cazenou

Miss Quail Goes to the Auto
  Show
Mother Hubbard—Then and
  Now
My Little Grey Home in Escrow
Paprika
The Quiz-Whiz
Sparrow Pie
Spri'g So'g
Summers at Miss Plummer's

Duets, Trios, and Ensemble Numbers

At the Beauty Shoppe
Book-Ends
The Date
The Doge's Dilemma
Harry and Margaret and Bess
Since Our Daughter Hazel
    Started Singin' Nasal
The Hoodunits
The Lady Who Swung by Her
    Knees
Lo, the Poor Indian
Medea
My Sister and I

The Pipes of Pan
Pity Me, a Wandering Maenad
Radio Sketch
Remember How the Lilacs Grew
    Back Home
Salute to Spring
So Little Time
The Swing Song
The Television
The Village Clock
We Met in Westlake Park
You Can't Be Sonorous in the
    Chorus

Finales

This, My Friends, Is the Finale
Magic in the Air
Time to Say Goodnight Again

Thanks for a Lovely Evening
Goodnight Again
Christmas Finale

New Year's Eve

INDEX

Since the names of Harry Burnett, Richard Brandon, and the author appear so frequently in this book they have been omitted from this index.

A

O

R

P

S